Praise for The Chosen Son

This book, the words, the expression, the pain and the love clearly comes from a place of knowing. The author's experiences, although a mere fragment of The Stolen Generations history of being a white child born into a white family following the forced removal of an Aboriginal boy, has never been explored like this. An essential component for all to learn and understand the importance of accountability.

Robyn Newitt,
Yorta Yorta and Tharawal woman and
Monash University Lecturer

Written from the perspective of the younger sister/daughter, with the insights of an academic mind, *The Chosen Son* is profound, painful, and informative. The subtle and ethical way the author has negotiated the fraught and challenging nexus of personal story, Indigenous histories and the ramifications for us as a nation deserves a wide audience.

Distinguished Professor Lynette Russell AM,
Monash Indigenous Studies Centre

The Chosen Son is a beautifully crafted book. It is a story of familial relationships lived through the cruelty of colonial policies of First Nations child removal and placement with non-Aboriginal families. Although there may be no equivalence between the coloniser and the colonised in the pains and horrors suffered through colonialism, as the author writes, 'we are all part of the same unfolding story'.

Professor Chris Cunneen,
Jumbunna Institute for Indigenous Education and Research

In memory of my brother Len
15.4.1954–20.3.1980

And now, for Arthur

Leanne Weber

The Chosen Son

A memoir of love, loss and colonisation

G
P

Paperback ISBN 978-1-74027-011-3
ebook ISBN 978-1-74027-015-1

First published 2024 by
Ginninderra Press
PO Box 2 Bentleigh VIC 3204
www.ginninderrapress.com.au

Contents

That's the problem with history, we like to think it's a book – that we can turn the page and move the fuck on. But history isn't the paper it's printed on. It's memory, and memory is time, emotions, and song. History is the things that stay with you.

Paul Beatty,
The Sellout

Prologue

When it comes down to it, the stories we tell about our lives often turn out to be just a series of fragments. Some are barely remembered, confused and dreamlike. Others are vivid and full of meaning but difficult to connect. Sometimes the fragments are just a jumble, as if time's been put in a spin cycle. You try to patch them together the best you can, often with holes a decade wide, blasted through by emotion. The story eventually comes to an end, but it's hard to figure out how you got there. That's how it is with my story of Len and me, so I might as well start in the middle. That's the time when everything began to fall apart.

I am sheltering in the centre of our rambling old house huddled up against a wall, restrained by an adult's strong arms (perhaps my German grandmother?). We are like people hiding in a bomb shelter; on-edge, listening, waiting. But the exploding sounds are not artillery. In the kitchen, my brother Len has gone berserk. He is flinging open cupboard doors and sending crockery crashing to the floor. Someone is trying to calm him (my mother? father? neighbour?) but a primeval anger is erupting from the core of his being and there is no reasoning with him. Debris piles up on the chequered linoleum as more cups, plates and glasses shatter. Len is shouting, but it is not words coming from his mouth but an inarticulate fury. I don't remember how it ends. Perhaps Len runs out of ammunition. Perhaps the police come, although I don't think that started until sometime later. Perhaps his inner torment subsides. If Len had wanted to hurt us, if we were the target of his anger, he could have stormed through the house and unleashed his violence on us. The real war is raging within him. Everything is broken.

In my ten-year-old-mind, this was the beginning of the end. But it's not the beginning of the story. For that, we need to travel back to just before Christmas 1956.

Part 1

Piecing together

Remembering was a more active experience than she had…
remembered. You could reconstruct the past only with the building
blocks of the present.

Lionel Shriver, *So Much For That*

Love

Love is all we have, the only way that each can help the other.

Euripides

At its heart, this is a story about love. About how, despite how many times we've heard those words from that famous Beatles song, love is never all that any of us needs. I know it sounds shocking, because how can anything as simple and pure as love ever be wrong? But this book is about the destructive power of Misplaced Love.

I have imagined this book a thousand times over. In the beginning, it was just jumbled-up fragments and chaotic memories spinning around in my head. Now I have decided to tame it by writing it down. The story starts in early December 1956, almost eight months before I was born, as a two-year-old boy is about to spend his second Christmas far away from his family in a medical institution. Since I wasn't in the world then, I had to read about this first part of my brother's life many years later in a newspaper. The article I found in the archive of the Adelaide Advertiser was headlined 'Lennie will walk this Christmas'. This 'little aborigine', the story goes, has been in and out of hospital since he was seven months old. Other patients are eagerly awaiting the arrival of Father Christmas and have produced their Christmas wish lists. But Lennie, it seems, doesn't speak much. Instead, he tells us with his big brown eyes what he wants and needs more than any of the other little patients. And that's a foster-mother.

As the article goes to press, I imagine my parents are already preparing their own festivities at their rambling old house in Adelaide's western suburbs. Christmas at their place was always a special time marked by decadent treats like sticky glacé apricots that appeared on our table only once a year, along with less hedonistic family traditions like Sunday school nativity plays, donations to good causes, and invitations to join us extended to anyone in danger of spending Christmas day alone.

This is how I imagine the scene. When my dad shows Mum the photograph of little Len in the Advertiser, it unleashes in her a powerful torrent of motherly love. They are both convinced that they have been called on this year to give the greatest gift of all. From that moment, it has been decided: Lennie will become the child they have longed for.

*

After my elder brother Neil was born in 1947, my parents Peter and Jean tried unsuccessfully to have a third child. More than a decade later, to my eternal embarrassment, after I had unexpectedly become the fourth, my mother would declare to anyone within earshot how hard she had 'worked' to conceive me. Neil was the second child born to Peter and Jean, four years after their wartime daughter Beverley. He was a so-called blue baby, who was sickly from birth and prone to life-threatening episodes that sometimes resulted in emergency dashes to hospital and kept him isolated at home for long periods through his early years.

Our mother was no stranger to ill health herself. A congenital heart complaint had marked her for a childhood of physical restrictions and separation from her peers, and she had not been expected to live beyond her teens. Although she had defied those predictions, her frailty had derailed her dream of becoming a nurse. Instead, she had embraced with unbridled fervour the sacred role of motherhood, although the doctors warned her also against the risk that entailed. Ignoring medical advice to become a mother was for her a life's fulfilment, and possibly her one and only rebellious act. She lived for and through her children, summoning the full force of her nurturing power whenever someone in the household needed nursing care.

While the doctors viewed each of Jean's pregnancies as potentially fatal, for her the bringing into the world of a new life was an unparalleled human achievement. As Neil's needs became less urgent, she had longed for a third child to love and care for, but her second pregnancy had filled her bloodstream with destructive antibodies that for many years had snuffed out any flicker of life before it could take hold. It's easy to see how this newspaper appeal for a home for little Len must have been an answer to her prayers. A child who so clearly needed mothering. A mother who so desperately needed a child, and had the time, experience and patience to minister to his physical needs.

I don't know how much time elapsed from 8 December, when that article appeared, until Lennie became part of our family. That's another thing I can never know for sure. But it seems the anticipation of having a needy child to cherish unleashed some kind of 'fairy dust' that overcame whatever it was that had foiled Jean's many attempts to retain a pregnancy. By July of the following year, there was another addition to the Weber family. A miracle baby, late in life. Mum had spent the last months of her pregnancy laid up in hospital, but I was born without incident in the middle of winter, induced a month premature because of my mother's failing health, but robust beyond all expectations – so eager to burst into the world, Mum used to say, that I had cried out from the womb with indignation and impatience after her waters had been broken.

When he saw me, the family doctor had announced, to my mother's relief, that I was a good colour, by which he meant a luminous red, not an ominous blue. And right from the beginning – although no one ever said, or even thought, as much – my life was indelibly bound to Len's, linked through some mysterious alchemy that had been catalysed by my mother's love for him. I would not realise until much, much later that both my life and Len's were also embedded in a far bigger, more complex and much less happy story.

Loss

I understood, perhaps more than most, about loss, about how difficult things must be, and would continue to be. However much you loved someone, it wasn't always enough. Love alone couldn't keep them safe.
Gail Honeyman, *Eleanor Oliphant is Completely Fine*

When I was about twenty, I ran away to Melbourne on the pretext that I needed to go there to complete my university degree. It was not as glamorous or scandalous as joining the circus, but was a calculated act of independence nonetheless. Soon after, when I was part way through my Honours year, I decided to escape more comprehensively. I had not yet learned that the important journeys are the ones we take within ourselves. I quit my course and took a job in the Victorian snowfields, where my plan to save enough money for a one-way ticket to London quickly gave way to the necessity of late-night partying and expensive kamikaze attempts to ski. After the snow had melted, leaving me nothing to contemplate but an empty bank account, I embraced my overseas travel plans with a renewed fervour. I moved back to the family home in Adelaide for a short time and worked three jobs every day and night throughout the summer until I had secured the coveted ticket.

After a send-off at the airport, which I spent mainly in the bar with my friends while Mum, Dad, Len and the rest of the family sat dejectedly in the departure lounge, I flew to London with my childhood friend Debbie and began to hitchhike around Britain. In a turn of events that would be unimaginable to the constantly connected youth of today, I made my first contact with home after we had spent a full month on the road.

The slim envelope bearing my mother's handwriting was the first one I opened after collecting my poste restante mail. The letter it contained was brief. It said simply, 'Len, our beloved Len, died on the 20th of March.' I phoned my parents reverse charges to find out what had happened. They said he had fallen from a railway bridge in the city centre; had plunged into the bleak heart of the city in the dead of night and had not been found until morning. By the time I received that note, the funeral had already been held and Len had been laid to rest in the same plot as my paternal grandmother. All the collective business of dealing with death, all the practical and emotional rituals, had happened without me. There seemed no point at all in returning.

When I finally did go home two years later, I requested the coroner's report. It was the only thing I could think to do. The clinical language was mercifully detached. In fact, the whole report, like my mother's letter, was brief and to the point. It said that Len had suffered a sub-arachnoid haemorrhage attributed to the fall. His blood vessels contained less than 97% blood and more than 3% alcohol. Surprisingly perhaps, he had not fractured his skull. And when he was found, his body was said to be lying straight, with his limbs neatly aligned as if already awaiting his coffin. I remember thinking that falling from a great height should surely have been more untidy. But, in fact, what upset me the most in that official record of my brother's death was the passing mention of Len's greying hair. He had not even reached his twenty-sixth birthday.

One day, in what was for me still the near aftermath of Len's death, my mother caught me off-guard with the disarming news that she suspected someone had pushed Len from that bridge. Not being renowned for discretion, she simply blurted it out without forewarning, then launched another ambush, speculating that it might have been the police – maybe one of those 'bastards', she supposed, who 'knew' Len – in the way police say people are 'known to them'.

This had come as a shock, since I had never once heard my mother speak in that seditious way. We had all the usual trappings and illusions of a respectable white family. She would normally adhere to the conventional credo that the police were the ones to call on in a fix – that they were there to serve and protect us all. Although I doubt that we would have qualified as middle-class in the English sense, looking back it seems as though I'd been brought up in an Enid Blyton storybook where people were nice to each other, children were naughty in ways that never got them into real trouble, and authorities were there to be respected and obeyed. I had to wonder whether Mum had been a different, less conventional mother for Len than she'd been for me.

The whole issue was so raw and confounding that I never pressed my mother for details that might have provided some evidence either way, and she never mentioned it again. Nor could I bring myself to suggest to her that the fall might even have been deliberate, notwithstanding the strange observation about the position of Len's body, that – now I come to think of it – doesn't seem consistent with a catastrophic fall. I hadn't known at the time, as I was too busy trying to thumb rides from British truck drivers in the driving rain, but two weeks before his death, Len had slashed his wrists. I found this out from the coroner's report as well, where it was recorded matter-of-factly as background to the main event.

I'm sure you will think me hardened and morally remiss, but I confess that resolving these questions about how and why my brother died never seemed to be that important. I didn't embark on a quest to unearth the truth about Len's untimely end because it seemed to me that the greatest tragedy was not his death. It was his life. And I didn't know what on earth I could do about that.

*

After that day in 1980 when I telephoned my parents from England, I resumed my travels. I stumbled around Europe with my Eurail pass in a sort of daze, mechanically ticking off the places we planned to visit without truly experiencing any of them. After Debbie had returned home to get married and get on with having a proper life, I went on wandering around Europe on my own, taking all sorts of crazy risks. I found myself sleeping in caves on the beach and living in squats in Crete; drinking to oblivion with Swedish merchant sailors in Venice and waking up on someone's doorstep in the rain; smoking opium in the desert with Turkish men I'd met in a bar; jumping off balconies in Istanbul and out of moving trucks in France to evade would-be attackers. I put myself in mortal danger with as much thought as I gave to breathing and used up more lives than an extremely lucky cat. No serious harm ever befalls me. If I weren't an atheist, I'd say that guardian angels were watching over me.

Then one night, when I'm all alone, dossing in a disused house in a nondescript village in the Peloponnese, a real angel comes to me in my sleep. It must have been about four months after Len's death. I see him very clearly. More real to me than he had been in the last years of his life.

He is hovering brightly a few feet above me. My dead brother. I am only aware of his head and shoulders, so they seem disembodied, yet at the same time profoundly real. Although I'm asleep, I am conscious that he is with me and convinced I am not merely dreaming. The spectral presence evokes no horror or fear. Len's face is serene and loving and I understand he has come to release me. I feel overjoyed to see him and at the same time gripped by intense emotion that is part love, part grief and part relief. When I wake up, the pillow is soaked and I am literally awash with tears. In a sort of existential trance, I get out of bed, find pen and paper and scribble down a fully formed poem. It's not that great as poems go, but amazes me nonetheless. Where has it come from? I had forgotten that expressing my feelings in verse was what I had done right through my childhood. The poem is called 'A New Mourning'. It ends, 'How could I know the night would bring new life in death, new hope in grief, and the dawn, a bright new morning.'

Something inside me has sprung back to life, and it's both exhilarating and terrifying. I'm forced to confront the proposition that I have been living in a state of suspended animation for years – feeling almost nothing, sensing almost nothing, allowing only as much connection with the outside world as was needed to pass for being alive. I recognise immediately that it was an astonishing act of self-preservation in the face of everything that had happened to Len and therefore, vicariously, to me. Somehow, I have managed to safeguard my capacity for self-reflection and emotion, and my precious creativity, tucking them away in a hidden place until it was safe to come out again. My eyes are so wide open that the sun streaming through the window is blindingly bright. I'm surrounded by blazing colour. And the birds are trying to tell me something with their raucous chatter. It's like being born again, without the god bit. The world has come flooding back in.

Miraculous as that seems, I soon realise that my unconscious self-preservation strategy has come at a cost. I don't have a favourite colour, a favourite food, or an opinion about anything. I'm twenty-two years old and I don't even feel like I'm a person. I will have to learn from scratch how to become one, and the prospect is frightening. It might seem like a rare privilege to have the chance to reconstruct yourself. But identities don't come in handy flat-packs, complete with instructions. The most confronting truth I now have to face, beyond the finality of Len's death and my failure to prevent it, is that my life will continue to go on. And I will have to work out how to live it.

After the visitation, I will be gripped by the notion that Len and I had been bound together in some inscrutable way from birth; that while I owed my coming into the world to his arrival in our family, it was somehow ordained that his life must end in order that mine could continue. It made no sense at all, rationally speaking, and I was not at all inclined to magical thinking. And yet, at the same time, it presented itself as the inescapable truth. The injustice of it, and the realisation of my inculpation in the whole affair, was annihilating. From that moment, I would be haunted by the idea that perhaps our family had no right to have claimed Len as our own, and to shackle him with our love: that it was our family's Misplaced Love that had somehow killed him.

Blood

There are two kinds of history: official history, all lies, the history which is taught in schools, history ad usum delphini. Then there's secret history, which explains how things really happened; a scandalous kind of history.

Balzac, *Lost Illusions*

As Rumi tells us, 'A seeker of Truth looks beyond the apparent and contemplates what is hidden.' And so I need to tell you the other story of Len: the part that happened without us. A story also constructed from fragments because I can't really know what went on. This story comes mainly from books and government files and old handwritten records unearthed in the Lutheran Church archives. I know you might think you are way ahead of me, that you already know about the policies that took Aboriginal children away from their families. But I have tried to find out as best I can what this scandalous history meant, not just in general, but for Lennie in particular and for his first family. You might even think this story is not mine to tell. But I need to learn it myself before I can hope to understand what it was that made our love for him so lethal.

One thing I do know is that Len was born in 1954 on Koonibba mission on the far west coast of South Australia, the youngest of a family of at least seven children. It was an arid place where Aboriginal people lived, and city dwellers rarely visited. In fact, I doubt I ever thought about that place as a child. Why would I? But Len would have grown up there with the rest of his family if he had been born with proper feet. The mission hospital records his affliction by its medical name: talipes equinovarus. It was his club feet that sent him far away from his birth family, and into the dangerous unknown, for years of surgical treatment, therapy and institutionalisation in Adelaide.

At the time of Len's birth, the mission was run by the Lutheran Church. It's hard to know exactly what kind of place it was. Missions nowadays have a nefarious reputation as part of the colonial machinery of dispossession and control. But Peggy Brock assigns Christian missions a more ambiguous place in the history of Aboriginal adaptation and survival, observing that they 'simultaneously oppressed and nurtured the communities they confined'.[1] In contrast to the hostile world outside, missions sometimes offered a haven of sorts, providing a basis for community solidarity and survival. In other words, they were places for making the best of a very bad lot for people who had been left with few choices.

Koonibba mission was opened in 1898. Like other similar establishments, the objective was ostensibly to protect Aboriginal people in what was expected to be their declining years. But the regime of the Lutheran superintendents was strict. According to the Lutheran archives, a Reverend Sexton recorded on a visit to Koonibba in 1919 that it was a place where 'idleness was not permitted' and where the 'moral tone and standard surpasses anything I have seen in any other station'.[2] In a short time, or perhaps from the very beginning, the mission had become an instrument of 'civilisation' and control.

From the 1930s, the mission came under the oppressive regime of Pastor R.K. Traeger. His chronicler Cameron Rayne claims that mission residents were treated as if they had no rights at all.[3] Traeger worked closely with South Australia's Chief Protector of Aborigines, William Penhall, for several decades, enforcing a regime marked by rigid control and paternalism. A 1951 document I found in the Lutheran archives in Adelaide, commemorating fifty years of work by the church at Koonibba, notes approvingly that 'the man who acts as superintendent has duties towards [the residents] similar in many ways to those of a father of a family of under-age children'.

By 1958, after Len had been living with our family for just over a year, mission residents had had enough of this paternalistic control and staged a mass walk-off in protest at the poor living conditions and their lack of influence in running the establishment.[4] Just a few years later, in 1960, a report about Koonibba by the Board of Aboriginal Missions concluded that the mission was dying, despite the injection of considerable government funds to build cottages and raise educational and health standards. The document exemplifies the fusion of welfare and moralising control that had become the modus operandi at that point in the trajectory of colonisation. While older residents were said to be grateful to the mission for providing them with a home, standards of hygiene, behaviour and willingness to work were reportedly declining. The report's authors concluded that a police presence was necessary to restore discipline, noting that 'natives who have reached the status attained by our Koonibba natives are difficult to control anywhere, as Government experience also shows'.[5]

At Koonibba, control was exercised, in part, through the children's home which was established in 1914 in the aftermath of the South Australian Aborigines Act of 1911. Penny Brock notes that this institution was originally the only way Aboriginal parents could obtain a mainstream education for their children, and later provided some level of protection against forced removal under the Act to more distant locations.[6] The Bringing Them Home report[7] also acknowledged this double bind faced by Koonibba residents, concluding that 'a large number of parents relinquished their children to the care of the Lutheran mission, Koonibba, in South Australia to protect them from being removed by the Protector and placed further away'.

Finding strategies to keep families together must have been a constant struggle. While mission management denied forcing parents to surrender their children to the home, some commentators hailed the Koonibba Children's Home as the 'solution of the native-children problem' serving to 'mould the character of the natives' and make them 'reliable Christians'.[8] However, practices that included keeping older girls at the school to perform domestic work long after their formal education was completed, and after their families had expected them to be returned, have been described by more critical observers as no less than a system of slavery.[9] Eve Vincent concludes that a place that was originally conceived 'out of genuine concern, in order to circumvent aspects of the 1911 Act' had 'evolved into an institution with aims entirely congruent with nation-wide policies of Aboriginal child removal'.[10]

This is the place where Len's life started, and where his family tried to make the best of the survival strategies that were open to them. The Lutheran archives record both of Len's parents – Leonard and Clara – as Koonibba-born. Len's surname is identified there in a list of well-known Koonibba families, and members of his extended family are mentioned in several accounts of the history of the mission, where they are referred to as successful and respected community leaders.[11] I was happy to read that, and to hope that despite the undeniable hardships, some people had managed to live rewarding lives there.

When Len was born at Koonibba, the place was already considered by state authorities to be in decline. After a church commission of enquiry, the government took over the management of the mission in 1963, prompting another protest from residents who pointed out that, once again, they had not been consulted.[12]

Mission-dwellers had good reason to be wary about the new regime. The head of the South Australian Aboriginal Protection Board, who now had direct control over Koonibba and its residents, was said to have criticised the church for allowing the mission to be perceived as home, recommended the closure of the children's facility, and proposed the fostering of all children without immediate relatives to white or mixed heritage families.[13] It seems that life on the mission was about to become a whole lot harder.

By June 1959, 412 children from across the state were known to be in the care of the South Australian Aboriginal Protection Board, 260 of them in institutions and 152 placed in private homes.[14] Although he had an extended family at Koonibba, Len had become one of those 152. In fact, the Bringing Them Home report identifies 1954, the year of Len's birth, as the very year the Aboriginal Protection Board began placing Aboriginal children in foster homes rather than institutions, no doubt because of the life advantages they believed a white family environment such as ours could offer.

To assist in the assimilation process, a list was compiled by Koonibba's administrators in which all residents were ranked according to their perceived capacity to merge into white society.[15] If this process followed the conventions of the time, it would be reasonable to surmise that the ranking was driven largely by the colour of their skin. Len had a well-established extended family living on the mission to care for him, and no known European heritage. Had he still been living with them, perhaps he would not have been considered an assimilation prospect. But in any case, his fate had already been decided according to other parameters that were driven by his medical needs. Len had been thrust down the assimilation track from the moment in which his photograph appeared in The Advertiser. And there was to be no easy way back.

*

It must be during lunchtime or recess at primary school, this memory. I am sitting on the steps to one of the demountable classrooms, engaged in an awkward exchange with some schoolmates. I don't think they are kids I know very well. I think they might be boys. They have approached me because they want to settle something they believe to be important. They are throwing out a challenge – 'How can Len be your brother?' I don't know what to say. 'Because he just is.' They all agree he can't be. Although they're not openly hostile, their scepticism is unsettling. 'Perhaps he's your half-brother,' they persist, 'or your stepbrother?' 'I don't think so' is all I can think to say. I had never stopped to consider what kind of brother Len had to be. But the boys are still not convinced and continue their probing. Finally, to put an end to the interrogation, I agree with their proposition that Len must be my ex-brother. I was not to know then how prophetic that label would prove to be.

23

While Len was alive, I gave no thought whatever to his origins. To me, he was simply a permanent feature of our family landscape, the brother who had always been there. As far as I recall, it was not until after Len's death that my mother told me he had been a 'proud Aranda man'. This remains for me one of the biggest mysteries about Len's identity, since I now know that Aranda or Arrentje[16] country is far to the north of Koonibba over the Northern Territory border in central Australia.

As with other projects of dispossession, people from many different cultures were thrown together unceremoniously at Koonibba, without consideration for the social tensions and cultural dislocations that might produce. The original inhabitants of Koonibba mission are recorded as Wirangu, Gugada/Kokatha and Mirning people from the west coast, and Yirgala people from the far west coast of South Australia.[17] Over time, specific events in the colonisation process forced other groups of displaced people to move even further from their ancestral land to seek refuge there. By some accounts, this eventually forced mission-dwellers to try to develop a regional Aboriginal identity to accommodate the imposed diversity.[18]

The Lutheran archives record that Antakarinja and Pitjantjatjara groups from the western desert began to arrive at Koonibba from the APY Lands in the 1930s. These groups might be considered near neighbours of the Arrentje considering the vast scale of these territories. By the 1950s, there was a constant influx of newcomers from the north and west.[19] In 1947, there was said to be a major drift of people from Ooldea to Koonibba in search of work. Ooldea had been a vital crossroads and meeting place for Aboriginal people on the edge of the Nullarbor Plain. The mission at that location was closed in 1952 and many residents relocated to Yalata station for work.[20] These groups then suffered a further and more catastrophic disruption following the nuclear tests at Maralinga between 1952 and 1963. The state archives hold a letter dated 14 January 1954 from the chairman of the Koonibba Mission Board, Pastor Kriewaldt, to the secretary of the Aboriginal

Protection Board, noting that mission-dwellers were leaving Yalata and 'causing some anxiety' – he doesn't say to whom – 'in the districts through which they are travelling'. The anxieties driving that forced migration do not feature in the official record.

None of the sources quoted above mentions large-scale movements from Arrentje country to Koonibba. However, the meticulous mission records, kept with a Germanic eye for detail, reveal an intriguing possibility. Len's father Leonard is recorded as the child of a Wirangu man and a Kokatha woman – both groups that are local to the west coast. But, crucially, the records state that Leonard had been adopted by that couple. If that is correct, it left open the possibility, although providing no positive evidence, that Len's father did have more distant origins through his own birth family. I was to find out more later about Len's ancestry, but the records that do exist tell the tale of a family that had been fractured many times over, long before Len was sent away for hospital treatment in Adelaide.

In the years preceding Len's birth, it seems that the lives of his parents and older siblings were coming under considerable strain. Correspondence I received long after Len's death from the Adoption and Family Information Service at the South Australian Department of State Aboriginal Affairs notes that the whereabouts of Len's parents at the time of his placement with our family were unknown. Clearly, if there had ever been a time when Koonibba had provided a safe haven for Len's family, that time had passed. A search of state records for Len's name turned up several index entries for Leonard senior. The official notations are brief, declarative and coldly instrumental, retaining the same bureaucratic tone to record events as disparate as the issuing of blankets, requests for dentures, and the removal of children. Even without regard for the content, the tone of the official record conveys with breath-taking assurance the department's seemingly ubiquitous control.

In April 1945, the superintendent of Koonibba complains that an older sibling of the as-yet-unborn Len is not receiving an education (GRG 52/1/1945/18). A few months before, Leonard senior had been advised not to return to the mission without permission (GRG 52/1/1944/10A), a ruling that might reasonably have been expected to detract from his children's school attendance. Indeed, a further note in the state records indicates that Leonard challenged his expulsion, arguing – with obvious merit – that it would have a detrimental impact on his children's education (GRG 52/1/1945/18). It seems that the un-named child in question may have been placed in the children's home at the mission as a result (GRG 52/1/1944/10A), although the Lutheran archives hold no record of their admission. The fact that Len's father is recorded as having requested the placement conforms to the well-documented pattern of Aboriginal parents being manoeuvred into circumstances in which they had little choice but to hand their children over to institutional care, although whether this eventuated remains unclear.[21]

Not surprisingly, the order for Len's father to leave the mission had long-lasting ramifications for the entire family. Later entries in the state records note an alcohol-related offence in Ceduna, the region's main township, which resulted in a prison term for Leonard senior in 1960 (GRG 52/1/0/0/1956/51). The family's lives seemed to be unfolding according to another inexorable logic in which public drinking and other petty or non-existent public order offences were used to control Aboriginal people once they had been forced onto the fringes of settler towns.[22] There is a brief report from October 1966 of the family 'camping in substandard conditions' some distance away at Port Augusta, a place that has always been a significant crossroads in South Australia for Aboriginal people on the move. And in 1967 the records show that Leonard wrote to the Department of Aboriginal Affairs enquiring about the status of his trust account (GRS/6624/1/12/221/1967), although no details are recorded about the outcome or nature of that dispute.

Even based on these cursory and disjointed fragments, the story of Len's family bears all the hallmarks of Australia's secret history of dislocation, stolen children, resistance, pilfered wages, criminalisation, despair, conflict and survival, all permeated by calculated bureaucratic control exercised from a distance over every aspect of Aboriginal lives.

So it was that Len's need for long-term medical care led to him being sent far away from home as a tiny baby. He had at least one other set of foster-parents before he joined our family as a toddler. It must have been a painful and unwarranted separation, but Len did not lose contact entirely with his birth family. His parents never gave him up for adoption and Len never took on our family name. But beyond that I can't know how or why he was not returned to them, or what anguish his parents endured in the hope of getting him back.

Sometime after Len's death, my father told me that Leonard senior had thanked him for providing a secure and loving home for Len. I did not feel as reassured by this as my father clearly did, given the way it had all worked out. As a young woman, I also struggled to grasp how a loving father could ever accept that his child had been sent to live with strangers. I still understood so little about the realities of the scandalous history I have just recounted; about what it was really like to live through it; about the devious ways in which it distorted all the rules of everyday human relations. I must at that time have been what the great African American writer James Baldwin described as an 'innocent', giving the term a meaning that makes the inverted commas essential. In other words, a white person who failed to appreciate the reality of my country's racial divide.[23] Confronting that history made it possible to grasp how families who were struggling with the burden of endless, unresolvable dilemmas, who had run out of viable options, could be forced to come to terms with what would otherwise be unthinkable.

Many years after his death, I tried to uncover the most secret and personal parts of Len's own history by requesting the records relating to his fostering. I was told that most of the files dating from that period had been deliberately destroyed as a space-saving measure. Only a small number had been randomly selected for preservation in case they were needed 'for research'. Clearly, the emotional needs of the actual people whose lives were documented in the files earmarked for destruction did not feature in this bureaucratic reckoning, or at least were judged not to outweigh the considerable benefits of freeing up floor space that would presumably be used for storing more files.

I had hoped to find answers in those records – possibly distressing ones, but answers that would surely be preferable to remaining in a state of 'innocence'. There could have been harrowing letters from Len's mother or father politely requesting that the authorities restore their youngest child to them. Maybe social workers' reports on how Len was faring in the Weber household, and why they thought he should stay there. Possibly – and this would have been the most confronting – statements of some kind from my own parents. Certainly, I had expected to find official documentation of the many institutions Len had passed through later in his life, although he had always come back to us. Instead, some bureaucrats whose sense of compassion was eclipsed by the dictates of sampling theory had decided this information was of no further relevance.

Other obstacles I encountered as I tried to piece together an understanding of my brother's life served to reinforce the circumstances that had propelled me on this quest in the first place. A letter I sent to the South Australian Adoption and Family Information Service in early 2003 following a series of unproductive telephone enquiries illustrates the point. I wrote, indignantly, 'I have been informed that I am not entitled to have access to his records as I am not a biological relative. This is unfortunate, as it seems to denigrate the very relationships which your service is involved in establishing.' This prompted an apologetic reply listing a few dates at which legal decisions had been made about Len's life and the lives of his birth family, most of which I have already woven into the story I have told you so far.

The letter advised me to contact SA Link-Up if I wished to find out more about Len's Aboriginal family. But when I enquired at their office, I also found that I did not fit the expected profile. The service was intended to help those who had themselves been removed from their birth families, and the organisation's limited resources were already stretched to breaking point trying to meet the growing need.

I understood and accepted this reality. But it only served to reinforce how I was condemned to find myself – inescapably, forever – on the wrong side of history.

In 1963, the gates that spelled out the name of 'Koonibba Lutheran Mission' were reportedly 'torn down' by some residents as the state government took over the running of the community.[24] While it appears that some mission-dwellers were glad to see the end of the Lutheran administration, the new arrangement still ignored their calls for self-determination. Many residents left during that time, although it seems that government plans to actively 'disperse' occupants never came to fruition. It was not until January 1976 that responsibility for a wide range of services on the former mission was transferred to the Koonibba Aboriginal Community Council. Title over the land was granted to the Aboriginal Lands Trust and the land leased back by the community council. Residents purchased the land through the Aboriginal Development Commission in 1988 and, as far as I can make out, Koonibba still survives as a self-governing Aboriginal community. Quite a lot will have changed since the dark days in the 1940s, 50s and 60s when Len's parents struggled to keep their family together, watched over and seemingly undermined at every step by mission authorities and the Aborigines' Protection Board. Today, the community has a website[25] and boasts a women's group, childcare centre, health service, regular sporting competitions and a community development employment programme.

No doubt many individual and collective struggles persist for the families that live there. The events of the past are not that easily put behind. As one literary luminary pointed out, 'The past is never dead. It's not even past.'[26] Although I have demystified it in my mind to some degree, Koonibba remains a place that I am yet to visit. I am waiting for the time when, through some process that is yet to materialise, I might be invited – will have a legitimate reason to go. If that happens, my hope is that when I go there, I will find that something of Len has remained. I hope, even in that unfamiliar place, that I will feel like a secret part of me has found a connection.

Belonging

Refugees do not change places; they lose a place on earth, they are catapulted into a nowhere.

Zygmunt Bauman, *Society under Siege*

In some ways, colonised peoples might be thought of as refugees within their own land. This is exactly how the Larrakia people described their predicament in a petition they presented to Queen Elizabeth II in 1972, capitalising the most crucial words for emphasis: 'Today we are REFU-GEES. Refugees in the country of our ancestors. We live in REFUGEE CAMPS without land, without employment, without justice.'[27] Sociologist Zygmunt Bauman has likened this condition to being catapulted into a nowhere – not only banished from one's homeland but potentially denied a sense of secure belonging anywhere. I don't want to say that this has been the fate of Aboriginal people in Australia who, through unremitting struggle, have retained an unassailable understanding of where they rightfully belong. But colonial policies of dispossession from land, and separation from family and culture, have been designed to have that effect. Wiradjuri author Anita Heiss speaks in one of her novels of the 'misery being no one in your own land can bring'.[28]

My mother told me, sometime after Len's death, that all Len had wanted was to find a small piece of land in the countryside where he could build a hut and live in peace. This was not a politicised vision of securing land rights and reclaiming sovereignty over ancestral lands. It was a more modest and personal desire to find a refuge away from the hostility of the outside world: a place of tranquillity at least, if not of deep-seated belonging.

My parents dealt with Len's visible difference from the rest of the family by calling him their 'chosen son'. It was their way of trying to make him feel special and wanted. They also called him, playfully, their 'brown boy' – thinking, I suppose, that it would help him to love his own skin. When I was small, they gave me a beautiful brown-skinned doll I named Wendy, presumably to ensure that I learned to love brown skin as well. At the time, I paid no attention at all to her skin colour and would have had no idea that it had been a deliberate strategy. When he was older, Len would play along with the 'brown is beautiful' theme, insisting, with a mischievous grin, that he took his milky coffee brown rather than white.

This approach seemed to work within the confines of our loving home, but did not travel so well outside. Many years after Len's death, when I was helping my elderly dad in the supermarket, we came across an elegant white woman almost Dad's age who was wheeling a dark-skinned toddler in her shopping trolley. She may have been the child's grandmother, or someone babysitting their neighbour's child for all we knew. But my beaming father marched straight up to the pair, tickled the little boy tenderly under the chin and announced with pride that he too had once had a 'little brown boy' of his own. Mercifully, he seemed not to register the look of dismay on the woman's face, as I disappeared into the next aisle, consumed with shame.

I have a dog-eared black and white photograph of Len and me as small children riding on a tricycle on the cement path near the grape-vine trellis in our old family home. I suppose I'm about two years old, which would make Len around five. He's in the driver's seat and I'm standing behind him on the running board, my chubby arms clamped around his chest. It's clear that the picture has captured the innocent and loving bond between us. But it also captures something that seems to be at odds with the usual childhood scene. Instead of smiling at the camera, the sombre little characters appear to be in a world of their own. And yet neither of us is watching where we are going. Instead, we both seem transfixed by a spot on the ground just out of shot, as if something serious is going on there that no one else has noticed. As if we already know that the road ahead will be no laughing matter.

As far as I was concerned at that tender age, Len was simply my big brother. When we were small, our mother would bathe us together. While Mum did battle with the endless knots in my fine blonde hair, Len would scrub and scrub at his skin trying to make it white. His feelings seem to have been shared by other Aboriginal children (dis)placed with white families. Lance told the national inquiry that produced the Bringing Them Home report that, even though his adoptive parents had tried their best to make him feel a part of the family, he had wished that 'God would make me white and these people's son instead of an adopted son'.[29] Ironically, as a teenager, I would risk a nasty and premature death from melanoma by sunbaking for hours on end until my pale skin turned a deep burnished bronze.

Another childhood memory. This time a dream in which nothing much happens. In point of fact, it is really just a vision: a kind of tableau. Standing before me is a large gathering of ferocious-looking people, arrayed in orderly, military-style rows. I think of them as the 'Half-and-half People'. They could be carrying spears, or that might be an embellishment I've added later. They look exactly like the miniature troll dolls that are in vogue at the time – little squat creatures with brightly coloured topknots sticking straight up from their heads. In my dream, they don't have technicolour hair. The only colours I register are black and white. The Half-and-half People look like white troll dolls that have been dipped head first into molten chocolate, leaving them dark from the waist up. Or they might be dark brown trolls that have been dipped into white chocolate. Whichever way it is, they are all two-tone. Despite their warlike presence, I feel totally at ease in their midst. When I wake up, I know it's important that I have seen the Half-and-half People, important enough to remember them always, although at the time I have no idea why. Looking back, I wonder whether what I was doing was inventing a tribe in which Len and I could both belong.

*

People would sometimes mistake Len for being Indian. I don't know if he would put them right or take the pragmatic route of accepting that exotic identity, and the denial of Indigenous heritage it entailed. Rightly or wrongly, our parents encouraged Len's pride in being 'full-blood' Aboriginal. The inescapable implication – that this was some-how more desirable than being a 'half-caste' – was never articulated and probably not really thought through. Such a notion would have been inconsistent with their sincere commitment to values of universal love and acceptance. I suppose if their foster-child had been of more visibly mixed descent, they would have encouraged his pride in that background too.

Despite his seemingly impeccable Indigenous credentials, Len was sometimes labelled a 'coconut' when he returned in later life to visit family on the west coast: acceptable on the basis of skin tone, but not in terms of culture. The mission was not immune to its own hierarchies of discrimination on the basis of skin colour either, as Dylan Coleman chronicles in her semi-biographical novel set in Koonibba where the young protagonist Grace is often ostracised for the whiteness of her skin.[30] As it turns out, while Len always believed that he came from

33

an unbroken Aboriginal line, I later found out from state records that Len's family name originated from a white farmer who had married Len's paternal great-great grandmother at Poonindie mission near Port Lincoln towards the end of the nineteenth century.[31]

There must have been some reasonably happy, uncomplicated years when I like to think that Len thrived on the love and care he encountered in our family. Our parents saw Len through a series of operations and corrective treatments, and Mum would spend hours on end massaging his legs and supervising exercises devised to sculpt him some functional feet. I don't remember much about those early times. As far as any small child can know, I'm certain that I loved my brother, that we played together, and I remember no jealousy or acrimony of any kind. There are some old black and white snapshots taken on our family's Kodak Instamatic showing Len and me playing happily with other kids in the shallows, possibly at Henley Beach, our local retreat from the summer heat; or maybe further down the south coast where the whole family would relocate to a rented beach house for our annual summer holiday.

At home, our favourite game for a while was playing circus. I would put on my gymnastics leotard and swing like a daredevil from the exposed rafters in the shed or dress up in a cowgirl outfit and ride bareback on an old dappled grey rocking horse while Len, fitted out as an Indian chief, kept his feet planted firmly on the ground, both of us utterly unaware of the colonial stories we were acting out. Len must have grown in physical confidence as he got older, as I remember the time he broke his collarbone after careering headfirst on his bike down the steeply sloping sides of the concrete drain that passed as 'the creek' in our humble suburb.

When it came to the distribution of material goods within the family, our parents were meticulous in ensuring absolute equality between all four of their children, down to the infuriating habit of insisting that our gifts at Christmas time or birthdays must be of exactly the same monetary value. This often meant some random small object – a chocolate bar or plastic toy – would be wrapped up along with the main gift to make up any shortfall. The result, as far as I am aware, was a total absence of sibling rivalry, which I later understood to be quite exceptional. I'm told that Len used to hit me with his callipers, perhaps with good reason – a practice he did not reserve for me alone. In turn, I left a permanent scar in the middle of his forehead where – showing a precocious ability with my throwing arm – I hit him fair and square from across the room with a rubber tomahawk. But none of these childhood incidents left significant emotional scars. More likely they contributed to the building up of sibling bonds in the usual rough-and-tumble way.

But our temperaments began to diverge noticeably as we grew. While I devised a system of neatly labelled paper bags into which I would divide my pocket money each week, to save mainly for sample bags and rides at the Royal Adelaide Show and to buy gifts for birthdays and Christmas, Len lived without any apparent thought for tomorrow. He was clearly a one marshmallow child, whereas I would have held out for the two (see the Stanford marshmallow experiment if interested).[32] In other words, Len either lacked self-control (if you favour explanations based on personality traits); or he had no reason to trust that the promised reward would materialise in return for his restraint (if you prefer, as I do, an interpretation based on social learning).

One time, I recall blurting out self-righteously at a family gathering that it had in fact been our mother who had bought the birthday gift that bore Len's name because, unlike me, Len had spent all of his pocket money on himself. The reproachful looks directed from all corners of the room signalled my fall from grace. These sentiments did not accord with the values of loving acceptance that were expected in our family, and I was engulfed in an invisible cloak of shame. I can recall no other time when I felt resentful towards Len, even though, of necessity, he attracted the lion's share of our mother's attention. And certainly, as his life began to disintegrate, there was nothing whatever to be jealous about.

*

35

Like many families where there is a large gap in the children's ages, our family functioned almost as two separate units. My older sister Beverley and brother Neil were married and out of the family home by the time I was twelve, whereas Len and I were contemporaries. If Len was the chosen son, then I had been the surprise in the family, although not unwanted by any means – my arrival being viewed as a 'blessing' long after our mother had given up hope of bearing another child.

My mother was often unwell, and in the early years much of her energy was spent ministering to Len's special needs. Although she was only in her mid-teens at the time of my birth, my sister Bev would often be mistaken for a young mother as she pushed my pram along the street. It's to her I remember running in the morning, or sometimes my live-in grandmother, to have my hair braided for school. It is only now that I realise my sister's disappearance from the household – effectively from the time she went away to teach in a mission school in the New Guinea highlands when I was ten – must have seemed like the loss of a parent.

My brother Neil had also played a role in my early life, channelling his artistic sensibilities into the creation of custom-made, haute couture outfits for my dolls using scraps of ribbon and lace and leftover fabric from Mum's sewing projects or playing the piano while I sat transfixed on his knee.

Looking back, it seems as though my older siblings had grown up in more innocent times. I suspect it always seems that way when people gaze back across generations. Family life, when Len and I were small and my older siblings were becoming young adults, was approached from a conventional and communitarian perspective. Everyone's business seemed to be out in the open. Bev's latest dress or glamorous hairstyle would be an object of admiration and a talking point for the whole family, while Neil's brief foray into the unchartered world of university was a constant source of wonder. When he returned from a trip with the Adelaide University Choral Society telling debauched tales of dancing hand-in-hand around a public toilet in the rural town of Dubbo singing 'here we go round the Dubbo dub', we all marvelled at the wit and audacity of such a prank. When he told us an offbeat riddle that was going around campus at the time – 'Q. What's the difference between a duck? A. One of its legs is both the same.' – we were astonished at this rare glimpse into a seemingly impenetrable, intellectual world.

Although not without their own dramas and detours, it seemed to me that Bev and Neil's lives unfolded largely according to the expected script. The individualism and non-conformity of the 1960s would not infiltrate the suburban backblocks of Adelaide until at least the next decade, just as I was entering adolescence. So my older siblings grew up within the tightly knit church community and emerged into a world of confirmations, glory boxes, diamond rings and engagement parties, got married at the West Richmond Methodist Church within a few months of each other, and moved out of home to create their own families. Len and I featured in both wedding parties: a twelve-year-old me as my sister-in-law's bridesmaid with hair in honey-coloured ringlets, wearing a daffodil-yellow shift trimmed with vertical lace; then in deep purple crèpe for my sister, with long flared sleeves and hair piled high in a nest of pinned-up curls that made me feel unbearably grown-up; while Len smiled shyly at the camera, looking stiff and self-conscious in his formal suit.

The year they both married, 1969, proved to be a turning point for the family in many ways. First of all, we had seen off my older siblings. Then my paternal grandmother, who had always lived with us, suffered a fatal stroke, reducing the family left at home to Mum, Dad, Len and me. And all of these events, two weddings and a funeral, happened just as we moved into the newly built house our mother had dreamed of ever since the day of her wedding, and I prepared to start high school in a brand-new suburb, far away from the close-knit neighbourhood and childhood friends I had known until then.

This new start was not destined to bring happy times, and before long the atmosphere in our shiny new home grew joyless and oppres- sive. As the troubles mounted, we became increasingly estranged as I retreated into myself, and Len disappeared into the system. He spent much of the time away from home in various institutions and grew into a man without me, as alcohol, confinement and mental illness transformed him. When he was home, we would barely talk. It pains me to think that I can't recall the substance of a single conversation with my brother. He was often sullen and withdrawn, spending hours in his room playing records, with Mum his main point of contact. Why didn't I ever sit with him, I wonder, and ask him about the music he loved? About his family on the west coast? About how he felt about his life? Although no one seemed to notice, I was far too immersed in my own Deep Thinking to venture into anyone else's inner world.

As the baby of the family, and as the cherished chosen son, Len and I had both enjoyed an unquestioned place within an abiding circle of love and acceptance, with the church community at the outermost boundary of our world and our family at the core. Still, for quite different reasons, and in very different ways, both Len and I were marked by an indelible difference that would make it hard for each of us to figure out who we really were and to discover where we truly belonged.

*

Apart from the time he spent in hospital as a small child, Len's most significant exposure to the world outside our family home would have been at school. As far as I know, Len was the only Aboriginal child in our relatively multicultural school, and for most of the time the only dark-skinned pupil there. In most classes, the majority of pupils were either Greek or Italian, reflecting the large waves of migration from southern Europe in the 1950s and 60s to our part of Adelaide. The government referred to these migrant children and their parents as 'New Australians', as if the rest of us weren't. With hindsight, I understand that many of these kids had a very difficult time themselves. As well as having their schooling to contend with, many were required by their parents to attend language classes at night and extensive religious instruction on weekends – imposts that the Australian-born kids regarded with pity and disbelief. Most of the Italian and Greek girls were not allowed to attend camps or even school excursions. For some reason, many of them seemed to get their periods early, in some memorable cases in spectacular and highly public fashion. One tall, sad-eyed girl called Milagros from a poor Spanish family, stood out because she brought nothing but thick slices of dry bread to school each day for lunch.

All of these things set the migrant kids apart. There seemed to have been no obvious support for these young people who needed to catch up with language so they could avoid humiliation inside the classroom and develop strategies for surviving outside it. Over time, the older Greek and Italian boys, many of whom had been left behind by their year groups, began to organise loosely into gangs in an effort to redress the balance of a system stacked against them. They would ambush Anglo-Australian kids like me on their way to and from school with itchy powder from pods plucked from the trees, or sometimes with heavier artillery. Who knows what villainy was directed against them by others more combative than me? By the end of my primary school years, the skirmishes had descended into serious tribal warfare, and police cars would sometimes pull up at the gate to take one or more of the combatants away, most memorably after one of them had stabbed the deputy headmaster.

Although I harboured no feelings of either animosity or superiority towards the kids who were marked as outsiders, I don't remember feeling any requirement to intervene in solidarity with them. I fell into the general schoolyard dynamic, which was for the southern European and Anglo-Australian kids to hang out with their own kind. The children I met playing in our street, on the sports field, and at Sunday school were the ones who became my closest friends, and they were, without exception, Anglo-Australian or at least of northern European origin like me. I simply, and without reflection, took the line of least resistance.

I do recall, to my abiding shame, that when a new boy from Papua New Guinea started primary school in the year above me, my mother had me select some coloured pencils that could be spared from my own collection, sharpen them carefully and secure them together with a rubber band, before delivering them to his classroom as a welcome gift. This was a one-off gesture, and not intended to signal the beginning of an enduring friendship. The Christian message was that it was the responsibility of 'those who have' to share with 'those who have not' —and the question of who was to give and who was to receive was determined on the basis of skin colour.

Even in the midst of this diversity, Len would stand out, or be made to stand out, from the others. For one thing, his special boots and inability to join in running games must have marked him as both different and defective. The only good friend I remember him having in his school years was a quiet and shy pale-skinned boy whose family were from the country. Peter wore a rope around his waist to hold up his trousers, had a slight facial tic, and kept homing pigeons.

Being several years behind Len in school I have no insights at all into how his classmates behaved towards him. But insensitive teachers reinforced his outcast status by setting up thoughtless rituals of humiliation. My mother used to recount a story about Len being directed to inform the class, with the help of a calendar, how many days were in the current month. When he started to move his finger from one date to the next, counting out each of the days in turn rather than skipping to the final number, the class had erupted with laughter. I now recognise the calendar-counting episode not merely as a one-off act of insensitivity, but as part of a process of 'systematic inferiorisation' through which denigrated groups come to internalise their subordinate status through repeated humiliations.[33]

Although I shared her outrage, my mother's explanation was just as unsettling to me as the incident itself. In traditional societies, she ventured, precise counting was not necessary, so Aboriginal languages typically contained only the words for 'one', 'two' and 'many'. Nowadays, Aboriginal writers and activists work hard to dispel these myths, pointing to well-developed systems of Indigenous mathematics, not to mention architecture, agriculture, physics, astronomy and natural science.[34] Even supposing my mother's understanding to be true, it relied on the magical transmission of this cultural knowledge into Len's brain. It seemed to me that years of disrupted learning, especially those crucial first two years at the start of life when Len was institutionalised and traumatised by loss and dislocation, would go further in explaining his educational difficulties.

*

In a statement that resonates with the idea of being 'catapulted into a nowhere', one man who told his story to the Stolen Generations Inquiry explained that lack of knowledge about his birth family had left him feeling like he had 'just come out of nowhere'.[35] Len's circumstances differed in at least this respect from some other casualties of forced removal, since members of his immediate family were able to maintain some contact with him in a variety of ways.

As if following a familiar colonial script, Len's older sister had come to help in our family home soon after I was born. No doubt, Mum had more work on her hands than she had anticipated with two very young children to care for and bringing me into the world had taken a heavy toll on her already compromised health. I recall nothing of the time that Nora spent with us, but she remained part of our family folklore long after she had left. She and my sister Bev, who were about the same age, had been close companions. There's an old black and white photo of the two of them fashionably dressed in slim-waisted dresses with flared skirts and matching hats and gloves, sporting meticulously teased and lacquered hair, probably on their way to a church social.

I can't know what Nora thought of the experience of living with our family. While I would like to think there was some other meaning to the arrangement, it's possible she had learned her domestic skills and been formally offered as a domestic worker from the children's home at Koonibba. Although these may not have been the circumstances in which Nora would have chosen to seek proximity to her small brother, that prospect must have been something of a drawcard. It seems unlikely that she would have felt overworked, undervalued or exploited in our home. For one thing, our mother was the sort of woman who would insist on dusting before the cleaner came, washing her hair before going to the hairdresser, and making the beds herself on the rare occasions when we stayed in a motel on holiday – partly in order to keep up appearances, but also because of a genuine reluctance to place herself above others. I expect that Nora would have been loved and embraced within the family at the same time as we were all unwittingly playing out a deeply entrenched colonial dynamic.

Len's older brothers never lived with us but would become big influences in his later life as Len regained contact with more of his family. Arthur, the closest in age to Len, maintained a connection with my parents long after Len died, and Mum and Dad became like honorary grandparents to his daughters. While I don't remember meeting Len's father, Leonard senior, I was always told by my parents that he was a good man who loved Len and had Len's love and respect in return. Len's mother Clara came to visit several times, but I only remember one occasion when I was quite young. I recall feeling confused and – to be totally honest – rather indignant at her presence. I couldn't understand what this strange lady had to do with our family. She stayed for dinner, but didn't eat much, explaining that 'I don't like meat to my stomach of an evening'. For some reason, that unfamiliar construction – meat to my stomach – stayed etched in my immature brain, signifying something that was out of the ordinary and slightly alarming.

It would never have occurred to me, had my mother not mentioned it once in passing, that Len had felt rejected by his own mother. I don't think for a moment that my mother would have cultivated such a cruel and unjust idea, but she may have been told that by others in authority. Even if those feelings of abandonment came from within Len himself, I wonder how she would have responded when he expressed them; whether she would have been able to find some kind of explanation. Admittedly, an explanation may not have helped in any case, since feelings of abandonment can't easily be talked away. But I can't forget that my mother once said to me – naively, I believe, and completely without malice – that Aboriginal people, living a harsh nomadic existence, would have had no choice but to leave behind a disabled child like Len. She had no doubt heard that from someone claiming to be in the know. But in any case, it hardly seemed relevant to life on Koonibba mission in the 1950s, where residents were no longer subject to the pressures of an unforgiving environment but were exposed instead to the relentless power of colonial administrators.

*

According to the Bringing Them Home report, many foster-parents in the cases brought before the inquiry 'did not respond appropriately' when children experienced prejudice and came to appreciate the enormity of what they had lost. In his autobiographical book Australia Day,[36] Stan Grant recounts such an experience. He writes how his childhood friend Owen had lived next door, in a home 'of great love', where a Presbyterian minister and his wife, having raised their own children, had taken seven Aboriginal children, including Owen, into their family – no doubt motivated, I can't help thinking, by the same Christian values of loving service to others espoused by my own parents. Grant describes the household as a 'world apart', as a place where 'you could even say colour disappeared'.

Confusingly, while acknowledging these practices would not be encouraged today, he considers the adopted children to be 'all the better for it'. But when put to the test, this apparent colour-blindness proves problematic. Facing their first encounter at school when another pupil points to differences in skin colour within the family, Owen's adoptive mother assures the two boys that they are not black at all but have 'lovely olive skin'. Owen's mum, Grant explains, although seeking to protect her adopted children from racial sleights, is just as 'trapped in the prism of race' as the schoolboy who had precipitated the incident.

Former leader of the opposition, Kim Beazley, in his parliamentary response to the Bringing Them Home report, commented on this lack of understanding about identity and the politics of race.

> Many very decent people took up the fostering status, and they did so without maliciousness and with the very best intentions. This Report is not really about them. It does refer to them of course in the context of the extent to which those people nevertheless, without knowing it, were implicated in a de-culturalisation of a race, with all the loss of identity that

flowed from that and the extraordinary difficulties that they confronted.[37]

Ngarrindjeri/Kaurna woman Veronica Brodie recorded in her memoir the problems that arose for children who were denied early opportunities to learn the strategies needed to live as an Aboriginal person within settler colonial Australia:

> We've got kids who have suicided because they can't cope in a mixed world. They just can't cope with the transition of being brought up in a white family, and then suddenly being introduced to a world of Aboriginal culture. They get totally lost. They can't seem to pick up the pieces... These stolen children often have the added burden of trying to understand why they were taken away. Sometimes they prefer to believe the government departments rather than believe what their own people tell them.[38]

The crucial importance of cultural identity to a sense of security and belonging is now widely understood. Perversely, we know this mainly because 'cultural traumatisation' was used deliberately as a tool of colonisation.[39] I know my parents did their best to expose Len to what they understood to be his cultural heritage. One of our most celebrated family possessions was a glorious set of hardcover books purporting to tell Dreamtime stories. They were full of mysterious spirit characters beautifully illustrated by Ainslie Roberts in ethereal, elongated forms. Because of the need to accommodate their supernatural stature, the books were so enormous they couldn't fit in the bookcase and had to be kept alongside it propped up against a wall. Years later, I heard a radio interview in which an Indigenous commentator dismissed with contempt the Westernised packaging of a homogenised 'Aboriginal culture', which these cherished books no doubt exemplified. In their innocence, it seems my parents had fallen into the category of foster-parents who had failed to respond appropriately to the separation of Aboriginal children from their cultural heritage.

My parents were certainly not alone in their inability to fill this crucial acculturation gap. Even children living in loving homes with their own birth parents could experience trouble with identity. One contributor to the Growing up Aboriginal in Australia anthology explains how their mother missed out on learning about her Aboriginal heritage in the first part of her life because she was raised by her white father:

> Despite being raised by her birth father in a home filled with complete and utter love, unconditional security and protection, the one thing he couldn't give my mum was the knowledge of who she was as an Aboriginal woman.[40]

Other contributors to Growing Up Aboriginal in Australia identified challenges that arose for them after being raised within loving white families. One author acknowledges the love she still feels for the foster parents she calls 'Mum' and 'Dad', but is conflicted by the emotional costs to her birth family:

> [My foster parents] couldn't have children of their own and were given the opportunity to do so, but obviously this came at the expense of others' hardship.[41]

Another author explains how, in his adoptive family, their undoubted love could never be enough:

> My adoptive parents grew me up with all the love and material comfort that was theirs to give from when I was seven months old. They loved me, and I loved them as a son should. However, like so many people in Australian society at that time, my adoptive family had little understanding or factual knowledge about Aboriginal people and cultures. Consequently, I had to wait several years before I came to know what it meant being Aboriginal in Australia.[42]

Mum and Dad also tried to build Len's self-esteem by encouraging his interest in art. This translated into the learning of Western artistic techniques since my parents' idea of Aboriginal art – no doubt shared by the majority of Australians at the time – was exemplified by the revolutionary work of Albert Namatjira. Len tried his hand at crayon and charcoal drawing, some Namatjira-inspired painting that rendered Indigenous landscapes in non-traditional style, then dabbled in ceramics. I still have two pieces that he gave me. One is a cup and saucer finished in a dazzling blue-white glaze; the other a large oval plate in natural earthy tones with the wistful figure of a lone emu wandering a rich brown landscape. While the first of these objects speaks to me of sanitised whiteness, the other suggests the idea of home that Len may have imagined.

One testimonial recorded in the Bringing Them Home report stands out to me because of its uncanny parallels with the imagery I employed in 'Feet on the ground' – the original poem featured at the end of this chapter. This witness gives a moving account of a reunion with her biological family, saying:

> For the first time I actually felt like I had roots that went down into the ground. But not only into the ground – that went through generations. And it was like I was connected through.[43]

For Len, having had at least some contact with his birth family had still not been enough to provide this sense of connection. In adult life, he began to see-saw precariously between his two worlds. He would disappear regularly back to the west coast to spend time with his relatives. These forays took him to a place of love and belonging, but also to a world in which there were many dilemmas and hazards. Sometimes he would come back to us in a sorry state following weeks of binge drinking. Always he would return without some item of value such as a record player or item of clothing that had been his gift from Mum and Dad at the previous birthday or Christmas. At least it was always easy to know what to give him next time as there was an endless stream of re-homed presents to be replaced. Dad tried to arrange jobs for Len in Adelaide, always somewhere not too far from home so he could ride there on his gearless, black and white pushbike. Len would give them a try, but nothing ever lasted for long. On the other hand, nothing seemed to hold him at Koonibba either and he would always come back to us, long after he was in a position, legally at least, to decide his own fate.

By adulthood, the only place where it seemed that Len felt secure was the space in our house between his bedroom and the kitchen. He would pace back and forth day after day chain-smoking, playing tracks from his massive record collection that charted Black musical history from traditional delta blues to rock-and-roll and disco, including albums by Jimmy Hendrix, Sam Cooke, Janis Joplin and other defiant voices of the outcast and oppressed, moving in a constant orbit around our mother as she prepared food in the kitchen, like twin pulsars locked into the pull of each other's gravitational waves, Len at the centre of her universe.

I still have some of those classic albums – a testament to my brother's inner life. It was only recently that I appreciated the significance of something distinctive about them. On every record sleeve, Len had written his name in indelible marker pen in the top right-hand corner, right there on the front cover in full view. I recognised it as the sort of declaration I had felt compelled to make in all my books when I had first reached the point of being able to buy them. This was not a stamp of ownership so much in the sense of having made a purchase: more a statement of identity. 'This is me', I think Len and I were both saying. 'This is what defines me, and what I care about'.

It has been observed with respect to missions that these places of sanctuary were also a form of imprisonment. I would come to think of that space at the heart of our family home between Len's bedroom and the kitchen as the physical manifestation of the Love Trap our family had inadvertently created for him; a place to which he was tethered by unbreakable bonds of love, where the perils of the outside world could not touch him, but where he was also cut off from the things that most defined him and could perhaps have given his life meaning. Not long before he died – during the most tormented years – Len burst outside late one night in a drunken fury, bellowing out to the sleeping neighbourhood and the complacent world beyond, 'FUCKING WHITE CUNTS! FUCKING, FUCKING WHITE CUNTS!' It was only while writing this book that it finally occurred to me that perhaps he wasn't talking about us.

*

In the mid-1980s, several years after Len's death, I visited Uluru for the first time and went on a food gathering walk led by Anangu female elders. The experience was profound and gave me my first insight into the prodigious level of knowledge, fortitude and collective effort required to survive in such a challenging landscape, and the deep connection to country this forged. To my shame, I also climbed the sacred rock in a state of ignorance, learning only afterwards that the traditional owners objected to the steady stream of climbers that stretched up the steep face each day, which they referred to dismissively as the munga – or ant – trail. When I arrived back home, I was moved to write about what I had experienced. It would be many years later that I realised that the poem also expressed my own profound sense of alienation. Without realising it, I had written about the power of belonging.

Feet on the Ground

Your dress isn't worn in that neat European way,
as it was, I suppose, by its first owner.
It hangs freely on your frame as if
ready to catch a passing breeze.
You move with sure steps through the spinifex,
then drop to unite with the welcoming ground
and draw in the sand with your finger.

Life is your poet. The rhythm of the digging stick
sends music in search of goanna.
Your stories are history, religion and science.
And art is carved, without affectation,
into The Rock.

There is no mystery in this to you –
that witchetties live in the roots of the acacia;
that the barren grass, beaten, sheds seeds for a damper;
that the flowers of the corkwood may be ground
to a black drink that tastes, of all things,
like Coca Cola.

But I, who burn with ignorance,
revere this truth. Yet could
not be content with its veracity.

For this place does not belong
to me, who came here
on the highway strewn with upturned carcasses
of cars and kangaroos; who walked
with sand-shoed sacrilege
on the munga trail,
then washed the red earth from my skin,
and carefully scraped it
from my shoe
and thought I could cleanse myself this way;
who existed only from the moment
of
my
birth,
plunged into a cold, disinfected world
attached by such a fragile cord,
indirectly,
to the meaning of things.

Who must build my own connections.

And I, who once saw
my family tree,
drawn in thin black lines on a
piece of paper,
am drawn to your thin brown feet
planted firm in the earth
as if you had grown there.

It is I who roam
a desert.

And I must also tell you
that I had to run to my safe place,
encased in concrete to keep out the dust,
before I could write down this story.

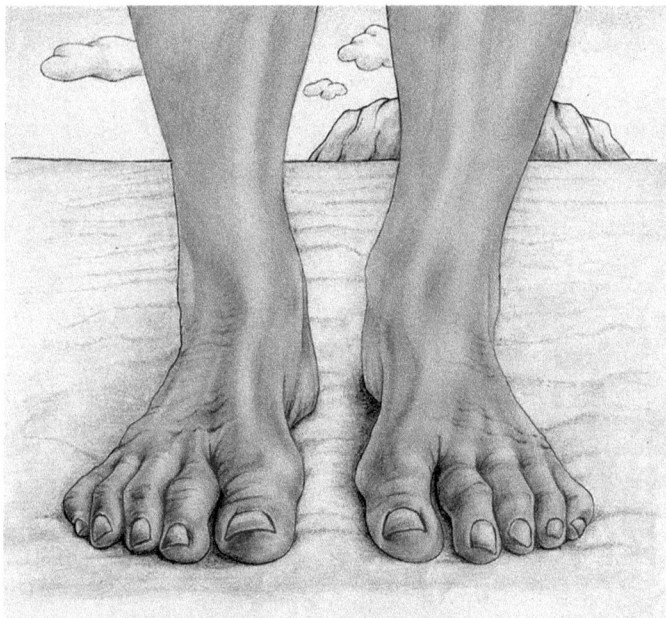

Law

Justice? You get justice in the next world. In this one you have the law.
William Gaddis

When we were very small, Lennie and I played together, were bathed together, fought together, slept in the same room and spent holidays at the beach together. Since he had been there before me, there was no reason for me to ask how he came to be in our family any more than I wondered at that age about where I had come from. For my parents and older siblings who had known life without him, I suppose the story of his coming into our family was a simple tale about love and the desire to care and provide, to live out their deeply felt Christian principles.

But lurking behind that personal story is a different one about the devastating power of colonial law. A woman named Sarah told the Stolen Generations Inquiry that her institutionalisation had been an experience of naked, arbitrary power: 'it just seemed to be that the power was enormous. We were able to be dealt with just like that.'[45] This chapter is my attempt to understand the unfettered colonial power that shaped my brother's life.

From 1940 to 1953, while William Penhall was South Australian Chief Protector of Aborigines, Aboriginal children were removed from their families even where no legal power existed, a practice that is said to have continued up to four years after the end of Penhall's reign.[46] This means that Len's fostering into our family towards the end of 1956 might have been, amongst other things, without legal foundation. Following the repeal of the Aboriginal Affairs Act in 1962, the Aboriginal Protection Board's automatic guardianship of all Aboriginal children in the state lapsed. But colonial governments invariably find ways to govern the colonised, so individual removals continued under general welfare law. There was a brief return soon after to policies favouring institutionalisation which was reportedly thought to promote positive Aboriginal identity, although it's not clear what sort of white institutions would be likely to produce that effect.[47]

The policy shifted again in 1967 towards placements with Aboriginal families, although no doubt what was happening on the ground did not change quite as rapidly. This new thinking apparently arose from a growing body of evidence that children raised in white foster homes almost invariably experienced problems with self-image, mental health and family formation.[48] The Aboriginal Child Care Agency that was charged with putting this new thinking into action was not formed in South Australia until 1978.[49] It was not until 1983, three years after Len's death, that the Department of Community Welfare adopted as official policy the Aboriginal Child Placement Principle that enshrined the importance of Aboriginal children being raised in Aboriginal families. Full incorporation into legislation wasn't achieved until 1988.

Len's initial fostering with our family occurred under the Aboriginal Affairs Act, at a time when the state government exercised absolute power over the lives of Aboriginal people. It's unlikely that later reforms brought any benefits to him or his birth family. Throughout the 1960s the governor retained the power to make regulations for the 'care, maintenance and education of Aboriginal children'.[50] Oppressive powers, such as expulsion for minor offences, were still exercised by mission superintendents, as Len's family at Koonibba knew from personal experience. Although different sources agree that 'full-blood' Aboriginal children were seldom removed from their families, the Bringing Them Home report notes that Indigenous children with disabilities, such as Len, were over-represented in welfare statistics and were particularly likely to be placed with non-Aboriginal families.[51] Clearly, Len's birth defect had placed him doubly at risk.

On the other side of the removal laws, it was white families who were given all the choice. The cover of a published collection of stories given in evidence to the Stolen Generations Inquiry shows a chilling photograph of six little girls in identical white smocks that appeared in a Darwin newspaper in the 1930s.[52] In the accompanying story, the Minister for the Interior is appealing for charitable white families to take in these 'half caste' and 'quadroon' children 'to rescue them from becoming outcasts', presumably from their Aboriginal communities. The reader of this copy of the paper has drawn a cross on the chest of one child – notably the tallest and the fairest – and written, 'I like the little girl in centre of group, but if taken by anyone else, any of the others would do, as long as they are strong.'

A quarter of a century later the language may have changed, and possibly the motives driving removals, but the technique of using newspaper articles to offer children for fostering and adoption into white homes was still in play. When my parents saw the heart-melting photograph of little Len in the Adelaide Advertiser, he was certainly neither strong nor fair, and their intention was not to cultivate him for a life of domestic servitude. Nor had they selected him from a line-up of children on offer to the highest bidder. Nevertheless, they chose him, no doubt believing that was what god intended. This sense of Christian duty to help the less fortunate was compounded, I suspect, by my mother's compulsion to reproduce the kind of protective mothering she had experienced growing up as a physically vulnerable child.

At this point, I need to explain that I'm setting this out as an attempt to understand everyone's point of view. But no doubt you are burning to interject, 'What about Len's own mother? What choices did she have?' Extremely few, it would seem. The Bringing Them Home inquiry never heard Len's particular story. And there is no possibility of finding out his parents' views about it now. But the inquiry report has sometimes helped me think through fundamental questions like these. First, it distinguishes between 'forcible removals', in which coercion was obvious, and those that were 'truly voluntary'.[53] In the space in between, the inquiry found a murky area in which all the duress of social and economic marginalisation, of inequalities of power, and of racist, ill-informed, moralising judgements were played out in decisions made over Aboriginal lives. Aboriginal parents might submit to separation, the inquiry found, because they were invited to believe it was 'for the best', given the precarious positions they occupied within a white-dominated society. Or they might be lied to, tricked or misled about the nature and longevity of the placement.

Nowadays, the best children's hospitals tend to have brightly coloured animals painted on the walls, host visits from children's entertainers, and offer spaces for families to stay when their children are gravely ill. But hospitals were a place of particular vulnerability for Aboriginal parents in the 1950s and 60s. Many children were taken away after being sent for treatment, often in circumstances in which the wishes of parents were ignored or misrepresented. The national inquiry reported cases in which children were removed without permission after their parents had freely consented to their hospital treatment. In other cases of extreme duress, proposals about placing children into care 'were presented in such a way that families could not refuse them'.[54] At other times, the lack of parental choice was even more blatant. Bruce Trevorrow, Australia's first successful Stolen Generations litigant, was described by one legal commentator as being taken from his family in South Australia 'by stealth' when he was just over one year old and without legal authority; he 'simply disappeared from hospital' and was placed with a white family who, like ours, had responded to a newspaper advertisement.[55] Another strategy reported in the Bringing Them Home report, was the 'permanent retention of children who were voluntarily placed in respite care, in educational institutions or in hospital on the understanding that the placement was temporary and for a specific and defined purpose', often procured by what the inquiry described as 'a false promise or a lie'.[56]

It seems likely that this was the sort of choice facing Leonard and Clara. My mother told me on more than one occasion, with an air of regret rather than judgement, that Clara had experienced problems with alcohol. Supposing that were true, it is difficult to untangle whether this contributed to, or resulted from, the loss of her youngest child.

The Bringing Them Home report points out that Aboriginal parents might resort to alcohol, in large part, because they were undermined in their social roles by the loss of their children. In the cruellest twist of all, judgements about 'problem drinking' might then work against the family's chances of regaining custody.

Despite the separation from their birth families, the Bringing Them Home report acknowledged that Aboriginal children sometimes came to love their new legal guardians, an outcome that was at once a blessing for the fostered child and a further tragedy for their first families. The inquiry acknowledged that foster-families might also be considered to be victims of assimilationist policies and the targets of official dishonesty. One mother, who was wrongly told that the child she had adopted had been sick and not wanted by her birth family, told the Inquiry:

> We would never have deprived any mother of her child, nor any child of its mother. This business has been very painful to us, ever since his natural mother told us she had asked for him back... We have the saddest situation one could possibly imagine...somehow someone made this decision and ruined his life.[57]

*

Eventually, the law that had brought Lennie to us took him away again. I would have been nine or ten years old when things started to unravel. It was around 1967, I would think, the year that Australia voted to have Aboriginal people recognised, for the first time, as part of the population. But for me it was the year that the world as I knew it came crashing down. Something that had been simmering in Len finally erupted into a volcano of anger and confusion. He began to run away from school and from us, and external authorities entered our lives. His rage and rebellion were no longer confined within the walls of our kitchen, and I began to be called to the headmaster's office for interrogations about my brother's whereabouts. Me, who is always the first to finish my work in class; who then sits quietly so as not to attract attention or disrupt the others; who is captain of the netball team; who is always asked, to my eternal shame, to mind the class when the teacher is out; who, notwithstanding concerted efforts at times to break the rules, never seems to get into trouble.

The spaces into which I somehow mould myself – unenthusiastically, but with a certain degree of success – have no room for Len. He becomes overwhelmed by the need to escape from the life that he is at once trapped in and excluded from. At some point, it is rumoured that Len has set fire to the school shed. I don't know if that is true. He starts going missing from home as well and, sickened with worry, my parents resort to calling the police to bring him back.

Len starts to build up an impressive juvenile record. Not for theft or joyriding, as far as I know. Not the kind of collective thrill-seeking associated with high-spirited lads from the wrong side of the tracks. I don't know exactly what he is supposed to have done wrong. His life just becomes perpetual trouble. There is some alcohol-fuelled, frustrated violence. This might be cause, or it might be effect. There is a series of boys' homes and training centres, where much of the training seems to take the form of brutality and abuse.[58] A letter I received from Family and Youth Services (FAYS) in South Australia in 2003 informs me that Len was admitted to Windana boy's home in 1968 for 'safekeeping'. Within the same year, he is sent to Glandore Boys' Home, then to Brookway Park, until his eventual 'placement' in Magill Training Centre. It seems he has been convicted of something. Having achieved all the usual milestones along the 'youth justice' conveyor belt, he has now graduated to the serious reformatory. All that I know is that he is gone from home for long stretches of time. I don't really want to know more.

I go sometimes with Mum and Dad to sit with Len in visiting rooms that have scuffed linoleum floors, plastic tables and chairs, and windows that are installed high in the walls (to avoid glimpses of the world outside, perhaps, that might create hope or invite disorder?). We take him family-size bottles of soft drink and large blocks of Cadbury's chocolate that he devours while we are there. (He's still a 'one marshmallow kid', it seems, or maybe it's just too risky there to keep that kind of currency on you.)

Although it's not mentioned in the official records, I know from conversations at home that Len spends time at some stage in the notorious Mount Barker Boys' Home run by the Salvation Army. That home was also known as Eden Park and was later the subject of a class action to compensate survivors of physical and sexual abuse and the subject of a memoir written by a survivor.[59] Mum tells me, many years after Len's death, that he had bad experiences there. I ask my brother Neil about it much later still, who says that Len came home from there with a back bruised from beatings, and who knows what other invisible scars. Neil says he thinks the incident may even have been mentioned in state parliament, possibly after Dad had appealed to our local MP. None of it is discussed with me at the time and I remain cocooned tightly in my protective shell.

When he is not institutionalised, social workers are called in to keep Len on track. He's in his late teens by now, and falls in love, inappropriately, with one of them. Apparently, he throws a knife at another one. At some point, Len becomes a ward of the state. The letter from FAYS states that he was 'committed into the care' of the department on 9/7/1968 and 'released from its care and control' on 14/4/1972, the day before his eighteenth birthday. While he was often away from home by that time, either in some kind of institution or on the west coast with his relatives, he remained part of our family as far as we were concerned, in the same way that he always had been. But as a state ward, I suppose Mum and Dad had no more say in decisions about his life than his birth parents. This legal status seemed to mean that Len could be locked up, not because he had broken into someone's house or stolen someone's car, but simply because he was resisting the fate that had been ordained for him.

By my late teens and young adulthood, I had started to dabble in what would be described today as 'risky behaviour'. Nothing too dramatic. While I'm consciously trying to shake off the 'responsible' image that has always attached itself to me, I actually dread the intervention of authorities of any kind. I suppose, to paraphrase the late and great Leonard Cohen, I was trying, in my way, to be free. But no matter how reckless I become with my life, the law in its many guises never bothers with me.

It all starts innocently enough: I sneak out of the high school biology lab on a regular basis (the long benches make for good cover until the final dash for the door) and take my friends to the drive-in bottle department in the ancient Morris Minor my parents bought me for my sixteenth birthday. The teachers don't seem to notice. In my matriculation year when I should be studying for exams, I spend most of 'swot vac' playing cricket on the beach with other disaffected kids from my class, pretending I don't care about doing well. My results still put me on the state's honour roll and get me into university. On my eighteenth birthday, I get so drunk in the Adelaide Uni bar that I drive the Morris Minor over the kerb and into a flower bed on the banks of the River Torrens, coming to rest just before what would have been a final death plunge into the water, then reverse out and somehow find my way home. I manage to escape drowning, culpable homicide and drink driving charges, on that and many other occasions. I appear to be protected by an aura of respectability, normality and whiteness. I am simultaneously powerless and indestructible.

In my philosophy tutorial, I think it's smart to reply 'hedonist' when each of us is asked to describe our personal value system. Even as I say it, I know this is just a cynical label to cover the cavernous void inside. Despite my disdain for religion, I have unconsciously internalised many of my parents' Christian values. They linger subcutaneously, always threatening to spoil the party. But, lacking any alternative plan, hedonism is what I settle on for the next few years. I just like the way that it sounds and it has the added merit of not requiring any self-examination.

Like many young women growing up in the post-pill, pre-HIV 70s, I have my share of sexual adventures. I show more restraint with respect to mind-bending drugs, which consist at that time primarily of alcohol, hash, weed and – for the truly hard-core – speed. Despite cultivating a veneer of casual recklessness, I sense that the fragile balance of my mind would not survive the assault of psychotropic substances. I am the only person in the world – or so I think at the time – who can become paranoid rather than mellow after taking a harmless draw on a bong – so the prospect of tripping further into the depths of my psyche on anything stronger is terrifying.

Although I don't emerge from this period completely unscathed, I somehow manage to hold together the appearance of a normal life and, most importantly, avoid intrusions of any kind from formal authority. In contrast, Len's entrapment by the law is encapsulated in this single sentence written to me by child welfare officials in 2003:

> During his placement with your parents [not his?], Mr & Mrs Weber [missing second comma! – my annoyance is making me pedantic now] he went in and out of Windana and Magill Training Centre because he absconded from either foster care or institutional care [indignant italicisation and square brackets definitely not in original].

Joseph Heller could hardly have concocted a more dazzlingly self-justifying statement for his Catch-22 narrator. According to the official script, Len had to be confined in one kind of institution because he had escaped from another kind. Worst of all, in the departmental files, our family home counted as one of those institutions, a disturbing revelation that was later confirmed in South Australia's Supreme Court.[60]

Medicine

The diagnosis of paranoid schizophrenic was not offered me where I could look kindly back onto the earnest practitioner and say, 'you're wrong. It's really just a lifetime of grief'.
        'Hope', quoted in Judith Herman, *Trauma and Recovery*

Apart from religion (more about that later), illness was the lens through which our mother viewed the world. Doctors were figures of supreme authority in her life and their proclamations were followed to the letter. During my teenage years, Mum consumed a small mountain of prescription pills each day – yellow ones to regulate her faulty heart, white ones to thin the blood, red ones to drain the fluid that would otherwise collect in her lungs, and an assortment of other potions to alleviate ailments that were real enough but had probably been caused by taking the other pills. Whenever her doctor recommended an antibiotic for one of the children or a change in her own medication, she would comply without question. I suppose that was not so uncommon in a less sceptical era before Dr Google when doctors were looked up to in working class communities like ours as all-knowing demi-gods.

When Mum was advised by her family doctor to eat six serves of vegetables each day for the sake of her cholesterol, she really took it to extremes. Thereafter, preparations for our family dinner had to commence in mid-afternoon so that an enormous steamer could be filled to the brim with vegetables of every hue. And when men in white coats began to appear on our black and white telly warning us that our homes were teaming with deadly microbes, my mum's cupboards filled up with liquids, powders and sprays of every description.

It might seem pointless to record these trivial observations. But I have come to understand them as indicators of what I would now call – very grandly – obedience to authority.[61] This is not surprising considering that Mum's formative years had been largely governed by medical pronouncements. With doctors predicting that she would not live beyond her teens, and with no effective treatments available for her condition, she had been subjected to a cosseted childhood, where she was prevented from participating in energetic pursuits. While other kids were playing boisterously in the schoolyard, Mum would be made to sit alone on the veranda and read a book – a not unpleasant pastime when engaged in voluntarily, but otherwise a bitter restriction. When she showed every sign of defying her prognosis and living into adulthood, medical opinion once again put an end to Mum's dream of becoming a nurse, also advising against marriage, especially the rigours of childbirth.

In a rare act of rebellion against the strictures imposed on her life, she did marry and devoted herself with passion to the vocations of home-making, caregiving and mothering, which she elevated to the highest pinnacle of human achievement. She made clear to her children her disapproval of corruptions of the hallowed word 'mother', but her pro-testations fell on deaf ears and she was destined to endure a lifetime of 'mumhood'.

She filled my early years with a constant stream of propaganda about the sanctity of motherhood, with tales about nursing her ailing mother until her death, and of the joy of bringing a new life into the world to brighten her declining years, which was apparently my designated role. Until I was old enough to declare that I wanted to be an archaeologist – purely for the pleasure of showing that I knew such a sophisticated word – I would obediently answer 'a mummy' whenever an adult posed the obligatory question about what I wanted to be when I grew up. And I didn't mean the sort of mummies that attract the attention of actual archaeologists.

The failure of the medical profession to predict the course of Mum's life, and her avoidance of premature death, might have been enough to convince other people of the fallibility of medical opinion. Instead, doctors remained amongst Mum's staunchest advisors, and dealing with ill health – her own and others' – became her vocation. Sickness brought an opportunity to unleash her most intensive form of mothering which, as a ferociously independent child, I was more inclined to think of as smothering. Fortunately, my robust health meant that being bought an ice cream as a reward for submitting to an injection was the most extreme form of maternal attention I was likely to attract.

Despite my cynicism, I will concede with the benefit of hindsight that my strongest memories of maternal nurture arise from the rare occasions when I found myself home from school due to illness. I would spend those sick days propped up in bed, reading voraciously, having damp cloths applied to a burning forehead. Once the fever had passed, Mum would bring me boiled eggs with funny faces drawn on in biro, which I would eat by dipping strips of buttered toast that we called 'soldier boys' into the runny yoke. If I was lucky, lunch would be a meat pie fetched from the deli across the road that I would eat by carefully peeling off the lid, adding tomato sauce then scraping out the filling with a spoon, leaving the pastry for last. If I was very lucky, Mum would bring me a tray filled with colourful home-made play dough for me to mould into lumpy works of art.

While these were rare experiences for me, my older brother Neil, born nearly ten years before Len joined the family, had been the kind of child described in those days as 'failing to thrive'. I don't know how well his condition was understood at the time, but he undoubtedly had serious, undiagnosed auto-immune complaints. This resulted in regular emergency dashes to the hospital following life-threatening convulsions, and long periods at home being nursed by Mum and separated from other children his age. While not exactly a cause for celebration, Neil's ill health had enabled our mother to fulfil her nursing aspirations. It also, unwittingly, provided an opportunity to reproduce the patterns of her own restricted childhood.

Len's arrival into the family brought a new range of medical challenges. When Len and I were very young, the Adelaide Children's Hospital van – painted all over with iconic Australian animals – would pull up outside our house several times a week to take him for treatment. Mum would continue the therapy at home, massaging and manipulating his surgically sculpted feet for hours on end, fitting the various medieval contraptions that he wore for sleeping, and supervising the exercises devised by therapists. Later, it would be his emotional and mental health that would take precedence, although the remedies in that case were less clear and definitely beyond the grasp of any of us.

The multiple challenges that faced Len as he matured could be viewed, if one chose, through a medical lens. As Len's emotional and behavioural problems mounted, his explosive childhood aggression would be labelled 'epilepsy', his self-destructive teenage drinking 'alcoholism', and the damage this eventually caused to his developing brain 'Korsakoff syndrome' or 'wet brain'. Finally, we were told that his psychological disintegration had resulted in 'schizophrenia'. These labels imposed some kind of order onto the chaos his life had become – but offered few solutions and still further disempowerment.

The medical labels attached to Len's predicament appeared to be accepted without question within our household. Len was behaving as he was because he was sick. Although I couldn't have articulated why that explanation made me uneasy. It seemed to me that illness became just another form of entrapment. At university in the late-1970s studying psychology, philosophy and genetics, I had landed in the centre of the nature-nurture debate. I intuitively rejected both deterministic extremes on the same grounds that had led me to reject religious dogma. I was deeply suspicious of certainty. While I didn't feel I had the answers to many of life's fundamental questions, my studies made me dubious about cut-and-dried opinions that seemed too neat, too narrow, too superficial and altogether too complacent to capture all of life's messiness and mystery.

Various canons of accepted wisdom that I heard my parents repeat – such as Aboriginal people being vulnerable to alcoholism due to a deficiency in a particular enzyme – seemed simplistic and possibly even racist. Even if it was part of the story – and I didn't know one way or the other – it could not surely be all there was to know about why the lives of so many Aboriginal people, along with non-Aboriginal people, descended into alcohol-induced oblivion. R.D. Laing's existentialist views on the social construction of schizophrenia provided an extra layer of scepticism and convinced me that labels offered no kind of explanation at all. While there was no denying the associated symptoms and behaviour, Laing saw them as 'normal' human responses to being placed in impossible situations – a psychiatric version, perhaps, of what Judith Butler has referred to as 'unliveable lives'.[62] This perspective, whatever its limitations, at least invited scrutiny of the wider circumstances of sufferers' lives. Even Len's supposed epilepsy looked to me like an eruption of authentic, suppressed anger, rather than just a random brain malfunction. I did not fully grasp at the time the reasons for this anger, but when I looked back later, they were not hard to find.

In 1997, the Bringing Them Home report concluded that 'welfare departments continue to pathologise and individualise protection needs of Indigenous children'.[63] This is problematic, they argue, because a medicalised approach locates problems solely within individuals themselves and, by focusing the microscope within, may divert attention from a toxic external environment. The words of Hope – a survivor of childhood abuse interviewed by trauma researcher Judith Herman – point to the underlying harms that can be left unexamined if medical labels are treated as ends in themselves:

> Long ago, a lovely young child was branded with the term paranoid schizophrenic…the label became a heavy yoke… Somehow the dreaded words got sprinkled on my cereal, rinsed into my clothes… The words 'paranoid schizophrenic' started to fall into place, letter by letter, but it looked like feelings and thoughts and actions that hurt children, and lied, and covered disgrace, and much terror.[64]

By the 1970s, knowledge was accumulating about the types of experiences that could create lasting damage in young children. Psychological and neurological studies pointed to the crucial importance of the first two years of life in particular, initially to the physical development of the brain and later to the formation of personal and collective identity. The Bringing Them Home report noted that early separation could result in fragmented identities and problems with attachment. Self-harm, risk-taking and substance abuse were likely to follow in order to ease feelings of hopelessness, marginalisation and lack of self-worth. As with so many of the other problems identified, the inquiry found that foster-carers of Aboriginal children rarely responded appropriately to trauma reactions and signs of grief associated with loss of family.

No doubt ours was one of the many families who failed to react appropriately to these signals. The first two and a half years of Len's life were spent mainly in medical institutions and in at least one failed foster placement. One would think that the seeds of insecurity and emotional detachment had already been sown, even before Lennie came to live with us. My father and sister told me, long after his death, that even as a toddler, Len's mood would swing abruptly from a broad smile one minute to unprovoked anger the next. The 'Cross Nennie' photos are a case in point.

*

When I was about a year old and Len around four, my parents paid a professional photographer to take some portraits of the newest members of the family. The pictures that went on display in the family home showed a cherubic and inquisitive little girl, and a beaming little boy with mischievous sparkling eyes. But the full set of thumbnail prints tells a different story. While the first and last few frames show little Len smiling radiantly for the camera, in the shots in between his features are fixed into a determined scowl. When he was shown the thumbnails later, Lennie replied that the ones in the middle were 'Cross Nennie'. The term became part of our family folklore – along with my big sister saying, 'No, my naughty little fingers did it' when asked whether it was she who had scratched a piece of furniture, and calling her dressing gown her 'gownigan'. 'Here comes Cross Nennie' became the catch cry whenever little Len was transformed by the melancholic mood that often overtook him.

*

Len's destructive drinking began when he was not even into his teens. Although my parents did very little recreational drinking (my mother's daily shot of brandy, she would remind us with a mischievous smile, was for medicinal purposes only), they were not narrow-minded about alcohol in trademark Methodist fashion, and always kept a few beverages in the house for guests or special occasions. What started with a youthful Len pilfering sweet liqueur from the cupboard to pour onto his ice cream ended only a few years later with the family having to hide or lock away anything in the house that contained alcohol, including aftershave, cough medicine and methylated spirits. Len was never a happy drunk. Our parents suffered broken ribs on more than one occasion trying to pacify him. Sharp knives had to be hidden to prevent him from harming himself. They had to be stealthily retrieved when it was time to prepare dinner, taking care not to reveal the latest hiding place. A heavy atmosphere descended on the house, thick with foreboding and worry.

I came to dread the sound of the telephone ringing in the dead of the night. It was the usual endgame of Len being 'out on a bust'. If it was a drinking mate of Len's calling, our gentle dad, who hardly ever entered a pub, would quickly pull on some clothes and drive to the Carrington Hotel in the south end of the city centre to extricate Len before he got himself in trouble. At other times, it would be too late for pre-emptive missions. If it was the police who called, Dad would go and collect Len from the city watch house. Or sometimes a taxi would pull up in the middle of the night, the driver would ring the doorbell for the fare, and Len would stumble in, sometimes aggressive, sometimes on the point of losing consciousness. Once, not so late at night, I answered the door myself to find Len with his face swollen beyond recognition following a beating by members of the 'local law enforcement community' (to steal some Blues Brothers terminology). Perhaps on other occasions a kindly cop might have been the one to put him in a taxi, but that's not something I ever saw for myself.

Against a backdrop of pointless, revolving-door incarcerations on public drunkenness charges, Len started to accrue time away from home in mental health facilities and alcohol rehab centres as well. When I returned home in my early twenties after a short spell of living interstate, I found him to be unrecognisable – bloated from alcohol and prescription drugs; sporting a full-face beard that might be fashionable in hipster circles today but made him look like an unkempt elderly man; and with defeated, downcast eyes. From time to time, the alcohol would unleash all the frustration that had built up in his body like a volcanic eruption – all the hatred of himself, of the black world that he thought had abandoned him, the white world that had rejected and tormented him, and of our family who had wedged him between the two in our Love Trap.

I don't presume to know what was going on in Len's mind during all those tortured years. I don't recall ever trying to talk with him about any of his troubles. I am still trying to work out why not. But I think the story of Eric, recounted in the Bringing Them Home report, would approximate Len's state of mind. Like Len, Eric had been institutionalised and then fostered from the age of two and a half. His psychiatrist testified to the inquiry as follows:

> He says looking within himself that he's a kind-hearted person, that it's not him to be angry or violent, but he certainly recalls a period of time in his life when it was the only behaviour that he felt able to use to protect himself.[65]

This of course makes perfect sense. And so it was that Cross Nennie continued to live with us alongside the gentle and kind-hearted Len that was his true self.

As Len's mental state deteriorated and he began to hear voices urging him to kill us, my dad fitted chain locks on the bedroom doors and insisted that I barricade my door with furniture at night for extra security. Despite that, I don't ever recall being afraid of Len, and the fortification of our family home only increased my anguish. It was a torment to hear Len prowling up and down the corridor late at night, physically and emotionally separated from people who loved him, as he had already been from his first family. Len had become exiled within his own home, the place that had once been his sanctuary. Sometimes he would talk to us, without threat or anger in his voice, through the locked door. But my parents by this stage would never risk opening it, not out of spite but for the sake of self-preservation.

I am a young adult now, having moved back into the parental home for a short while after some years away at university. I'm woken in the middle of the night by the sound of agitated voices in the corridor outside my bedroom door. Len has come home after a drinking session lasting several days. I put my head under the pillow and try to block out the voices, but something about their tone and pitch disturbs me more than usual and I decide I must investigate. I turn on the light and slide back the dressing table I had pushed across the doorway before I went to bed. I undo the security chain and fling open the door to find all three of them not more than a metre away: my mother, father and Len. Len has a huge kitchen knife in his right hand and is hacking into his left forearm with great sweeping strokes that look crazed and mechanical. My parents are standing either side of him trying their best to stop him. Blood has spattered all over the walls and is trickling down between the leaves of the fleur-de-lis wallpaper. The unexpected opening of the door startles Len. He stops and looks intensely in my direction, then strides towards me with the knife raised high above his head and a demonic expression distorting his face. I back as far as I can into my room until I hit up against a chair that is pushed against the wall. I'm trapped, yet strangely calm. It's not that I'm frozen with terror. I'm frozen with trust. It is not possible for me to form the thought that my brother could hurt me. Len is right in front of me now. Our tiny, frail mother has launched herself onto the arm that is wielding the knife and has been lifted completely off the ground. The weight of her acts as a circuit breaker, and a miraculous transformation occurs. Len's face visibly softens. His eyes and mine are locked, and what I see now is not hatred or murderous intent. It is recognition and love. He has seen me. The energy drains away from his body as he collapses into my arms. I stagger under the burden of his weight as the knife falls harmlessly onto the floor. It is over.

That was the first time I realised there was something constructive I could do to help. I suppose it was a coming of age. I wrapped Len's arm tightly in a towel and prepared to help our father get him to hospital. While I was tending to Len's bleeding, I noticed that Dad was busily wiping the blood off the wallpaper. I was horrified about his priorities, but too stunned to say anything. Not until many years later would I come to realise that this intensely pragmatic response, this attempt to render horrific events normal, was Dad's way of coping with years of relentless strain that would have broken a less stoical man. At the hospital, I try to defend my brother from the unsympathetic nurses who see him as 'just another drunken Aborigine'. They smirk when I demand to know why he is not being given painkillers while they stitch his lacerated arm back together. 'He's already well anaesthetised,' they say.

*

Sometime before I made my final escape to England, not long after the episode with the knife, Len and I went to the pictures together in town. It was a simple enough thing to do, but we attracted curious glances from passers-by who seemed to be wondering what relationship there could possibly be between us. I felt uncomfortable and exposed to unwanted scrutiny. But I also felt like an adult, deciding. For the first time in my life, I was doing something independent and planned with my brother. Getting to know each other again after becoming estranged, first by his absences, and then by mine. We were just trying to be normal, and it felt empowering. But it was only a matter of months before I was at the airport with a few possessions hastily stuffed into a backpack, five hundred dollars in a bum bag and a one-way ticket to London. 'Following my star' was how our mother described it, the biblical reference not lost on me. But from where I stood it felt more like I was clinging to a passing meteorite that was hurtling towards a gigantic black hole. I don't think I ever said proper goodbyes to my family, although I had given them no indication of when and if I would return. I have an image of Len sitting alone in the departure lounge, looking downcast and drawn into himself. I hope at least I paused long enough to give him some recognition and a hug. As it turned out, I would never see him again.

Religion

Aborigines have suffered almost as much over the past two hundred years from misguided benevolence as from the actions of those with evil intent.
Henry Reynolds, *Aboriginal Sovereignty*

As you may have gathered by now, the church was the centre of our family's world. My parents were founding members of our local Methodist church, and in the years before I was born and before the church hall was built, Sunday school classes had been held in our home. When the church was finally built, it was within walking distance of virtually everyone we knew. It was a close-knit and homogeneous community, and we called our parents' friends Auntie and Uncle. Every Sunday, Mum's trained soprano voice would soar majestically above the mewling of the rest of the congregation. It was her domain. At Christmas time, while other kids were out at daybreak riding their new bikes or playing football in the street, Len and I would have to content ourselves with a peek at the Christmas tree through the keyhole of the lounge room door just to be sure that Father Christmas had delivered the presents. Religious observance and restraint came first in our household and presents had to wait until after we returned from church.

Our pleasures were all simple and family-oriented, but it was a happy enough childhood. Each year, our parents would rent a beach house at one of the pristine beaches south of Adelaide for the long summer holiday. Once his allocated leave was up, Dad would sometimes travel from there into the city and right across the sprawling suburbs to Elizabeth in the northern outskirts of town to do his job helping people find work in the car factories and shops, while the rest of us took turns paddling our old wooden surf-ski in the calm waters and ate sandy ham sandwiches on the beach. At other times of the year, our treats would be Sunday drives to see the autumn leaves in the Adelaide Hills in our FJ Holden 'Bluebird', or to Flash Gelati in Hindley Street for cones piled with the most eye-watering lemon sorbet in town. Only once did we holiday further afield, driving all the way to the glamorous Gold Coast with Len, me and our toy poodle Jacques in the back seat of Dad's beige Kingswood, stopping at small towns along the way and waking up to delicious country breakfasts. Most memorable of all, although for all the wrong reasons, was driving across the Sydney Harbour Bridge on the way home (our only attempt at sightseeing in the nation's most populous city), all of us rigid with stress while Mum shrieked at Dad not to collide with the fast-moving cars either side of us.

Once a year, Mum would stay up all night with her mother-in-law, my live-in German gran, baking cakes, pies and rock buns that would be loaded into brand-new plastic bins to be devoured the next day by hordes of kids at the Sunday school picnic. Picnic day was one of the most exciting days of the year, second only to Christmas, and without doubt the best thing about church. We had a ramshackle old house that had once been a suburban farm from which my widowed grandmother and her son had eked out a meagre living. During my childhood years, the house was still surrounded by a large block of land filled with almond orchards and grapevines and chicken coops tended to by Dad. Although much of the original acreage had been sold, it remained the epicentre for many community activities that required that kind of space. Early in the morning on Sunday school picnic day, two or three chartered buses would pull into our backyard and would quickly be filled with excited kids carrying jam tins with string handles and kitchen strainers they would use to catch tadpoles in the stony creeks that trickled through the Belair National Park.

My older siblings had grown up within this religious community, been confirmed and become Sunday school teachers, played in church sports teams, won anniversary day prizes, played the organ or sung in the choir, attended church socials, met prospective partners and, in my brother's case, married within the church. If truth be told, the main attraction for my musical brother Neil was probably the opportunity to play the organ and manage the church choir. But my sister's religious devotion was real and enduring. After the disappointment of a broken engagement, rather than go on a backpacking tour for consolation or embark on an ill-judged affair – either of which would have been more likely choices for me at the same age – Bev signed up for a stint of voluntary teaching in a religious mission school in the remote New Guinea highlands. I was separated from my older siblings, not just by half a generation, but also by a profoundly different world view.

My life had largely revolved around the church as well until I reached my mid-teens and had to confront the thorny question of confirmation. Perhaps there were nascent signs of an irreligious nature even earlier, such as my choice of material the time I decided to sing to my primary school class during show and tell. The song was on the radio at the time and was called 'It Ain't Necessarily So'. I still remember the tune, and the chorus that cautioned listeners not to believe everything they found written in the holy book. The teacher cut short the performance and hustled me back to my seat.

I don't think my parents' brand of Christian belief was any crazier than the other kinds on offer – based, as they all are, to varying degrees, on the reification of faith over reason, a belief in immaculate conception, salvation through human sacrifice, and the promise of life after death. They were not in the ranks of the happy clappers awaiting rapture every Sunday with eyes and arms raised to the heavens that have now come to dominate our public life, even beyond the pulpit. My parents would have been horrified at the exclusivity and hatred these beliefs have sometimes engendered, and rejected any notion that personal prosperity was a religious virtue. Their Methodism was simple and unassuming, based on humility, service to others and a belief in a just and universally loving god.

But I had known from my early teenage years that path was not for me. There seemed to be better ways of answering life's questions, and more important questions to ask than the ones posed by the earnest men dressed in 1970s pastel suits who spoke to us from the pulpit every Sunday during my early adolescence. For one thing, I could never come to terms with the idea that the meek would inherit the earth – which seemed to be a very convenient let-off for the ruthless, who seemed always on the lookout to exploit them.

The depth of my resolve to avoid confirmation was partly a matter of conscience and partly because church bored and mortified me in equal measure, particularly where symbolic feasting on the body of Christ was concerned. And that's exactly what awaited me at confirmation. For the teenage me, religion was, at worst, rather creepy; but even at its best, a complete waste of precious time.

One evening, sometime after my heathenism had been fully revealed, my mother crept into the darkened room and sat on the floor beside my bed. It was unusual, and filled me with foreboding. She had come to convey to me her despair that, while the rest of the family would be joyously reunited in the world beyond this one, I alone would be missing. In her mind, I would be lost to them for eternity in the afterlife, even more comprehensively than Len had been lost to his own mother in this one. It was indeed a desolate prospect if that's what you believed. I suppose that moment of excommunication from the family marked a turning point in my life, although I understood it at the time merely as another source of inescapable misery. No doubt she had meant it as a plea – although it sounded more like a threat - that she hoped would bring me into the fold. Instead, a huge abyss opened up between us and I fell in head first.

*

There are many ways that someone can be marked as an outsider. Differences that set you apart can be in your own mind or the minds of others. Whereas Len faced his biggest challenges regarding acceptance in the world outside our home and religious community, it was within my own family that I experienced my most abiding sense of non-belonging. While Len's skin marked him outwardly as different, I carried the internal mark of the perpetually unforgiven. I went through a stage where I delighted in telling people that I was adopted. Perhaps it was mainly to test their reaction, but I think I suspected at the time that there had been some kind of mistake and I had been assigned to the wrong family. Later, as Len began to retreat further into the sanctuary of family and church, I came to think only of separating myself once and for all from the alienation I felt there.

I wake up in the bedroom I shared with my grandmother when I was aged about ten, when we were still living in our old house. This is strange because I clearly remember going to bed that night in the modern bedroom I have slept in since I was twelve when we moved to our new house by the river. In fact, it is more than strange. It is not possible. And yet it is really happening. It's dark, and as I get up, I see the light is on in the dining room and is spilling out into the corridor. I can hear voices, so I walk towards them. The whole family is gathered around the dining table. My parents, grandmother, Bev, Neil and Len. No one turns to look at me when I enter the room. I say something to get their attention, but nobody hears me. My brain registers that things are becoming increasingly odd. Perplexed, I walk up to my dad who is sitting at the head of the table and touch him on the arm. No response. He can't feel me either. Lightning bolts of horror surge through my body and lodge deep inside my gut as I realise that this is what it is like to be dead. Being invisible. Disconnected. Perpetually separated from people you love. Then, more horror as I'm led to the only explanation there can be when the impossible actually happens. Clearly. I am. In fact. Dead.

I wouldn't want to paint a picture of my parents as either bug-eyed zealots or narrow-minded bigots who imposed their religious strictures on others and were prone to harsh judgements. These are the caricatures that often inhabit the minds of those not raised in a conventionally religious family. Our parents were neither of these things, and in some ways were quite the opposite. For one thing, our home was often filled with music and dancing. They may not have been exactly debaucherous, but in their heyday Mum and Dad's New Year's Eve parties had been legendary amongst members of the West Richmond Methodist Church, and really were a whole lot of fun even for a kid. Dad would spend the day blowing up balloons to hang from the Hills hoist and spreading quicklime over the concrete slab underneath which, by evening, would be filled with foxtrotting members of the congregation. Len and I would be put to bed before the guests arrived with a view to being woken up before midnight in time to welcome in the New Year. There may have even been champagne for the toast, but, if not, some sparkling grape juice would have sufficed. On one memorable occasion, the more energetic guests had danced right through the night, then sat down at daybreak to breakfast cooked by my mother and gran, each choosing from à la carte menus written out by hand in Mum's meticulous copperplate writing.

Our mother liked to tell the tale of the only time her teetotal father, the Reverend Ernest George Neil, had been driven to drink. It was the day of her wedding, no less – Boxing Day 1941, right in the middle of wartime austerity. The day was not in the least auspicious. The weather in Adelaide was brutal, with the thermometer surging past a hundred degrees Fahrenheit. In the inferno, sandwiches were curling, icing was melting, tempers were flaring, and bride and bridesmaids were wilting while trying their best to glow in a ladylike fashion. Worst of all, the Reverend E.G. Neil, who was to perform the marriage ceremony, was nowhere to be found. It seems that whatever form of public transport he had relied on to convey him to the church had also succumbed to the heat, and he finally arrived red-faced and panting, having been forced to cover the territory on foot. By all reports, he strode straight into the kitchen and, to everyone's surprise, downed a bottle of Cooper's ale in a single gulp. It seemed to revive him, and the ceremony soon got underway, but nobody could remember afterwards whether he had actually pronounced Peter and Jean married – an embarrassing oversight, if true, that was universally blamed on the weather.

Although my grandfather had only broken his rule of abstinence out of dire necessity, he was relatively open-minded about the choices made by others. When the family was posted to a country parish in her girlhood, Mum had scandalised the parishioners by striking up a friendship with the publican's daughter. When a deputation of moral campaigners arrived at the door of the manse demanding that the unsuitable liaison be terminated, the reverend thought it the perfect opportunity to deliver a short sermon on the loving acceptance by god of each and every one of his children.

Following his lead, our parents also reached out and embraced others with an inclusiveness that I found excruciating. I mean, what teenager wants to have a twenty-minute conversation with the waitress, including detailed enquiries about every member of her family, every time she is dragged out to lunch with her parents? In return, intimate details of our family life would be shared with virtual strangers. I soon learned to reveal as little as possible, knowing that even my most private details could be offered up for mass consumption. It seemed there were no boundaries to our mother's gathering of people into the fold. Christmas shopping became more of an ordeal each year as her gift list expanded to include everyone from the doctor's receptionist to her hairdresser's new baby. It was as if my parents could only relate to people by incorporating them into their extended family. The individuals concerned appeared to be quite willing to be adopted into the fold. But to me it was an unwanted intrusion and a constant source of embarrassment.

Rather than living narrowly by a set of unbending rules, Mum and Dad conducted their lives according to broad Christian principles that were sincerely and deeply held. They believed in the redeeming power of a loving god, and in lives spent in the service of others. They taught us by example rather than through harsh indoctrination that it is more blessed to give than to receive. My father would be quizzed by the tax office each year as he indicated, truthfully, on his tax return that he had given ten per cent of his modest earnings to charity. The centrepiece of our dining table at Christmas would always be a large receptacle into which each member of the family was encouraged to place donations, however meagre, to the Christmas Bowl Appeal. Christmas was, first and foremost, a time to spare a thought, and a coin, for those less fortunate.

Our dad's honesty was without parallel. When he was young, another child had offered him a penny on the proviso that he shift his allegiance to the Norwood football club. Dad took the penny gratefully and kept his word throughout his lifetime, despite no one in the family having any connection to that distant, more privileged suburb. Even at work, Dad knew no other way to respond to others than through kindness, and many of the people he had supervised remained loyal to him long after he retired. My siblings and I met some of them for the first time at his funeral, which was attended by hundreds of people, many of whom were strangers to us. Dad was devoted to his semi-invalid wife and performed many of the household chores, such as food shopping, which would have been too much for her. At the same time, he was stoical beyond belief about his own afflictions. No one but close family members would ever have known how his body had been assaulted by disease, much of it brought on by internalised stress. The string of ailments he'd survived included polio, skin cancer, tuberculosis, debilitating dermatitis, serious ischemic heart disease and stomach-consuming ulcers, all of which he faced with a sense of acceptance that was underpinned by his unerring faith in god.

If there is one biblical verse that summarises my parents' world view, it would be the well-known maxim from Luke 6:31 which is commonly paraphrased as 'do unto others as you would have them do unto you'.[66] The Reverend E.G. Neil himself had followed this rule to a fault. During my mother's childhood in the Depression years, her father would sometimes give away one of Mum's favourite toys at Christmas to a needier child or literally take food from the family table to give to a jobless swaggy who had knocked on the door of the manse. Despite this austerity, or rather because of it, Mum considered her father to be a saint. And my dad, who had lost his own father in a farming accident while he was still a babe in arms, idolised his father-in-law too as the loving father figure he had never known. In that respect, it was a marriage made in heaven.

*

The Reverend Neil had served as a missionary in Samoa in the early part of the twentieth century. My mother – like me, the youngest in the family by a very long stretch – was the only one of his four surviving children not to be born there. Although I never knew him, the stories of his heroic exploits and self-sacrifice acquired a mythological status in our household which at first intrigued, then later disturbed, me. Who can say how much of the content was true? Without doubt, the most exciting tale of derring-do was when a volcano erupted near the mission at Satupa'itea and Papa Neil crossed the red-hot lava flow with banana leaves strapped to his feet, leading his flock to safety. There was a back-story too about how the Catholic priest had foolishly remained in the church with his flock, having put his faith in the Lord to save them. I always suspected that was just a piece of internecine propaganda, but I visited the ruin of that church over a century later and saw that lava had flowed right through the middle of it, hopefully after the congregation had decided to vote with their feet.

Then there was the time while crossing between islands in a raging storm when Papa Neil was flung violently to the bottom of a dugout canoe, causing his eardrum to burst. He was apparently trying to bring medical care to someone in urgent need, as he had done on many occasions before, although he was never trained as a doctor. Moreover, because of his knowledge of the German language, the Reverend E.G.

Neil was reputedly called upon to mediate when a German gunship steamed into Apia harbour during the escalation of tensions before the First World War. In addition, there was Papa Neil's crowning achievement – the one story for which there is material evidence – the building of the imposing chapel at Piula Theological College that sits high on a clifftop on the main island of Savai'i, after which my mother, Piula Jean, was named.

There is no doubting that the Reverend Neil was an impressive man. Born into a farming family so poor that as a young child he was forced to sleep amongst the agricultural machinery, he found a way to obtain a belated education through a scholarship to Prince Alfred College, one of Adelaide's premier schools. He then trained for the Methodist ministry at Way College, having elected to turn his back on the prospect of a university education, or so my mother always said. His form of Christianity was of the practical, no-nonsense type. Following the 'manly' tradition of Way College, he trod the path of the 'godly mechanic' – so much so that he was chastised by the church hierarchy in the first year of his missionary work for spending too much time mending mission buildings and too little time saving souls. With no training whatever in medicine or architecture, he set about administering talavai (medical care) to the local population and planning the construction of one of Samoa's iconic Victorian buildings, buoyed by the conviction that he was doing god's work. No doubt he saved as many souls along the way amongst the canny Samoans as wanted to be saved.

In my cut-and-dried teenage mind, the label 'missionary' cancelled out all those achievements. I'm not sure I fully understood at that point the role that missions had played in the colonial project, either in Australia or elsewhere, but since I'd felt personally oppressed by the requirement to attend church, I didn't much care for the idea of inflicting that impost on others. Much later, as my mind began to open to life's nuances and ambiguities, I turned to the leather-bound journal that my grandfather had kept in the first year of his missionary work, looking for insights into his thinking. It was beautifully written in careful copperplate script, starting from the time the freshly ordained minister had set sail for Samoa with his new bride Ethel. In an early entry, he explained that, while it was difficult for the pair to leave behind the land of their birth, 'the love of Christ constrains us to take the light to the world's dark places'.[67] This terminology, invoking the innate superiority of the light and white world of Christianity, immediately confirmed my worst fears. But as I continued reading, I also detected the dedication to service, humility and love for humanity that I recognised in my own parents.

Samoa must have been an eye-opening experience for an unworldly young Methodist. It's not hard to find unpalatable examples of paternalism in the pages of that journal, accompanied by an inability to understand alien cultural practices and their significance for the local people. It has been said that Aboriginal people in Australia were often regarded by church officials as 'irresponsible and unreliable in an unredeemable state of inferiority'.[68] Judging by the pages of his journal, the Reverend Neil may have agreed at times with the first two counts in relation to his Samoan charges, but certainly not with the third. On the 12 May 1903, he wrote:

> These native boys and girls have the knack of winning one's affection, with all their faults they are a loveable race of people. Probably their redeeming features are so good that one cannot long dwell on the darker side but is obliged to forget it in promise of the bright elements which are so unmistakably revealed in most of them. Surely there is plenty of scope for the grace of God to develop much beauty of character out of such promising material.[69]

While this concession – framed as it is, in a culturally bound and unwavering Christian perspective – is still not enough to absolve him in my view, my research into his time in Samoa gave me some measure of comfort about his missionary exploits. True to the universal principles of the Bible Christian movement which set great store in the involvement of the laity, history records that he agitated for greater equality for Samoans within the structure of the church,[70] and was devoted to enabling as many people as possible to experience what he saw as the love and saving grace of the holy spirit. Given that it was the only pathway to salvation he could recognise – and therein lies the problem for me – at least it is some consolation that all followers of that pathway, without exception, were to be valued as equals in the eyes of god.

My parents visited Samoa once as guests of the Samoan Methodist Church in the company of Mum's older brother Charlie, who had been born in Samoa and spent his childhood there. For them, the visit was a homage to all that Papa Neil had achieved. Some church members remembered my Uncle Charlie, whom they had named the 'Little Chief' when he lived as a child among them. Because they were in the entourage of the Little Chief, my parents also became guests of honour at a celebratory feast and kava ceremony. My mother loved to recount how, after the ceremony was finally over, one of the chiefs complimented her on the regal air she had maintained throughout the proceedings. Little did he know that her rigid posture was in fact a desperate attempt to stem the onset of a nasty bout of diarrhoea.

I eventually visited Samoa myself, just a few years ago, in the company of my brother and sister, and her husband, having finally overcome my misgivings about embracing this aspect of my family's past. I managed it by transforming the event into an exercise in historical research, rather than a personal quest to connect with a family heritage I still considered dubious. Our party arrived at Piula Theological College at short notice – deliberately on my part, to avoid any risk of roasted pigs or kava – were greeted politely and invited to share the staff members' everyday lunch. I had brought along copies of our grandfather's sepia photographs that showed the construction of the magnificent chapel, including one in which an image of the Reverend Neil can be seen hanging in a prominent position on the chapel wall. I also had with me the original print of that portrait. We passed them around the table and made what conversation we could while theological students stood behind us and cooled us with enormous woven fans. I did a reasonable job, I thought, so as not to seem unappreciative, of suppressing my discomfort at this show of hierarchy and privilege.

After lunch, we toured the complex and Neil and Bev gave an impromptu performance in the chapel, my brother at the keyboard of the electronic organ while my sister sang a well-known hymn. A small crowd of theological students gathered in the wings and showed their appreciation with applause. Later, they came out to pose with the performers for photographs, while I scoured the interior of the church but was disappointed to find no trace of either the 'photograph-with-in-the-photograph' of our grandfather, or any other recognition of the connection he had once had to the place. The plaque that we had always thought had been erected in his honour on one of the outside walls was nowhere to be found. The world had moved along and left this part of our family history behind.

*

It seems to me that most people form their views about the probity of human actions, not through the judicious application of moral principles, but according to whether things do or do not turn out for the best. Some submissions to the Stolen Generations Inquiry had positive things to say about missionaries and credited them with enabling Aboriginal people to learn new ways of coping with their precarious position in settler society. Other accounts also give the missionary legacy some qualified praise:

> Grudgingly or otherwise, one can say this of the missionaries: they tried. And one measure of their endeavours is that so much of what they have tried to do in social or cultural work has been appropriated by those who regarded (and still regard) missionary work with no small contempt. For more than a century before it was recognised by State or Commonwealth governments or the general populace, missionaries were affirming that the first Australians were human and should have the same rights and dignities, the same opportunities and respect as were normally accorded to other Australians.[71]

This supposedly included the opportunities for redemption that were uniquely afforded by Christian belief. In a 1926 document from the Lutheran Archives which commemorates twenty-five years of work at Koonibba, the mission director acknowledged the prior possession by Aboriginal people of the 'country we now call our own', but concluded:

> Having occupied their territory, however, and having brought along with us treasures, spiritual and eternal treasures, unknown to the original dwellers in the land, what could be more natural for Christians imbued with the love of Christ than to share these treasures with those who have them not?... As people walking in the light we are to bring the light to those still walking in darkness.

My parents' Christian perspective imbued them with a similarly unquestioning and unshakeable belief in the universal power of god's love, coupled with an explicit notion of where the pathway to that love could be found. In contrast, the non-believers among us would agree with Henry Reynolds that attitudes like this amount to 'misguided benevolence'.[72] Many years after Len's death, and after our mother was gone as well, Dad confided in me that he wondered if 'we' – by which he meant non-Aboriginal Australia, I suppose – had done the right thing by converting Aboriginal people to Christianity. This questioning had arisen because he had come to believe, in his words, that 'their own Dreamtime stories are very similar'. In what respect he thought Aboriginal and Christian beliefs to be similar, I am not sure. But I can attest that Len shared with my parents an intensely spiritual world view. A painting of a golden-haired Jesus hung on the wall in his bedroom, apparently placed there with his approval. On occasions when I ventured in there, I found the piercing blue eyes unnerving, and his European appearance disconcerting, but kept my discomfort to myself.

Although he was shy and sometimes sullen in company, my mother liked to tell me in my teenage years how Len would astonish and entertain the ladies at Bible study class with the breadth of his scriptural knowledge and the keenness of his mind. I was unable to fathom why he would want to do that. I suspected my mother was only telling me in the hope of shaming me into similarly pious conduct, which was an exercise in futility. Whenever I think about the ladies at the West Richmond Church – many of whom, I hasten to add, were kind and reasonable people – other memories tend to be eclipsed by this one event, relayed to me via my mother. Just as the extent of Len's problems was becoming apparent, one of those very same ladies, while sipping tea after the Sunday service, had suggested to Mum that she should simply 'give him back'.

*

I think you will understand by now that our parents' responses to life's challenges were invariably based on their Christian beliefs. In fact, that was pretty much the only toolkit they had available to get through life. When Lennie was very small, and Dad found out he'd been trying to scrub himself white, he showed Len a well-known religious picture called the Hope of the World and asked him who was sitting at the feet of Jesus. It was a little dark-skinned boy. Jesus, dad explained, doesn't care about the colour of people's skin. All god's children are equally valued. While the message was one of universal love and acceptance, the incongruity of the saviour's own pallid complexion went unremarked. Even so, my parents' efforts seemed to be more honest than the response of the Presbyterian foster mother from Stan Grant's childhood, mentioned earlier, who resorted to denying the origins of her foster-son's dark skin.

Later, when the main concern was Len's unstoppable drinking, my parents turned again to a religiously inspired solution. Len joined Alcoholics Anonymous, and attended meetings whenever he was not on a bust or locked up somewhere. Mum and Dad became active members of Al-Anon, the organisation for families of alcoholics, in a loyal effort to support him. The Serenity Prayer became the favourite maxim in the house, and although I dismissed it at the time because it was a prayer, I later came to understand the wisdom of its core message: 'God grant me the serenity to accept the things I cannot change, the courage to change the things I can, and the wisdom to know the difference.' That last part, I have always thought, is the hardest.

While I was more attracted to criticism than catechism, religion and a broader spirituality bound Mum and Len together. 'Also Sprach Zarathustra' became my secret bible at university, although this godless creed would never have been acceptable to my mother. On the other hand, the ladies at the church would have been scandalised if they had known some of the unconventional topics canvassed by Mum and Len. Jean, the missionary's daughter, would listen with reverence to the stories Len brought back from the west coast about the Kadaicha men who walked without leaving footprints and could come in the night to spirit away a wrongdoer, leaving behind them only a trail of ice-cold air. She accepted without hesitation Len's conviction that the long-awaited home our parents had built on a brand-new subdivision alongside the River Torrens was located over an Aboriginal burial ground, and that he could feel the power of the ancestors rising up through his bedroom floor. And she took it in her stride that Len had the ability to communicate with the spirits of the dead and as-yet unborn.

I have just arrived home from netball practice on a Sunday afternoon. I've been selected in the under-16 state team, which has provided the excuse I've been looking for to absent myself from church. As I open the front door, I hear an eerie noise coming from the TV room. I reach the end of the long corridor and can't believe my eyes. My mother and Len are sitting around a laminex card table, their fingers resting lightly on the base of an upturned tumbler. The glass is spinning on the glossy surface in a perfect circle at an impossible speed, creating a high-pitched hum. I can't see how they could be pushing it, as it would surely catch on the surface. They invite me to sit down and put my finger on the glass as well, which I do reluctantly, expecting that the touch of an Unbeliever will bring the whole thing to a grinding halt. But the spinning continues, and I have trouble moving my arm fast enough to keep up with its frantic motion. Mum explains that Len has contacted the spirit of a relative who died recently on the west coast. Len begins to ask questions and the glass moves more slowly now towards letters that spell out something important that Len needs to do. He needs to tell someone that the death was an accident. The glass spells out that a gun went off unexpectedly when the crowded utility drove over a bump. The dead man insists it will be a grave injustice if anyone is charged with his murder. Len has been chosen to carry this message between two worlds.

Although organised religion was a source of angst and alienation for me during my youth, it appeared to be the glue that held Len together when everything else was falling apart. I am also certain that it was their faith in god that enabled my parents to retain their love and commitment to Len through pain and anxiety that many others could not have endured. On the other hand, I suspect it was their belief that they were doing god's will that blinded them to the part they were playing in Len's separation from his birth family and may have prevented them from questioning the official line that these practices were ultimately 'for the best'.

Politics

Far more, and far more hideous, crimes have been committed in the name of obedience than have ever been committed in the name of rebellion.

C.P. Snow

Ours was not a family where major world events, scientific or artistic innovations, political scandals or difficult social and moral conundrums would be canvassed around the kitchen table. Methodism formed a complete world view based on acceptance, faith, humility and caring concern for others. We talked, I suppose, about things that were happening in the family, church and local neighbourhood. I can't say I recall a single conversation. Thankfully, Mum and Dad's form of religion didn't promote the narrow-minded bigotry and politics of hate that is coming to dominate public life today; theirs was a god of universal love. But neither was their brand of Christianity of the lefty liberation theology kind. Although the teachings and life of Jesus inspire in some people a progressive politics directed to the pursuit of social justice, my parents' religious faith seemed to promote a deferential reluctance to rock the boat – an unquestioning acceptance of authority.

I would come to interpret this world view as one of stultifying conformity. Mum and Dad's humble Methodist values served them well at an interpersonal level, and they were kind and generous and truly cared about others. My father in particular approached his life with a rare and genuine simplicity that endeared him to all who knew him. But these values did not lead them to question wider social inequities or push for political change, beyond a generous commitment to charitable giving. By the time I got to university, I started to realise how little I understood about the machinations of the complex world around me, and that I would have to be responsible for my own, belated, political education.

Although neither of them would ever have wished harm to a single living soul, their religious outlook also made my parents unlikely to challenge the judgement of those in authority. They thought it unbecoming to have ideas beyond one's station and asserting one's rights – or even someone else's – appeared unseemly and confronting to them. Even complaining about receiving the wrong meal in a restaurant was thought to be making a terrible fuss. I think many people would agree that a parent's foremost responsibility towards their children is to love and nurture them, but after that to prepare them for surviving in the world. My parents excelled at the former but, due to their own restricted childhoods perhaps, were less adept at the latter. Mum's aspirations to become a nurse had been thwarted by her ill-health and the gender expectations of the day; and my dad's educational prospects had been similarly restricted by hardship and poverty. Despite their best efforts, none of their children entered adulthood particularly well prepared for the challenges of life beyond home and religious community.

For one thing, having been inculcated with the notion that 'Christian children all must be, mild, obedient, good as he' – none of us was geared up for the increasingly competitive world of work. My calm and capable sister completed teacher's college and became a primary school teacher, a profession she abandoned after marriage even though she had excelled and risen quickly to the position of deputy headmistress. Perhaps it was dictated by the gendered policies of the day, but she never returned after those barriers were removed and remained a homemaker and willing helper in her husband's business. My intelligent, but highly strung, brother was encouraged to study medicine because of his academic ability, whereas his true talents and passion lay in music. He proved to be a fish out of water amongst the privileged medical students at Adelaide University and soon dropped out, then did not return to complete the music degree he should have taken in the first place until many difficult decades had passed. We were not, any of us, early bloomers.

For me, although I was at ease in the world of education, the prospect of having to choose a public role in life, take on everyday responsibilities and routines, and account for myself in the world at large evoked a sense of terror that has taken a lifetime to overcome. This ordeal of transition into the outside world can only have been magnified for Len. For reasons that should be clear by now, Len had been in no position to even begin his high school studies, and the countless other obstacles he faced were beyond the resources of our family to deal with, or even recognise. Without the support and understanding he needed to guide him, it's easy to see how he could become lost in the world, with none of us able to rescue him.

*

Dad's forebears had arrived in the wheat belt of South Australia among the nineteenth-century migrations of ethnic Germans from Silesia. They were stern and hardworking Lutheran folk who eked out a living from the dusty soil of the Murray Mallee. Even Dad referred to them, affectionately, as rustics. When Pete was just a babe in arms, his father was killed in a farming accident while loading grain onto a horse-drawn cart at a railway siding. That tragedy, and the resolve of his stolid mother never to remarry, sentenced my father to an early life marred by hardship. My grandma Nell moved alone to her family's suburban farm in Adelaide to raise her only son. Throughout his childhood, to make ends meet, Dad would get up before sunrise to gather eggs and milk the cows, then help his mother deliver fresh produce and baked goods around the neighbourhood by horse and cart. He was regularly chastised for being late for school until the teacher finally thought to ask him the reason.

The deprivations he endured were not just material. In later years, Dad's lack of technical know-how became a source of bemusement for me. Even the simple task of hanging a Christmas wreath on the door could result in a tangle of wires and screws that resembled a Heath

Robinson cartoon. I was well into middle age before it occurred to me that my dad had never had anyone to teach him such manly skills. And while that absence might have turned another man into someone directionless, angry and harsh, our father was so gentle and caring that his pale blue eyes would fill with tears at the slightest hint of injustice or suffering.

Despite the many limitations of his upbringing, Dad was not without accomplishments. In his early years, he had been a capable horseman, having learned how to ride from visiting his uncles' farms as a lad. I only found this out towards the end of his life. My dad on a horse? I could never have imagined it. A child like myself, at the tail end of the family, can grow up completely unaware of her parents' youth. Dad had been a promising violinist as well, who was regularly the runner-up for his age group in state music competitions – second only to Lyndall Hendrickson, who later became a celebrated performer and teacher in South Australia. I know this because it was significant enough to find its way into our family mythology.

Dad told me himself that he had contemplated studying pharmacy but a combination of mediocre grades and the need to earn a living prevented him from pursuing that path. When he was discharged from the army after the Second World War, Dad considered himself blessed to land an office job with the newly formed Department of Veterans Affairs. Thus began a lifetime of public service that brought a level of financial security for his family that he would not have imagined possible. But he never again played the violin in public, and by the time I came along, his playing had almost disappeared from the family home as well. I think I have a memory of him in tennis whites, but for as far back as I can remember, his life was dominated by duty towards his family and church community. While our mother lived through her children, Dad unflinchingly lived for us.

As an officer of the Commonwealth Employment Service in the days when governments actively helped people to find work, Dad had first-hand dealings with union representatives and disliked what he saw as their strident, self-serving approach. My pious mother associated the Australian Labor Party with Marxism, and therefore godlessness, apparently oblivious to the strong influence of organised religion – albeit of the wrong kind – within the ALP. No doubt she was encouraged in that belief after attending a mass rally at the Wayville showgrounds in 1959 for the American evangelist Billy Graham. At some point in his world crusade, Graham is said to have issued the following ultimatum: 'Either Communism must die, or Christianity must die, because it is actually a battle between Christ and anti-Christ.'[73]

So, notwithstanding their own impoverished origins, my parents both did their utmost to keep the anti-Christ at bay by voting conservatively throughout their lives. They felt uneasy about any kind of protest or troublemaking at either the personal or political level. My mother, who possessed a genuinely life-threatening heart condition accompanied by a theatrical disposition, would often react to my teenage attempts to provoke a debate of any kind by collapsing dramatically into unconsciousness. This tended to bring an abrupt end to any discussion of controversial topics, particularly as I started university and began to broaden my mind in troubling directions. By our family's humble standards, I had always been a 'Deep Thinker' – that is still the term my older sister uses – but it wasn't viewed as a wholly positive trait. As a troubled adolescent, my excited (and perhaps too strident) attempts to impress on Mum the awesomeness of Nietzsche or the finer points from Hume's Dialogues Concerning Natural Religion would invariably end in tears and sometimes in emergency calls for an ambulance. In theory, people were to be universally loved and accepted as human beings, but their ideas were viewed with alarm and suspicion if they deviated too much from what was safe and accepted.

In his later years, my gentle father abandoned the Liberal Party because of what he saw as the unprincipled cruelty of John Howard's policies towards refugees and turned instead to the Liberal Democrats. That party was led in South Australia by political prodigy Natasha Stott Despoja, who was clearly a much nicer person. I was extremely relieved

and immensely proud of him. Filial love and an intense protective-
ness prevented me from ever asking my father whether John Howard's
refusal to apologise to the Stolen Generations had any bearing on his
decision. I will never know if he was even aware of that controversy or
saw our family as occupying a place in that national debate.

As for Len, he did not survive to see the heyday of Aboriginal politics, the open celebration of Aboriginal identity, the landmark victories
on land rights, and the gradual emergence of Aboriginal self-determination as a goal at the individual, community and national level. The
political milestones of the 1980s and 90s also passed by the rest of our
family. None of us joined the protests in 1988 to mark the bicentenary
of European invasion. Those actions seemed very far away from where
I was at the time, both geographically and in my own head. I was even
further away, living overseas, when former Prime Minister Paul Keat-
ing delivered the celebrated Redfern Speech in December 1992. I was
still missing in action in the year 2000 when Australians from diverse
backgrounds walked across Sydney Harbour Bridge in support of the
emerging goal of reconciliation, and when the National Inquiry into
the Stolen Generations began to hear testimonies of family disruption
and separation. When I finally returned to Australia after ten years in
the UK, I opened the cover of the Bringing Them Home report with
some trepidation to read what the inquiry had found, wondering if I
would find our family's situation represented in its pages.

By the time Prime Minister Kevin Rudd delivered the nation's
apology for the policies that had devastated Aboriginal families and
communities, both my parents had passed away. I thought of them
often in the days following that historic speech, as apologists for the
policies lined up to observe that many foster placements and adoptions
had worked out happily and remind us that the people involved had
generally 'meant well'. It can be hard to explain to those people what is
wrong with that way of seeing things. These acts of rationalisation and
denial are precisely what James Baldwin meant, I think, when he spoke
of a 'chorus of innocents screaming'.[74]

I can only speculate as to how my parents would have responded to these events. I suspect they would have been bewildered at the thought that Len had been stolen, and deeply wounded by any accusation that their devoted parenting had caused him harm. But there is one thing I know for certain: the humility that they practised in their everyday lives would have prevented them from believing that their own hurt feelings were important enough to divert the nation's attention away for one fleeting moment from that long-awaited acknowledgement of those who had suffered.

What was missing in my parents' simple, Christian approach to life was the ability to view individual events as part of a larger socio-political pattern. I can only wonder how our lives might have been different if our parents had possessed a more nuanced understanding of the politics of colonisation – if they had questioned, rather than accepted, the events that had placed Len's family and ours in such different situations. Would they have spoken out against the ignorant teachers, officious bureaucrats, bigoted nurses, brutal police, abusive staff and violent inmates at prisons and reform centres whose everyday brutalities eroded Len's dignity and self-respect? Would they have ventured more actively into Len's cultural heritage, rather than assuming that he and his family would operate within theirs? Would they have reinterpreted what was happening in Len's life and discussed the underlying issues more openly? And would they have seen the perverse possibility that seeking to help others could, in certain circumstances, cause them harm? When life is seen as the natural unfolding of god's will – which, to be fair, is not the sort of fatalism I ever heard my parents express openly – it makes it difficult to see how performing acts of kindness could be construed by others as wrong.

And yet Christianity has been made to carry much of the blame for the destruction of Aboriginal civilisations. William Richard Penhall, Chief Protector of Aborigines in South Australia during the 1940s and 50s, whose name has appeared at several points in this story, is a case in point. Penhall's enthusiasm for the removal of Aboriginal children from their parents is said to have stemmed from his Christian world view that generated enthusiastic support for the 'civilising' work of Christian missionaries.[75] While not proposing any direct connection between Christian doctrines and beliefs in racial superiority, his chronicler argues persuasively that the framework of certainty provided by Christian belief had the secondary effect of preventing the development of a more culturally, politically and historically informed understanding. In an argument that reappears depressingly often in the political debates of today, we are told that it was 'entirely possible that he believed he was doing the right thing'.

This certainty about his own moral rectitude, however, was far from justified:

> [I]t is clear that Penhall failed to come to a sympathetic, intelligent understanding of Aboriginal people and their complicated plight in the context of colonial history. This failure of imagination, intellect and feeling allowed him to act as if his Aboriginal charges were themselves responsible for their own condition. The negativity towards them that he cultivated and encouraged allowed him to disregard their wishes, hopes and dreams, and to consider them as something lesser than the general, white population.[76]

This sounds like a much narrower and more judgmental variant of Christianity than that practised by our parents. However, their sincere adherence to the 'do unto others' principle was a recipe for paternalism, due to the implicit assumption that what we believe is good for ourselves is necessarily good for others. Revered Gangulu activist Lilla Watson famously threw out this challenge to those who, with the best of intentions, sought to intervene in the lives of Aboriginal people: 'If you have come here to help me, you are wasting your time…but if you have come because your liberation is bound up with mine, then let us work together.' It is difficult to meet this standard while at the same time holding the unwavering conviction that one's own belief system or way of life is the sole pathway to redemption.

I doubt very much that the racial politics of empowerment and self-determination that is prevalent in political debate today, although still unrealised in practice, would have been intelligible to my parents. Looking back to the early days of black and white TV, I can recall watching The Black and White Minstrel Show as a family, oblivious to the role those portrayals had played in the history of American racism. In the absence of any discussion between us on the subject, I can only offer this tangential speculation. When Venus Williams had begun to dominate women's tennis, I once said something admiring about her to my tennis-loving dad, which I expected him to endorse enthusiastically. To my surprise, his response was somewhat diffident, although he was reluctant or unable to say why. His face took on a puzzled expression and he flailed about for a while as I gently pressed him on it, until I opted to change the subject. To me, quietly spoken Venus was an inspiration: in fact, true to her name, something of a goddess, who had triumphed over adversity of epic proportions. Most important of all, I thought, from my dad's point of view, she had remained gracious, polite and god-fearing (although in a distinctly un-Methodist, Jehovah-praising way) throughout her rise to superstardom. I could only imagine how he would have responded to the subsequent ascent of the not-so serene, although also Jehovah-praising, Serena.

I know that my parents valued simplicity and humility above all else, but it was not hard to find much less accomplished sporting heroes who possessed egos the size of a planet. Did Dad feel uncomfortable about all of them? Or maybe it was a religious objection that influenced his opinion. My grandfather the Reverend Neil, while always welcoming and kind to the hungry and homeless, had been known to send packing any hapless Jehovah's Witnesses who knocked on his door, considering them to be 'home wreckers'. This was in reference to the conversion to that faith of his wife's sister, a catastrophe from which the family apparently never recovered.

Perhaps I'm overthinking it, but I had a terrible feeling that what was actually gnawing at my dad, what he couldn't quite put his finger on, was a gut feeling about the natural order being disrupted. Despite all his genuine and loving acceptance of others, I suspected that some unexamined assumptions were at play. Venus and Serena were out there doing it for themselves: conquering the world on their own terms. And neither of them needed a white person to give them some second-hand pencils. My parents' brand of kindly paternalism was driven, not by a sense of superiority over others, but by a more humble inability to imagine an alternative ordering of things.

As my own adult life began to stabilise into some kind of coherent narrative, and I was attracted to what has often been described as the 'secular religion' of human rights, my parents finally revised their opinion on the state of my soul. My father once told me that he and Mum had come to realise that, despite my determined atheism, I was in fact 'more Christian', as he put it, than many of the people who made up the congregation at what was by this time the West Richmond Uniting Church. It seems my parents had found a place for me amongst the angels after all. But my redemption was only imaginable by transforming me into an honorary Christian. Through this device, it was possible for me to be incorporated into their cosmos: but it would remain an insurmountable hurdle for them to venture into anyone else's.

*

The Stolen Generations Inquiry concluded that adoptive families often failed to respond appropriately when Aboriginal children in their care suffered identity problems or encountered racism. I don't doubt that this is true, but it's also difficult to envisage what kind of response would have been right at the time, save the obvious one of returning children to their rightful families wherever possible. I have only ever found one hint at an answer, and it comes, once again, from real-life testimony published in the Bringing Them Home report. The passage is so instructive that it is worth quoting at length:

> I was very fortunate that when I was removed, I was with very loving and caring parents. The love was mutual… My foster mother used to take me and my sister to town. Mum used to always walk through

Victoria Square and say to us, 'Let's see if any of these are your uncles'... I used to get so frightened and could never understand why my mum would do this to us, when it made us upset. Only when I was near 29 did I realise why... I remember one day I went home to my foster father and stated that I had heard that my natural father was a drunk. My foster father told me you shouldn't listen to other people: 'You judge him for yourself, taking into account the tragedy, that someday you will understand.'[77]

Politically aware parents such as these understood that love wasn't all their foster-children needed. Although it was unsettling, they openly confronted the historical tragedy that had brought them all together. And these parents chose to meet their children's original family on their own turf, no doubt hoping that one day the children they loved might feel strong enough to reconnect with their heritage.

No doubt, this is a small success story in the face of so much misery. Even this level of openness and understanding can never replicate the bonds that are formed by confronting a shared adversity together. Anna Haebich has likened growing up within the 'overlapping circles' of traditional kinship ties to a form of life insurance for young Aboriginal people living on the margins of a settler society:

> Drawing on a wealth of experiences, Aboriginal families teach their children how to survive racism – how to feel strong about their Aboriginal identity in the face of racist taunts and slurs, and teaching them that there are whole networks of relatives who will uncondi- tionally back them up if trouble breaks out.[78]

This description of the resilient Aboriginal family may not be uni- versal, and families under duress might sometimes be unable to provide that level of support. But the arguments about safety in numbers, shared experience and the protective value of cultural and kinship bonds, are compelling given the pervasive bigotry in Australian society at large.

I am in a restaurant in a picturesque part of the country that is popular with retir- ees. Two of my partner's relatives have moved there to live in the mountains, and we've been invited to dinner with their new friends to mark a significant birthday.

Suddenly, the conversation takes a dangerous turn. 'Isn't it absurd,' says one, 'how Pauline Hanson has been gaoled for three years when a rapist just the other week only got two.'

I pitch in – not sensing the danger. 'Then again, Pauline Hanson has been quite prepared to see Aboriginal women put in prison for lesser misdeeds on the three strikes you're out rule.'

'Ah yes,' says the woman, 'but what you don't realise is that most of "Them" have committed fifty other crimes before getting caught for that third one.'

Her particular expertise on the matter derives from having grown up amongst Them in a small outback town. In case We need further convincing that the entire Aboriginal populace is deserving of punishment, she is happy to describe at length the unruly behaviour, the arrival of hordes of relatives, and the wanton trashing of houses that have been provided at great expense by Us. She is confident that We would understand this too, if We had grown up around Them.

I want to tell her that in a way I have, and that I have a different view. I want to say that perhaps another, more thoughtful or open-hearted person might have lived through the same experience but drawn from it more considered conclusions. Might exercise some grace or humility. Might take into account the bigger tragedy. Instead, I'm overwhelmed first by anger and then by grief. I can feel the effort to hold it all in is turning my face to stone.

The woman is still launching forth with a confidence born of the belief that she is speaking an unassailable Truth. It is, after all, difficult to quarrel with direct experience. 'Some of the "full bloods" are OK', she is saying, 'but the "quarter casts", and "sixteenth casts" and "thirty second casts"'…she pauses for dramatic effect…'are just out for what –'

'They can get,' one of the other retirees chips in, just in case the rest of us do not follow where the argument is heading.

I hope desperately that someone from our end of the table – someone who has not been incapacitated by an emotional time bomb – will intervene. But they are all sitting tight-lipped, no doubt hoping she will stop of her own accord.

I try to conjure up some words so sharp, so penetrating, that they will cut through these people's complacency like a knife. How about 'FUCKING WHITE CUNTS – FUCKING, FUCKING WHITE CUNTS!' (That's not really what comes to mind, but it seems perfectly reasonable in hindsight.) But I know that at the crucial moment my outrage will dissolve into a blubbering grief that will be pathetic and ineffectual.

Another retiree has weighed into the melee now and makes things even worse. 'And then They go on about this Stolen Generations thing,' he says, 'when We all know it was meant for the best. Many of Them,' he explains, 'have clearly lived much better lives than They ever would have done if left amongst Their own kind.'

The whole situation has become unbearable. The only thing left to do is to flee – so I do, temporarily, pacing back and forth on the pavement outside, fighting back a tsunami of grief and hoping the chilly mountain air will have a calming effect. A few deep breaths and I struggle back to my chair, trying desperately to muster some composure. Our end of the table has made a belated stand.

'I just think you need to look much more deeply at these things,' my partner is suggesting, with an existential calm I wish I could have mustered.

'I think we should just change the subject then,' someone proposes, in another victory for peace over justice.

It will be me, I find out a considerable time later, who is thought to have spoiled the party.

This is how it perpetuates; this wanton and malign failure to understand, this blindness to the ongoing effects of the colonial project and the mundane privileges of whiteness. This is why Aboriginal people still need to find circles of safety from which to negotiate the settler world. And this is how we know our colonial past is not over. As James Baldwin has explained so perfectly, 'the occurrence of an event is not the same thing as knowing what it is that one has lived through'.[79] Therein lies the profound danger of populist belief in the superiority of unexamined experience over curated knowledge, painstakingly acquired from a range of sources. Baldwin knew that for populations to remain innocent of histories of racism and subordination was to be party to a collective crime. In his famous 'Letter to My Nephew', he said this of the white American population: 'They are in effect still trapped in a history which they do not understand and until they understand it, they cannot be released from it.'[80]

*

Unlike personal experience – which, by definition, simply happens – deep insights, empathy and knowledge can be elusive. At Cowandilla Primary School, which Len and I both attended, we learned about white explorers who had 'discovered' Australia, and other founding fathers whose names appeared on street signs and gave their names to Adelaide's city squares. If we heard anything at all about Aboriginal people, it was that they conveniently lived in the desert, out of sight and far away from our suburban existence. They didn't have many possessions, we were told, because the harsh climate meant they had to keep constantly on the move. It wasn't at all clear, in that case, what the Aboriginal people who gathered in the centre of Adelaide in Victoria Square, to sit, talk and sometimes to drink under the shade of the few remaining trees, were doing there.

What was deliberately omitted from school curricula in the 1960s and 70s, and possibly even now, was the history of the violent dispossession of the original inhabitants from land that white settlers now occupied: land that has since been transformed beyond all recognition by tubular steel and concrete. We learned nothing of the equally devastating destruction of cultural identity and Aboriginal family networks, an omission that the popular emphasis on 'cultural awareness' does little, in my opinion, to ameliorate. And we learned nothing about the knowledge systems developed over thousands of years of intimate interaction with the land: of Aboriginal astronomy,[81] mathematics[82] and agriculture.[83] Bruce Pascoe argues in his seminal text Dark Emu that early explorers knew about Aboriginal agriculture and recorded their observations in writing. But mainstream history later suppressed that knowledge, ensuring that generations of children were presented with a victor's version.

As a child, I had not thought of our family as part of the bigger historical canvas, and as my awareness grew I saw no sign that my parents had either. They would never have embraced the openly hostile views expressed by the gathering around that dinner table in the mountain retreat, would never have adopted such an imperious attitude towards those they considered to be 'less fortunate'. But neither do I think they would have had the means to counter such determined vilification, or to prepare Len for the pervasive animosity and rejection he must have encountered. A child and adolescent psychiatrist who had interviewed forcibly removed children reported to the Stolen Generations Inquiry that 'in none of these families was there a sense that one way to manage this situation was to recapture your sense of Aboriginality'.[84] One adoptive family admitted to the inquiry that they appreciated, belatedly, how their lack of political and cultural awareness had unwittingly contributed to their son's identity problems:

> We made a series of errors through our ignorance and paternalism. We brought him up separate from the Koori population...away from the Koori people. The ones we'd heard about in the papers were having big problems, so we thought we will keep him away from the problems until he matures. We didn't understand the full ramifications of invasion, of dispossession or disbursement. We learnt all this later. So we were – in the 1960s we're talking about – we were ignorant well-meaning whites.[85]

Another account that resonates to some degree with our family's circumstances appeared in a recent anthology Growing up Aboriginal in Australia. It was written by an Aboriginal man, John Williams-Mozely, who was raised in a loving white family, then went on to a series of highly successful careers in policing, academia and Indigenous education:

> My adoptive parents grew me up with all the love and material comfort that was theirs to give from when I was seven months old. They loved me, and I loved them as a son should. However, like so many people in Australian society at the time, my adoptive family had little understanding or factual knowledge about Aboriginal people and cultures. Consequently I had to wait several years before I came to know what it meant being Aboriginal in Australia.[86]

While Mum and Dad never tried to keep Len away from his

birth family and maintained active links of their own even after Len died, I had never felt comfortable joining in with these interactions. I couldn't have articulated it then, but I think the cause of my unease was an intuitive sense of the profound historical injustice and ongoing inequality that conditioned what was possible between us. I resisted being drawn into the relationships my parents had established between Len's family and ours because, although infused with warmth and loving concern, it seemed they could never be fully reciprocal. We were all of us operating in the shadow of an unacknowledged colonial past. I barely knew the history myself, but I somehow sensed the weight of it as we attempted to carry on as if everything was just as it should be.

Long after Len died, I asked my sister Bev about his funeral, which had been held in my absence. She told me that Len's family had come to the service and to the gathering at her house afterwards. They had chosen to stay outside in the garden, despite repeated invitations to come indoors. I was pleased that at least they had been there. But I also felt that familiar sense that something was profoundly wrong. Len is buried in the same plot as our paternal grandmother in a suburban cemetery. I visit there whenever I return to Adelaide, and if I'm alone, I kneel down and place my hands flat on the grass and send through my love, trying to feel some connection. A brass plate marks the spot, listing the members of Len's loving family – Peter, Jean, Beverley, Neil and Leanne – and, as always, identifying Len as our chosen son and brother. This is how the written record stands. But I can't help but wonder whether the family into which Len was born had any more control over what happened to him after his death than they had been able to exercise during his life.

You must discover ten truths every day, otherwise you will seek truth in the night too, with your soul still hungry.

Friedrich Nietzsche, *Also Sprach Zarathustra*

The Hungry Soul

Five times I woke
– I counted them –
in floods of fear that wouldn't wait
for day to come.
The day's last light, obscured
by clouds, grew dim;
an overflow of hidden fears
escaped the dam.

Soon, questions dragged up
by the squall
tossed helplessly like driftwood – all
unanswerable;
then, swamped beneath
a sudden desperate surge,

were swept up in a tidal wave
of inner purge.

The torrent's toll –
a soul laid bare.

A fragile vessel cast up on
a lonely shore.

And in its wake
remained a hungry fear.
A pleading
only introspective souls can hear.

Truth

*The heavier the burden, the closer our lives come to the earth, the
more real and truthful they become. Conversely, the absolute absence
of a burden causes man to be lighter than air...and become only half
real, his movements as free as they are insignificant.*
    Milan Kundera, *The Unbearable Lightness of Being*

When our father died in the autumn of 2006, my siblings and I placed
a death notice in the Adelaide Advertiser, describing him as the beloved
husband of Piula Jean Weber (deceased), and cataloguing the children
and grandchildren who were also mourning his loss. A few days later,
the younger of my nieces, who was born several years after Len's death,
expressed her dismay that Len's name had not been included in the
notice. At first I convinced myself there was a completely reasonable
explanation; that the notice in the newspaper was a communication
made on behalf of the living – those who were in a position to host the
funeral and invite others to attend. After all, the name of their chosen
son was etched on the memorial plaque on our mother's grave, where
our father would soon join her. He was not forgotten in our family's
most important historical record. There was no need, I reasoned, to be
so formal in the published notice, which served the entirely mundane
purpose of passing on practical information about our father's death and
the funeral arrangements.

I confess that I did not find my own rationalisation entirely convincing. For one thing, our mother had been included in the death
notice, although she had passed away five years earlier. Of course, it
would be unconscionable not to mention a person's spouse in their
death notice. But even so, this did not sit well with the 'on behalf of
the living' argument I had concocted. I can't say what explanation my

brother and sister would have given for their part in the oversight, and we never held a post-mortem about it, but I found it difficult to accept that I had simply forgotten about Len, even in the emotional turmoil following the loss of my beloved father. Len had been in my thoughts almost daily since his death, and was still frequently on my mind, even as the unresolved grief that accompanied his memory had slowly begun to recede with the belated help of therapy. Finally, I had to accept that, in leaving Len's name out of the funeral notice, I may have been activating the unconscious survival strategy I had adopted for so long, of writing Len out of my story. This strategy was only ever meant for the public realm – Len was never erased from my private thoughts. But publicly confronting the conundrum of his life with us would be like pressing hard on an emotional bruise.

A while back I saw the film Wonder, based on a book about a boy named Augie who is ostracised because of his severe facial deformities. His older sister, Via, loves and supports her brother, but has always lived in his shadow, since the family revolves around Augie's needs. Her artist mother has filled the house with pictures of her family, always with Augie at the centre of their universe. Faced with her first opportunity for romance, Via tells her flame that she is an only child. She is not ashamed of her brother, but senses that denial is the emotionally simplest route. I felt a weight lift from my shoulders as I watched that scene and knew that I was not the only sibling in the history of the world who had made that call. Via relented quickly, and decided to openly acknowledge and include her brother in the independent life she was building. The fact that I never had a chance to do that now feels like a moral injury.

*

Now I have told you the truth about Len's life as I understand it to be, it is no longer a painful secret eating away at my soul. I know it's only one version of the truth and that telling the truth entails the possibility of selective erasure and reinterpretation. Shamefully, I do not recall a single thing that Len ever said to me in person. I have pondered why that might be without achieving much enlightenment. Perhaps it was because my mother positioned herself as Len's Protector and, as our family relationships became more and more difficult, had somehow become the conduit for any information that flowed between us. Perhaps it was because both of us had become locked inside ourselves. And because Len was so often taken out of our lives. Whatever the reason, I failed to develop an adult relationship that would have allowed me to connect directly with my brother.

Writing this book has revealed many cracks that could only be filled by Len himself. But it has at least helped to let some light in. The process of recounting these events has forced me to position myself consciously in relation to Len's story, and to question the sharp division we usually make between victim and perpetrator. Rather than see Len as a victim and myself as a culprit, as I have done for so long, I see now that Len and I were both caught up in the relentless logic of colonisation – with mutually, although not identically, destructive consequences. While I was cushioned in many respects by white privilege, Len experienced its full force. But both of us, nevertheless, were crushed under the weight of this country's colonial history. This is not to suggest simplistically that we are all victims of colonisation to a similar degree, but to recognise that each of us is positioned somewhere within this shared narrative of ongoing dispossession, paternalism and control and continue to be burdened by the distorted human relations this history has imposed, whether we are aware of it or not.

*

When I began to rehearse the story of Len's life as I know it inside my head, I imagined that when I got to the end, I would have discovered some kind of answer about how to make things right. I envisaged a solution just as precise as the answer to the question about the meaning of 'life, the universe and everything' that was posed in The Hitchhiker's Guide to the Galaxy.[87] In case this wasn't an obligatory read in your youth, in The Hitchhiker's Guide the space travellers construct a computer called Deep Thought to calculate the answer to this ultimate question. It comes up with the solution '42'.[88] But Deep Thought also explains that the answer is meaningless, since the cosmic hitchhikers have not fully understood what they are asking. This is the kind of Black Hole into which Deep Thinking can lead you.

When I finally resolved to write this book, I went through the storage box containing scribbled notes on scraps of paper which I had squirrelled away over many years. I found two lists of questions that I must have thought at some point in time were important to ask: one list for my father – my mother had already died – and one for my older siblings. Beverley and Neil would have been almost fourteen and ten, respectively, at the time Len came into our family and neither of them had rejected our family's religious worldview in their adolescence. On this basis, I expected that their recollections might be clearer than mine and less bound up with complicated feelings of self-recrimination I held on so many fronts. On the other hand, they were no longer living at home during Len's most tormented years. Even so, I had hoped that, when provided with the answers to these questions, the missing pieces of the puzzle would fall into place. But the questions had remained unasked, and it was already too late, by the time I reopened that box, to put them to my father.

Here are the questions I had intended for him.

What was his and mum's expectation at the outset of how long Len would live with us?

What was their understanding of why Len did not go back to his birth family?

How and why did Len become a ward of the state?

Who initiated contact between Len and his birth family?

What made Len believe his mother had rejected him?

How much did Len know about his Aboriginal heritage?

Had Len's birth family been asked about their wishes for his burial and memorial?

Here are the questions intended for my brother and sister.

What did they think at the time about Len joining the family?

How long did they think he would stay?

What did they think about relations between us and Len's birth family?

Were they aware of efforts by Len's birth family to get him back?

What was our parents' understanding of the implications of Len growing up in a non-Aboriginal family?

None of these things, as far as I can recall, were ever discussed in my presence. But now that I am nearing the end of my attempt to reconstruct and deconstruct the past, I don't regret my failure to find clearcut answers. I realise now that these are not the most meaningful questions to ask, since they were driven by anxiety about how much each of us were personally to blame. The Sufi mystic Rumi is reputed to have counselled, 'Out behind the idea of wrongdoing and right doing is a field. I'll meet you there.' I'm not sure I am quite ready for that rendezvous yet or know exactly what promise it holds. There is something in both my Methodist indoctrination and the remnants of my rationalist individualism that make me want to hang on to the notion of right and wrong, and our duty to pursue what we believe to be right. Still, Rumi's ideal serves as a reminder of the potential destructiveness of becoming stuck in endless cycles of blame. I hope that speaking this truth about my early life with Len will transform the too-heavy burden of grief and shame that I have carried for so long into something still real, but at least a little lighter for being shared.

Moods

Sometimes I feel like a little grape
being crushed and squeezed
between treacherous toes,
till I run like a river of blood-red wine
that sobs and flows from an empty skin.
Insignificant.

But when I'm a magnet
I realise
the power of a compelling look
from fearless eyes
that tease and taunt and mesmerise.
And I stride away
feeling strong and wise,
with swinging hips
and arms that beat like drums
at my sides.
Magnificent.

Then sometimes I'm just a
drifting shape
suspended in space
in a lifeless case away
from sight – safe in a shroud of unknowing night,
not daring to turn towards the light.
Indifferent.

When suddenly –
in a fiery flash –
I burst my cage in a
surging rage and
frustration flows like
molten rock from
a seething core and
the steaming tears
come stinging down
and the anger boils in the
coiling depths
to a rushing roar –
and erupts
– unleashed –
from every pore.
Indiscriminate.

Responsibility

Life is always frightful. We cannot help it and we are responsible all the same.

Herman Hesse, *Steppenwolf*

It's a unique kind of agony to watch someone you love being slowly beaten down by life and feel powerless to intervene. It's an even bigger challenge to identify the wider forces driving their demise. But where does our own responsibility and power to alter the course of events begin and end? The great political philosopher Hannah Arendt made a crucial distinction between political or collective responsibility, on the one hand, and moral or legal guilt, on the other. For Arendt, while clearly there is a place in the world for both, none of us escapes collective responsibility for events in which we may have played no direct part, but which were nonetheless done in our name. She explains:

> This vicarious responsibility for things we have not done, this taking upon ourselves the consequences for things we are entirely innocent of, is the price we pay for the fact that we live our lives not by ourselves but among our fellowmen, and that the faculty of action, which, after all, is the political faculty par excellence, can be actualised only in one of the many and manifold forms of human community.[89]

This sets a high standard for communal life but should also free us from exaggerated feelings of personal guilt. We may need our burdens, as Kundera said, in order to be truly in the world; but we can also reduce their weight by sharing them.

The rush to attribute individual blame for wrongdoing seems to be characteristic of post-Enlightenment cultures, and one that is particularly emphasised in contemporary thinking. When my partner and I were living in England, a sixteen-year-old Nigerian boy who had arrived as an unaccompanied refugee came to live with us as a condition of being freed from immigration detention. During the course of a long legal battle to remain in the UK, Stephen became a beloved member of our family. I noticed that he would say 'sorry' whenever anyone suffered a slight mishap or misfortune, to which I would usually reply, 'It's not your fault', thinking I was reassuring him. I thought of Stephen's superfluous apologising as just another minor oddity with his English, along with his endearing habit of leaving notes alerting us that there were 'massages' on the answerphone. Stephen has since grown up and has two beautiful children of his own, whose mother came from his own culture. I realise now that my interpretation of his endless apologising was completely off-track because his wife would use 'sorry' in exactly the same way, as a simple expression of sympathy and solidarity in the face of hardship. And it mattered not at all whether anyone in particular was to blame.

Iris Marion Young, like Arendt another compassionate political thinker, was also convinced that we are collectively responsible for redressing structural injustice.[90] Young's position depends on the same distinction between individual liability and collective responsibility posed by Arendt, and requires a future orientation that is informed by, while not trapped in, the past. We may think that certain individuals should shoulder personal liability for harmful acts that they have knowingly perpetrated. But to dwell solely on the attribution of blame, she says, risks overlooking possibilities for collective action that might set things right. Those who have been harmed by unjust policies cannot be considered morally liable for them but, as respected and empowered survivors (not as hapless and helpless victims as paternalists may perceive them), she points out that they are best placed to guide the necessary change.

In a conclusion that could readily be applied to Australia's 'history wars' concerning the harms of colonisation,[91] this is how Young sums up our general human predicament:

A concept of political responsibility says that we who are part of these processes should be held responsible for the structural injustice, as members of the collective that produces it, even though we cannot trace the outcome we regret to our own particular actions in a direct causal chain. A concept of political responsibility fills this role without attributing blame.[92]

The proviso here, of course, is the capacity for settler Australians to see themselves as 'part of these processes'; to acknowledge the white privilege that has been a direct result of colonisation. This has never been required of us as a population, although the bitter debates that have raged around the Uluru Statement from the Heart reflect this kind of reckoning.[93] For those of us who already acknowledge our place in the nation's colonial history, but feel it as a too-heavy personal burden, a first step towards being part of a different future is to free ourselves from a stultifying preoccupation with self-blame, as expressed here by Carmel Bird:

If so many of us seem to suffer from psychic numbing, perhaps it is because we are afraid to acknowledge our need to be forgiven and to forgive ourselves. That story matters because it reminds us of our real task as human beings; not to be rich, powerful, famous or luxurious, but to know our place in the scheme of things, to live with respect for and with others, and for and with the earth.[94]

The transformative power of self-forgiveness is also expressed powerfully by a character in James Baldwin's celebrated novel Another Country:

[W]e all commit our crimes. The thing is not to lie about them – to try – to understand what you have done, why you have done it. ... That way, you can begin to forgive yourself... If you don't forgive yourself you'll never be able to forgive anybody else and you'll go on committing the same crimes forever.[95]

*

What is now widely known as 'survivor guilt' is a special kind of guilt borne out of the moral injury of failing to save others, or of continuing to live at the cost of others' lives. In Adam Haslett's novel Imagine Me Gone, which grapples with the inter-generational impacts of suicidal depression, the family matriarch has this to say after her son takes his own life: 'This is the thing I have discovered: Michael's being gone doesn't mean we stop trying to save him.'[96]

I am walking our dog in a leash-free park on the Georges River near where I live with my partner in Sydney. He is away on a golf trip. The previous night was stormy, and a baby galah has been shaken from its nest high in a gum tree. There is no sign of its mother. I arrive just in time to save it from the jaws of our kelpie. At home, I phone the RSPCA for instructions about how to care for the orphan. I'm told that since galahs are a protected native species, I'm not allowed to keep it. The operator asks for my address so she can assign someone to collect it, although without its mother she does not expect it to live. I terminate the call, mortified, without providing my details. My heart is set on saving that bird. I will nurse it back to health and everything will work out for the best. When Tony gets home, we'll make a perch for it in the backyard, and it will be free to come and go, but will always return to the sanctuary of our home because of our special bond. If we find that it is persecuted by the wild birds, we will make a cage where it will be safe from them but not permanently confined. I find recipes on the internet for various kinds of mash and feed the nestling with an eye dropper. At bedtime, I place it gently in a large cardboard box lined with straw. In the morning, it is dead. For days, I am inconsolable with helplessness and grief. It is all my fault. I tried to save it, but things have not worked out. How can anything – ever – be right?

Thirty years after Len's death I finally sought professional help to deal with crippling feelings of grief and guilt and serial attempts to posthumously save my brother. I started with a few visits to a counsellor. Diane was a wise woman with consulting rooms in a nearby suburb. She did not give me a questionnaire, or espouse any particular theory, or feel the need to enquire whether my relationship with Len had been anything beyond what was usually expected between a brother and sister. That is what I had experienced in one disastrous visit to a psychiatrist many years before, which probably set back my recovery by decades. Instead, Diane listened, and was kind, and made me feel acceptable in the world; and my thinking began to realign just a little, as if of its own accord.

Diane assured me there was nothing whatever I could have done to change what had happened in our family, since I was only a child. I knew she was trained to do exactly that: to validate the feelings and experiences of her clients. I tried hard to accept her messages of absolution, but there was no escaping the fact that as soon as that child became an adult, I had unwittingly used my white privilege to run away to the other side of the world, as far as I could get from the burdens of home, in order to save myself. Diane told me about 'radical acceptance' – that certain events that couldn't be changed simply had to be accepted. It was an idea I resisted from the start, being so mired in the illusion that humans possessed infinite capacities for change. I could not see myself as someone who needed to accept anything that had been done to me. Instead, what remained was the feeling I had always had, that I needed to do something to right what had happened to someone else. And I was not ready to let go of that feeling.

As the Buddhists say, 'When the pupil is ready, the teacher will come.' It was several years, after we had moved away from the city to live in the mountains, before the next wise woman arrived in my life. Kerry was a clinical psychologist who used the somewhat unorthodox technique of EMDR that aims to rewire the brain circuitry laid down from previous trauma.[97] EMDR stands for eye movement desensitisation and reprogramming – a phrase that instantly conjures up disturbing scenes from A Clockwork Orange. But once I met Kerry, with her vermillion pink hair and easy smile, I knew I could trust her not to mess with my head. It was a new feeling to let down the defences and give myself up to be helped. Rather than having to make a conscious effort to let things go, I found that EMDR did that automatically. Each session achieved a perceptible 'flattening out' of destructive stored emotions, and, with Kerry's gentle probing, brought new revelations about their origins and meaning. I remember waking up one morning feeling as though someone had 'ironed out' my brain. Funnily enough, it felt good, after having been somewhat crinkly for a very long time.

In a way, EMDR gives effect to the idea that, with help, we can sometimes rewrite our personal history. I picked up this inspiring idea from a book by psychiatrist and Holocaust survivor Victor Frankl.[98] I am usually suspicious of members of his profession, but I was instantly attracted to what he had to say. Surely you must take seriously anyone who can survive the horrors of a Nazi death camp with both their intellect and humanity intact. In contrast to other scholars of the mind who focus on the pursuit of sex (Freud) or power (Adorno), Frankl places the quest for meaning at the centre of human existence. Crucially, he sees the pathway to meaning as lying beyond our own individual psyches, involving devotion to a cause beyond oneself. He therefore incorporates ideas about collective responsibility, which are not usually emphasised in the individualistic world of psychiatry, and attributes to them significant powers of healing. Frankl believes that personal salvation can only be found against the backdrop of historical events that have shaped our lives. And he would know more about that than most of us. By confronting life-shaping events, he claims 'the past may well be changed and amended' – not literally of course, but in terms of how the past is perceived, and therefore the power it wields over us in the present.

Redemption

I always thought it was what I wanted: to be loved and admired. Now I think perhaps I'd like to be known.

Kristin Hannah, *The Nightingale*

After holding this story in my head for such a long time it is something of a surprise to see the way it has turned out. Along the way, it has been and become many things. It may have started out as a search for reasons about how and why Len's life went so badly wrong. Later, it became also a process of self-discovery and personal healing. And now I hope the book has become something of a treatise on the perils of benign paternalism; a warning of sorts against the Baldwinian 'innocence' of those who still claim that colonial policies towards Aboriginal people were, and still are, 'for the best'.

I also claimed at the outset that this was a book about love. So what – at the end of the day – can be said about that? First of all, however much we may wish it to be so, love alone cannot provide the sense of belonging and identity, self-esteem and acceptance that each of us needs. Because of the particular histories shaping our lives, the place of security and acceptance our family provided for Len also became a suffocating Love Trap, and none of us could help him navigate the hostile world beyond it. At the same time, Len was denied the love and security of his own family because of misguided policies that dictated that Aboriginal parents must forfeit their children in order for them to access medical care, or for any number of other purported reasons. And perhaps it was a different kind of love that lured my parents into accepting their place within this system rather than challenging its legitimacy: the kind that is fed by belief in the infallibility of a loving god who is guiding his followers to perform good deeds on earth.

Despite this gloomy conclusion about its manifold failings, writing this book has also restored my faith in love in many ways. Although I still harbour many doubts and regrets about our family's Misplaced Love for Len, his story would surely have been even grimmer if he'd been banished instead to a loveless institution. And I know that it was the inscrutable power of love that cut through Len's delusion that night he held a knife above my head. I can say from personal experience that it is literally possible to be saved by the power of love.

On a broader canvas, great intellectual leaders have attributed to love a unique social and political significance. The simple message from Mahatma Gandhi – 'where there is love there is life' – places love at the centre of all human existence. Civil rights leader Martin Luther King identified love as the only force powerful enough to defeat racial hatred when he said, 'Hate cannot drive out hate; only love can do that.' The celebrated writer James Baldwin – who saw race relations in the United States with an unparalleled clarity – wrote in his Letter to my Nephew, 'we with love shall force our [white] brothers to see themselves as they are, to cease fleeing from reality and begin to change it'. And Maya Angelou, renowned diarist and champion for the rights of African Americans and women, also saw the capacity to love as a force for liberation: 'I am grateful...to be loved now and to be able to love. Love liberates. It doesn't just hold.'

Although love can generate caring concern for others, I am more convinced than ever that worldly knowledge is needed to guide that concern along the right path: knowledge, that is, of a shared but differently experienced history, and the responsibilities this creates in the present. Love that isn't tempered by knowledge risks becoming the type of love that holds, rather than liberates; that creates a Love Trap. But, woven together, I hope that love and knowledge can create genuine human connections based on solidarity, rather than paternalistic efforts to help in the absence of understanding.

For me, what would help to rewrite the troubled past is to foresee a future in which relationships of genuine respect and equality are made possible between settler Australians and those who have been collectively wronged by them. Many people are walking towards that future now. I've taken my first step by telling this story, in the hope that telling the truth can open up a pathway towards personal and collective healing.

And I had to run to my safe place / encased in concrete to keep out the dust / before I could write down this story.

Interlude

Once I had pieced together all the fragments I could remember of my life with Len, it seemed as though there was no more remembering left to do. And yet I had not reached a place that felt like a proper ending. Then, unexpectedly, something happened that brought the story out of the past and right into the present; something that would help me take the next step from truth telling to healing.

We are sitting in the bath – Len and me —facing each other. The water is steaming hot. I am very small, maybe three or four years old. Our mother is bending over beside the tub, washing us. Suddenly, she jerks me out of the water by one arm, violently, and smacks me hard. My buttocks are already glowing red from the bathwater, and the slap is painful. But much worse than the pain is the shock. My mother is furious with me. I have done or said something terrible. Silent tears stream down my face.

'How do you feel?' says Kerry.

'Stunned.' I say. 'And confused. I don't know what I've done wrong.'

'Focus on the feelings,' she says as she turns on the chasing green lights and my eyes start to track them back and forth.

I feel intense pressure in my ears and forehead, like a volcano is trying to explode through my skull. When the lights go off, I ask Kerry whether I need to remember what I said.

'Probably not,' she says, 'but it's clearly an incident that started a lot of things for you.'

In the absence of memory, I have filled in the gap with my own suspicions. 'It must have been something awful about Len,' I say. 'It's the only thing that could have caused such terrible anger.'

Kerry offers the beginning of an explanation. 'At around that age, children are starting to notice difference. Len was a boy, and you were a girl. He had brown skin, and you were pale and blonde.' She pauses to let me ponder that.

She has articulated the same options that have occurred to me but has made them sound reasonable rather than blameworthy; has taken into account that I was only very small. I think about the time, around that age, when my big sister caught me with the little boy next door, both with our pants around our ankles. I conclude that I would have satisfied my anatomical curiosity then without needing to try it again in the bath. In any case, for all her stuffy Methodism, our mother was never, at heart, a prude.

'I think it's the second one,' I tell Kerry. 'I must have said Len's skin was dirty, or something like that. That would make sense in the bath.'

The tears turn into racking sobs, a solid burning sensation lodges in the front of my throat and Kerry switches the lights back on.

Once I'm calm, and the lights are off, I say, 'I don't think Mum ever explained what I'd done wrong. I'm sure I would remember if she had.' (It occurs to me later that, alternatively, with a calm explanation at the time, I probably wouldn't have remembered the slap at all.)

'She couldn't explain,' says Kerry softly. 'She didn't understand the innocent and natural way you related to Len.'

'But I think that must be the time when I started to think...' (struggling for words) '...that I was...just...all wrong.'

Later, I think of a third source of difference between Len and me – his club feet. I don't recall ever thinking of Len as disabled. It was just that he wore clunky metal frames on his legs to bed, and only in the very early years. I don't even remember seeing his malformed feet before they'd been surgically transformed. I'm not sure I would have said anything about that in the bath. Then again, I have no recollection either of being conscious when we were small of the difference in our skin. Our mother had never smacked either of us up to that point, and never did so again. It was not part of her parental repertoire, so the slap had been a memorable departure from life as I knew it. Whatever it was I had said, I just knew in my bones that it concerned Len, and it had been something unforgivable. This recollection could also explain why my attempts to soak in a relaxing bath as an adult were always cut short by panic and the urgent need to escape. From that day forward – I now realised – I had lived in mortal fear of doing the wrong thing, of somehow harming others, however inadvertently, through my thoughts or actions, and in the expectation that I should always know instinctively what was right.

We start the therapy again and a tingling sensation starts to travel up my body originating in my feet. Kerry has suggested before that this can represent a journey. Could it be an inner journey that is rewriting my acceptance of the past? Then comes a burning heat coursing through my core and into my shoulders. I know intuitively what it is.

'I can feel my power now,' I announce, somewhat dramatically, 'my capacity to accept responsibility.' My mind is scanning forward to young adulthood, to the time when I accompanied my bloodied brother to hospital. The only time I remember feeling like I was doing something right. 'I wasn't the sister I could have been,' I tell Kerry, 'And now I can't bear to think I might have hurt Len when we were small. And I'll never have a chance to make things right.' Then overpowering grief again – and the green lights come back on.

When the EMDR session is over, there seemed to have been something of a resolution; or at least a new idea had come into my mind. It was a plan about something I could do to try to make things better. I felt that I had to build a bridge between the past and the present.

'Somehow it feels like Len is here and has given me his blessing,' I say to Kerry, 'about something I've been thinking of doing.' I explain to her how I have started to imagine finding Len's brother Arthur and any other surviving members of Len's family. I just needed to be sure it was the right thing to do. I want to explain that grief and shame have kept me away for so many years, but now I want to be the sister I could have been to Len – the supportive, capable, adult sister. Since he is gone, perhaps I can be a sister to them instead, if that's what they want.

I explain to Kerry my fear that I have just made up this plan to suit myself; a white lady trying to soothe her own conscience, desperately seeking acceptance, like some phoney embodiment of white guilt.

'No,' Kerry reassures me, almost whispering, 'you haven't made it up.'

Part 2

Real Time

We have to hope...that the people who love us and who know us a little bit will in the end have seen us truly. In the end, not much else matters.

Ali Smith, *Autumn*

A reconnection

Today I'm feeling excited and hopeful, as well as a little apprehensive, because it feels like a whole new chapter in life is beginning. It began a month ago when I spent some time in Adelaide. I went there partly to enjoy my hometown in its annual moment of exuberance during 'mad March'. That's when the whole place throws off its sedate image and the Festival of Arts, Fringe Festival, Writers' Festival and Womadelaide converge in a perfect storm of contemporary culture. But I also went there with another agenda – to find a starting point in my search for Len's family.

The obvious method – looking in the telephone directory – hadn't amounted to anything, so I steeled myself and decided to approach SA Link-Up again. This time is more promising than when I'd tried several years before, only to be reminded – with good reason – that I was not in the category of people they were set up to help. The woman on the reception desk listens politely to my nervously truncated explanation.

'I had an Aboriginal foster brother. He was in the family before I was born so, to me, he was just my brother. It ended badly. I lost contact with his birth family and would like to get back in touch.'

She disappears into the office then returns with another woman, who introduces herself as a Link-Up researcher. What a wonderful job she has, I think, helping people to reconnect, or at least find out where they fit in the world. I tell my heavily abridged story again. Instead of sending me away, she asks for some names and starts to tap on her computer keyboard. I already know about the information that comes up but am grateful beyond words for her efforts. Both the women are sympathetic and want to help me. They treat me like someone who is worthy of receiving kindness, for which I am truly grateful.

I leave with a list of strategies for starting the search in earnest, the simplest of which is to visit the headquarters of the SA Electoral Office and use the terminals provided to look for addresses. I had looked in vain before that for an online version of the electoral roll and been surprised when I hadn't found one. In this online age, I had assumed that anything public was also going to be accessible via the internet, but the Link-Up researcher had set me straight. You had to go there in person and use their in-house system.

I manage to get there on my last day in town and log in to one of the terminals, expecting to be disappointed. Two of the names come up on the first search. The addresses are in Adelaide and look to be in areas where I know Len's family members have lived in the past. I feel sure it's them. I write down the details then see there is a browse function. When I put in Len's family name I get a large number of hits, so I settle in to work my way down the list, marvelling that I haven't thought to do this before. I notice lots of entries from Ceduna and some from Koonibba as well. They are bound to be Len's extended family. I look through all the unfamiliar names and wonder about their lives. Many of them must be growing up in a very different world from the one that Len knew. I wonder how many of the older ones might remember him. I find myself hoping that their lives are happy and fulfilled, wishing I knew them. There are many other names on the screen with addresses in Adelaide. I have no way of knowing which of those might be members of Len's family, but I read through them all, wondering.

Back home in the Snowy Mountains where I now live, quite close to the source of the Murray River that empties into the sea not so far from Adelaide, I sit at my desk and take out the paper where I wrote the addresses I'd found for Len's brother Arthur and sister Vonnie. I type out two separate letters containing what I hope are the appropriate words for each of them. I start with reminders to Arthur, who should remember me, about who I am and how much I loved his brother. For Vonnie, who I've never met, I start with an introduction and an apology for the unexpected intrusion into her life. I don't want to overdo it – to explain how I have grieved for Len all these years and blamed myself without really understanding why, to express what it would mean to me to reconnect with them, to join our families, but in a better way this time because the wrongness of the past is acknowledged and, in time, perhaps even put behind us. I don't want to scare them off – to have them see me as too needy or interfering or even a bit deranged; someone you wouldn't willingly let into your life. I'm sure they've suffered their own losses and tragedies, so they don't need to be burdened with knowledge of my own 'puny sorrows'.[99]

I keep the letters short and simple. In each of them, I say how much I would love to get back in touch and explain that grief and shame have prevented me from doing that until now. I print out the letters, then decide I can't send them in that form. They look cold and businesslike on the stark white page. The regimented typeface has stripped the words of the sincerity they were meant to convey. I pick out two sheets of decorative writing paper with matching envelopes – different patterns in case Arthur and Vonnie get together and compare notes – and copy out the letters by hand.

It was just over a week ago when I posted them. I had prepared myself for the possibility of receiving no response, whatever that might signify. Perhaps they've moved? Or passed away? Or perhaps they want to leave the past right where it is? But now it's Friday 13 April and it has turned out to be my lucky day. I'm on my way upstairs after a morning spent pottering happily in the vegie patch when I realise my mobile phone is ringing. I head towards it, lamenting the deposits of black soil I see embedded under my fingernails as I reach out my hand. It isn't a number from my contacts list, so I hesitate. Usually that means someone wanting money or inviting me to take a survey. But it rings out anyway before I can decide whether or not to answer. A voicemail announces itself a few seconds later.

I struggle to make out the message at first. It's a male voice I don't recognise, a bit muffled – sounding a little hesitant. Then I realise. IT'S ARTHUR. My heart begins to pound, almost out of my chest. He has called the number I included in my letter and taken the time to leave a message. I can't believe what I'm hearing.

'Would love to meet you again,' he says. I notice how he has emphasised the first word more than is usual. '*Would* love to meet you again.' '*Would* love to...' It's as if he realises how much I worried that he wouldn't. Then he adds playfully, 'It's been a while.'

Before calling him back, I listen to the message over and over again. I save his number securely in my phone contacts too and write it down for good measure, afraid that next time I look on my phone everything will have disappeared; that the whole thing will turn out to have been a figment of my imagination. A few minutes later, when Arthur answers the phone, everything seems perfectly natural. We reminisce about the few times when we met. Arthur remembers being at my parents' fiftieth wedding anniversary, many years after Len died. But he doesn't remember the time, much earlier, when we met up together in town, Len, Arthur and me. Incredibly, he even recalls that at the time of the golden wedding I was just about to leave for Cambridge to study criminology. It's as if I am a person in his life. I ask him how he is. I really mean it.

'How are you?' I say into the phone, wanting to convey how much I care about the answer.

He immediately talks about his family. I suppose that equates, for him, to an answer about his own well-being.

It's a struggle to keep up with all the information. There are four young grandchildren. And he just got back in touch with someone else's kids – I can't quite make out who. It turns out that Nora, who moved to Queensland a while ago, had one not-so-happy marriage then a good one. One was to a German.

'Same background as our family,' I say, making a feeble attempt at connection, and hoping that he was the good husband. 'Is Nora still alive?' I ask, knowing that must be wishful thinking.

Arthur confirms that she is not, but she's not forgotten. The family names live on in younger generations. Arthur lists them off – one child named Lenora after both Len and Nora, another one Monica, in memory of one of their older sisters. Although Arthur shares with me candidly some of the problems the younger ones are facing, it's clear that the family is strong and proud and tightly knit.

I also learn that Arthur's wife Elizabeth, who I remember well, died some years before. It's sad to think of Arthur living alone, but it turns out he's not. He has White Boy, his huge white bull mastiff who has one blue and one brown eye.

'He's so big,' says Arthur, 'that sometimes he knocks over the little kids. I have to tell them, "Watch out for White Boy."'

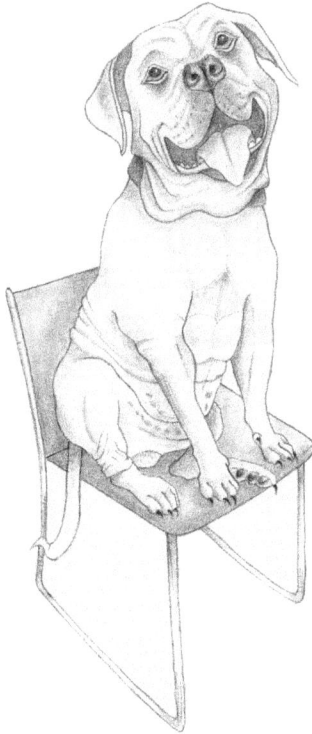

We both laugh and laugh at this, and all sorts of variations come to mind. 'Stop that, White Boy!' 'White Boy, get down!' 'Baaaad White Boy!' Sharing a joke makes me feel that things are going to work out fine. I foresee a future opening up where I will no longer feel trapped inside my own Deep Thinking or my family's small horizons. There could be fulfilment and acceptance. There could be responsibility. There could be heartbreak. But I feel ready. Some inspirational words come into my mind. I saw them once in someone's email signature, attributable – it turned out when I had googled – to a Christian writer Frederick Buechner: 'Here is the world. Beautiful and terrible things will happen. Don't be afraid.'

The phone cuts out and I can't get the call back. I text instead, saying, 'Never mind, I will call another day and make a time to visit.'

I go back over the conversation in my mind and marvel at the easy way in which Arthur imparted his family news, let me in, entrusted me with that special knowledge about his world. When I call him back later to make a time to visit, one of his daughters – either Jacqui or Jeannie – answers the phone. She seems to recognise my name. As I discuss with Arthur the dates when I could fly to Adelaide, it seems he intends to invite other people from the family. We agree a time, and he says he'll let me know the place.

'I only live in a one-bedroom flat,' he says. 'It would be better to meet somewhere else.'

'Please don't go to any bother,' I text him later. 'I'm happy to come to your place.'

In fact, I feel a need to see him in his home. Perhaps that will happen later when our meetings may need to be quieter. If all goes well, I'm hoping he will tell me what he remembers about Lennie's story, and maybe about his own, so I can record it in the memoir; so the book can become, to some extent, his story as well.

An apology

I had arranged to meet Arthur, and possibly other members of the family, on a Sunday in May. I fly into Adelaide the Friday night before and go to stay at my sister's place. Unusually, Arthur has not been answering my texts for the last couple of weeks so I am not confident that our arrangement to meet at his daughter's house is confirmed. Of course, I could have just gone there as planned on Sunday, and all would probably have been well. But I've waited so long for this meeting, and know that I have to be back in Melbourne for work on Monday, so there'll be no second chance on this visit if the meeting falls through. When I still haven't heard from Arthur on Saturday, I become anxious and decide I can't take the chance of missing him the next day. So I drive to his address, not expecting to find him there, intending simply to leave a note asking him to call.

I pull up in my hire car at the small block of one-storey flats and know immediately I am in the right place. An enormous white dog with a head the size of a bowling ball is barking at the screen door. There would be no option of leaving a note and sneaking away. Arthur comes to the door, looks at me for a long time, then invites me in. I instantly regret catching him off-guard. He had told me he preferred to meet me elsewhere. But instead, I've intruded into his personal space, uninvited. I curse my impatient and angsty nature, my desperate need to make sure that things work out as planned. I should have simply trusted him to be there the next day and taken things in my stride. Arthur does look slightly annoyed, as he has every right to be, and he mumbles an apology about not having had time to clean up the flat. I glance around and it seems tidy enough to me, if rather austere. There are very few furnishings and the walls are bare except for a set of family photos depicting an earlier time when Elizabeth was alive, and their girls were young. I make a mental note that Arthur would not have cultural objections to me showing him the photographs of Len I had decided not to bring this time, since I had wondered if they might upset him.

I make my own apology then. Although not the one I am planning to make at our scheduled meeting the next day in front of a gathering of Len's kin. I tell Arthur I'm very sorry to drop by unannounced, but I hadn't been able to reach him by phone and was just trying to confirm arrangements for tomorrow.

He glances at the phone on his table but offers no explanation. 'I didn't recognise you,' he says, looking back at me, seeming slightly disappointed.

It had been a very long time. I now wore glasses, and the trademark long blonde hair he would have remembered was cut shorter and temporarily coloured a pale shade of pink; grey showing through at the temples. For my part, I'm not disappointed. I am looking at a face that might have been Len's had he lived beyond his twenties. That recognition causes my heart to fill with love. But I also feel embarrassed and awkward about my unscheduled arrival and because of the luxurious car I've been assigned by the hire car company, an unasked-for upgrade on the budget model I had booked.

There is nothing at all luxurious about Arthur's living space. We sit down at the small table, occupying the only chairs in the room, and I ask about the arrangements for the following day. Would his sisters Vonnie and Judith be there? And their families?

'Oh yeah, yeah, I can ask them,' he says, but I can see he is only just contemplating that now.

'Do you still want to meet up at Jeannie's place?' I ask. 'And will Jacqui be there as well?'

My mind is bursting with things I've been waiting to ask and say, but I resolve to save them for the main event. They are things that can be said only once, and tomorrow would be the right moment. It begins to dawn on me that for some time I've been seeking an opportunity to make some kind of confession. It's a terrifying thought, and I have no idea how it will be received. But for now, I confine myself to practicalities, confirming Jeannie's address, checking the time for tomorrow, then filling the space with banter about White Boy, who is trying to break down the barricade he's been placed behind so he can land himself a pat. There's a little brown dog too, named Binnie, that I see has no hope of getting any attention while White Boy is around. Typical.

We start to relax a little as Arthur produces his phone and shows me photo after photo of his family members; many new ones from the younger generations, others old images of people who are gone that he'd photographed from archives. There seem to be hundreds of them, and he thumbs through, reeling off names and explaining relationships, as he had done before on the phone. Even in person, it's hard to keep up with all the details, and to take in the pace of change in Len's family. As he goes along, Arthur points out how pale-skinned many of his nieces and nephews and their children are. The family is transforming, outwardly anyway. The legacy of that German husband of Nora's, I surmise.

Arthur had grown interested in family history and this was his way of building a record, his equivalent of my memoir perhaps. His mission was clearly a documentary one, the creation of an historical record. Whereas mine had become more of an emotional journey and, as usual for me, an exercise in Deep Thinking. Arthur was also building a family tree and he tells me about various branches of the family – mostly people I've never heard of. And when he speaks about the place of his and Len's birth, I notice he calls it *Koo*nibba with the emphasis right at the beginning, instead of Koo*nibb*a as my family have always pronounced it. It seems like it will all be worthwhile – taking this leap into the dark – that I will learn a lot, and maybe unlearn some long-held misconceptions.

One is about Len's putative Aranda/Arrentje roots. Arthur looks at me askance when I ask him about that and explains that Aranda country is in the Northern Territory, nowhere near Koonibba, which belonged to the Wirangu and Kokatha people. I knew that of course, but for some reason Mum had told me there was a connection. The records I had found in the Lutheran archive had said that their dad had been adopted and I'd wondered whether his origin might have been from elsewhere. Arthur recalls being taken up north to Aranda country one time when he was just a young fella. He admits he found it 'scary' because he didn't understand the language. He isn't sure why his family had gone there – possibly something to do with a wedding. Did that suggest perhaps that there was already a family connection?

Despite all my clumsy directness, Arthur is beginning to open up now and tell me about his own life. That he'd had a good job for a while, ironically as a youth worker in the same detention centre where Len had been incarcerated many years before. Those were the jobs arising from colonisation where Aboriginal people were needed: liaison officers with police, courts or prisons, tasked with managing the punitive consequences of dispossession. Then he had lost his beloved Elizabeth, he says, and had fallen on hard times after that.

Arthur's eldest daughter Jacqui drops by then with her two sons, all smiles. She remembers who I am and has warm recollections of my parents. She even recalls that my dad had taught her and her sister to play carpet bowls and refers to them as Gran and Papa, just as my own nieces and nephews did. When I show my surprise, Arthur points out that Jacqui's younger sister Jeannie has been named after my mother. Her real name is Elizabeth, after her own mother. But they all call her Jeannie. I'd had no idea that the ties had run so deep.

Then we get onto the practicalities of catering for the next day, as women tend to do. It is agreed that we'll meet up at Jeannie's place.

'We could have a cup of tea,' suggests Jacqui, after she accepts my offer to bring some cake.

At the last minute, it occurs to me to ask whether Arthur will need a lift. I notice that Jacqui has arrived without a car, and Jeannie's place, although reasonably close, is too far for Arthur to walk. We agree I'll come back the next day and pick him up.

*

When I arrive at Arthur's place on Sunday, I find that Jacqui has stayed overnight with her two boys. I wonder where they'd all slept, as the flat is tiny and has no couch. I am learning fast that people manage somehow. We all bundle into the shiny hire car with one of the boys holding a squirming Binnie. I look around nervously for White Boy, imagining the outrageously inflated damage bill the hire company will send me if they find the tiniest scratch on the upholstery. Mercifully, Jeannie had come earlier that morning and walked White Boy around to her place. I have three luscious cakes in the boot that I've picked up from a fancy bakery in one of the leafy suburbs surrounding my sister's house. Three is probably more than needed – but I've bought them in case the extended family does turn up – plus a box of Cadbury Favourites for the kids. So all is in readiness for a modest celebration.

After a winding drive through suburban backstreets, we arrive at Jeannie's place. The house is in a modest suburb in a pleasant location with a football oval right across the road. Arthur's girls tell me later that Aboriginal teams often play there. The whole setting makes the place feel like a home, even though, at first impression, the house looks a bit run-down. My eye is drawn to the overgrown backyard where White Boy has been consigned. Following my gaze perhaps, Arthur explains that he 'tries to keep the weeds down' and I berate myself for appearing middle-class and judgemental. Or is that just what he has come to expect from white folks? The house itself is spacious and comfortable, with an upstairs part where the boys disappear from time to time. Every fibre in my being wants their lives to be happy and secure.

Although this house is handy to her dad's place, Jeannie tells me she is planning to move so she can be within the catchment area for the school that she and her sister had attended. I infer, without asking, that the attraction is a high enrolment of Aboriginal students, and a supportive approach to Aboriginal culture and history that is not necessarily to be found elsewhere. Later, among the many photos Arthur shows me that day, is one of a school-aged Jeannie looking stunning in her evening attire. The school had secured tickets for a few students to attend the Reconciliation Ball, Jeannie explains, and she'd been one of the lucky ones chosen to go that year. The contrast with Len's isolation at our primary school back in the 60s could not have been starker. Ironically, our school was named Cowandilla, which is derived from the Kaurna word – Kawantilla – that, on some accounts, equates most closely with that part of present-day Adelaide/Tandanya.[100] But no mention was ever made at school of the Indigenous connection, and we were never taught a thing about the existence of the Kaurna people in the seven years I spent there.

On the way in, I notice a dilapidated four-wheel drive parked in the driveway of Jeannie's house. I ask whether it's running, and Arthur tells me it needs about $2,000 worth of work to be roadworthy. They have considered doing it up and travelling around as a family. My mind immediately shoots down a well-worn path. I could come to the rescue. That amount of money is not small change to me, but I could find it, and would do so willingly for my newfound family. Fortunately, I check myself before this idea can come gushing out of my mouth. I know that these sentiments should be carefully managed. It was so easy to cross the line between generosity and paternalism, and not always easy to determine where the boundary fell. In any case, I judge it premature to raise the matter now. I have not yet earned the right to give to them without connotations.

Jeannie has made us cups of tea. The three boys pounce on the chocolate cake topped with lavish swirls of chocolate icing, while the adults, after a polite period of abstention, gravitate towards a more wholesome-looking carrot cake swathed in cream cheese frosting. It turns out that Arthur is diabetic, which I'd half expected, since the incidence of that disease is so high among Aboriginal people of his age. But that doesn't prevent him from tucking in to a second helping despite the protestation of his daughters.

It soon becomes clear that no other members of the family are going to appear. We spend some time looking at Arthur's photos and making small talk, until I feel the moment has come to make my announcement. I stand up abruptly to get everyone's attention – which is exactly what happens – then wonder how I can possibly start. Feeling a bit ridiculous, I seek out Arthur's gaze and lock on. I explain that, while our family had all loved Len very much, I'd understood for a long time that the policies that placed Aboriginal children with white parents were wrong and that I was sorry that Len had been taken away from his family.

Arthur looks bemused, then floors me with his response. 'You've been reading about that Stolen Generations stuff,' he says, intent on setting the record straight. 'Lennie wasn't stolen. Our mum give him away.'

The effect on me is seismic. I'd expected either a gracious acceptance of my apology, or maybe a confirmation of how much the family had suffered from the loss of their youngest son. It could have been the moment of absolution I had longed for, but I wasn't prepared to be let off the hook so completely. Trying to corral my turbulent thoughts, I realise that I must either stage a graceful retreat or continue along my intended path. I decide to persevere. Taking Arthur's hands in mine for extra emphasis, I explain that, even so, I believe it was wrong that Lennie had not been returned to them. This only prompts a further rebuttal.

'Peter and Jenny didn't do anything wrong,' Arthur exclaims, 'don't ever think that. We were happy that Len was in a good Christian home.'

I hadn't had the chance to show Arthur the first part of the memoir yet, although I had mentioned I was writing it. Was he reading my mind? Was this a reproach for all my politically correct, god-denying, Deep Thinking, which is how it felt to me? Had my parents' simple loving acceptance of the situation been reasonable all along? It seemed that Arthur considered them to be beyond reproach. Would he object to the forensic examination I'd made in the memoir of my parents' beliefs and actions? Had I got it all wrong? I had stepped unwittingly onto very thin ice.

It wasn't so much that I thought my parents had done something wrong – not intentionally at least. What troubled me most was that growing up with us had not been the right thing for Len, and that my parents had failed to see their role within a state apparatus that had caused so much harm. But neither, it transpired, had Arthur. He didn't seem the least bit interested in my confession.

Here's what I told myself when I was voicing my recollections into my digital recorder that night. 'It's made me feel like a bit of a drama queen – like maybe I've overthought the whole thing. But I know that it affected me emotionally from a young age seeing first-hand what Len was going through, although never really understanding it. The story I built up for myself over so many years seems to be unravelling. But speaking with Arthur some more might cast it in a different light, which can only be a good thing.'

*

After the apology, the conversation moves on to safer ground, assisted by further helpings of cake. Arthur explains how he was raised by his older sisters, including Nora. I know this was not unusual for Aboriginal families. These are the 'overlapping circles' of kinship that I had read about while writing the first part of the book.[101] But in Arthur's case, it seemed those circles had not included his mother at all during the crucial early years of his childhood. Coupled with the claim he had just made about his mother 'giving Lennie away', I interpret this as possible confirmation about Clara's problem drinking. That misconception will stay with me until the next time I see Arthur.

Arthur also says that he knew Len had loved us but was conflicted about his identity. 'Didn't know if he was black or white,' is how he puts it. 'Didn't know where he should be.'

This reminded me of times when Len had been called a 'coconut'; brown on the outside, but white on the inside. I'm not sure who had said this, but it was after Len started to reconnect with his Aboriginal heritage. I'm sure he'd been confronted with much worse while trying to find his place in the white world, but this rejection on what should have been his home ground must have been even more profound. Arthur relates how he and his older brothers would talk about Len's welfare once they had reunited with him as a young adult. They could see that he was 'getting confused'. I wonder how that confusion displayed itself when Len was with them. They would have seen the drinking, I'm sure. But I don't know how much they knew about the distress that had eventually been attributed to schizophrenia. I had expected that Arthur might link the deterioration of Len's mental health with the policies that placed a small Aboriginal boy in a white family, as I did. But in view of his response to my apology, I decide not to canvass that possibility.

As we continue to talk, it turns out that Arthur also has a different take on the time we had all met up in Hindley Street, when we were just youngsters. I had mentioned that occasion to Arthur the first time we spoke on the phone. In my mind, it had been a brief moment of togetherness as an extended family. I'd been disappointed that Arthur hadn't recalled the occasion when I'd mentioned it the first time. But it seems that he has remembered it now, and he mentions it in order to tell me an anecdote that he finds amusing. According to Arthur, I had left the two brothers in Hindley Street in order to catch the bus home from nearby Currie Street. I am impressed that he now remembers that degree of detail. After I was gone, Arthur told me he had said to Len, 'Aaaw, your sister's beautiful.' He is obviously enjoying recreating the scene and turns on a salacious and decidedly unbrotherly tone of voice to make his point. But Len had not been at all amused – had in fact become furious and told Arthur in no uncertain terms to 'keep away from my sister'. 'He was always protective of you,' Arthur adds.

I am slightly embarrassed about the circumstances, but it is the first insight I had ever had of how Len spoke about me outside the confines of our family. The words 'my sister' lodge in my heart, the more so because he had used the term without hesitation in front of his real brother. I realised then that, in the midst of my adolescent struggles to find my own way in the world, I had been truly unaware of how Len saw me or felt about our relationship. My mother had relayed Len's apparent fears about my safety, but I had interpreted that, cynically, as a maternal ploy to reinforce her own efforts to clip my adolescent wings.

Len and I had been just on our way to forging a more direct relationship of our own around the time that Arthur was recollecting, but I had put an end to that by buying my one-way ticket to London. With the newfound realisation of Len's brotherly devotion to me, the awful possibility arises in my mind that my abandonment of him could have been one of the precipitating factors that led to his death. I had always felt that I'd let him down by not staying to support him. But it would never have entered my mind, before hearing Arthur's story, that perhaps my brother might have needed me – a sister he could care for – to help him consolidate his own place within his white world. Instead of relieving myself of a burden, I begin to feel that the burdens are multiplying.

On the other hand, Arthur's telling of our shared story conveys very clearly that he has never thought of me as a sister. And why would he? I could see how the calculus might be different for the two of us. For him, a younger brother who had been absent for most of his life had recently reappeared and brought with him a white family with which Arthur had formed no childhood connection. For me, a brother who I had grown up with was starting to introduce me to family members I could only understand as extensions of him. I began to see how naïve I must have been to hope that my meeting with Arthur would create an instant and seamless connection between our families. I clearly needed them in my life far more than they needed me. The business of building bridges would not be easy.

*

One of the many things that had haunted me after Len's death was a concern about whether his family had been properly consulted about his burial. Having been overseas at the time, I had only a sketchy understanding of what had taken place. It turned out that Arthur had been heavily involved. I'd assumed that the funeral would have been held in our own local church that had been so much a part of our family life, and which Len had also attended. But Arthur tells me the service had been held in what was then the George Street Aboriginal Lutheran Church in Thebarton. It is another surprise, but this time it is something positive that corrects a longstanding misapprehension. Another revelation is that Arthur and his girls had continued to visit Len's grave, probably more often than any of our Adelaide-based family members, if truth be known.

I am intrigued to learn that Len had spoken with Arthur about where he was destined to be buried. I had come to appreciate how much this mattered to Aboriginal people, but it was disturbing to think that Len would raise the issue while so young, as if he were somehow expecting an untimely demise. Arthur says that Len had told him he had a place in his grandmother's grave, and that Len had been pleased about that. This was a prospect I could not have contemplated as a twenty-something-year-old who had barely given a moment's thought to my own mortality. Is it possible that knowing where he would be laid to rest was the only place of secure belonging that Len could envisage? That was devastating to contemplate. And why had our parents made this premature offer to Len, I wonder, and not to any other of their children? Again, my conversation with Arthur seems to be producing more questions than answers.

I finally have the chance to ask Arthur whether there is anything – maybe a traditional ceremony – that his family would have wanted at Lennie's funeral. I have in mind a smoking ceremony which might be healing for all of us.

'No,' says Arthur, 'we're urban Aborigines – Christians. Everything was done how we wanted.'

Clearly, I had underestimated my own parents all this time and also imposed my own image of the cultural preferences of Len's family. It occurs to me then to ask Arthur whether he and the girls would like to visit Len's grave that afternoon, while we have the opportunity to drive there in the hire car. Arthur and Jeannie agree to come while Jacqui looks after the boys. On the short drive to the cemetery, they tell me how they've often wondered where my mum and dad were buried and had tried to locate their graves. I realise with shame that they had not been notified when our parents had died. Admittedly, my siblings and I had no way of contacting Arthur. But to be perfectly honest, the prospect had not crossed our minds, perhaps because we had no idea how close their relationship had remained. I promise I will take them to see Peter and Jean's grave as well.

As we walk through the cemetery, Jeannie points out the headstones that appeal to her and seems to know quite a lot about them. It's as if she knows the place well and is pointing out the highlights on a guided tour. The headstones that catch her eye are like nothing I have seen before. They seem out of place in this sedate and tightly regulated space where the style of headstones, the placement of vases and planting of rose bushes are all carefully calibrated, with different rules applying in different sections. As far as I knew, the only exceptions to this conformity were the ornate Italianate memorials that lined the access road, topped with protective angels and plastic flowers, designed quite deliberately to catch the eye.

The section Jeannie is directing us through now seems to be newly established, and stands in marked contrast to the rest of the graveyard in terms of aesthetics. The oversized headstones are dazzlingly decorated in bright colours with personalised designs intended to celebrate the individual interred there – their heritage, personal qualities and lifelong passions. I spot a collage of high-powered sports cars in reds and primary colours, no doubt for a motor enthusiast. And a tropical design in brilliant pinks and aquamarine, perhaps commemorating a vibrant woman from the Pacific Islands. Whatever one thought of the aesthetic qualities, these are bold statements from people who embraced the inevitability of death and expected to be remembered by their kin. The images seem to be printed onto a glossy surface to create a 3D effect of the type you sometimes see on souvenirs. It is a revolution in memorialisation.

Jeannie points out the ones she likes, as if they are exhibits in an art gallery, and discusses with her dad the sort of designs they would like for themselves. I think about the unassuming plaque on my parents' grave that we had just visited, how it conformed to the expectations of that staid section of the cemetery, and how it reflected their own values of humility and simplicity. They would not have wanted to stand out from the crowd in death any more than in life. I feel obliged to explain that Peter and Jean had chosen their plain little plaque for themselves – noting that they were Methodists who were not interested in adornment – just in case Arthur and Jeannie thought we had not given them their due.

As we get closer to the section where my grandmother and Len were interred, the old order returns. This part of the cemetery, known as the Lawn Section, has even stricter rules than the part where my parents had been laid to rest. All the headstones have identical, low-level cement bases onto which bronze plaques of uniform size with standard gold lettering are attached. The regimentation is not unlike a war cemetery, but it has also created a sense of calm and serenity, which was no doubt the intention. The graves are punctuated at every third or fourth plot with a rose bush, white in some rows, pink or yellow in others. They are not flowering, and I struggle to remember what colour Lennie's rose is. I can't even be sure, in fact, that I've ever seen it in bloom.

When I visited Len's grave on my own, I usually dropped onto my hands and knees, pressing my palms flat on the grass, in the hope, perhaps, of detecting even the faintest vibration; longing for some kind of connection. But I stay on my feet this day and keep my gaze on the familiar words written on the commemorative plaque as we all contemplate the grave in silence. I'd read the inscription many times before – 'Esther Eleanor Weber, beloved wife of Christian Alfred (dec)'. Then Len's full name, 'Beloved chosen son and brother of Peter, Jean and family'. And yet I had never before seen what was so obviously missing. It comes to me suddenly. And then it is blindingly obvious. Shocking, in fact. Where is the mention of Len's Aboriginal family? Arthur may have been consulted about the service, and Len himself may have approved the choice of burial site, but no one had seen the necessity to acknowledge Len's birth family on the headstone – not then, and not during the course of all the years that had passed. This sent the message that my parents had claimed Len completely, erasing any record of his connection to the people who had brought him into the world and had loved him first.

A resolution begins to form in my mind. We needed to add a line to the plaque. A small act of acknowledgement that Len had had two families, not just one. We could at least rewrite this aspect of the past. I'd been wrong about just about everything in Arthur's eyes over the last few hours – things that I had thought about so obsessively over many years – so I'm reluctant to blurt out a thought that has only just popped into my mind. Arthur might say that he thought things were fine how they were, just how Peter and Jean had arranged them. Me over-reacting again. But I also sense that now, while we are standing there at the grave, might be the only chance I will ever have to raise this proposal. So I just jump in headlong.

'Your family name is not there,' I observe. 'Do you think we should add a line on the plaque to show that Len was the beloved son of your family as well as ours?'

Arthur and Jeannie exchange a look. 'Good idea,' they say in unison.

When I drop Jeannie back at her house, I leave two copies of what is now part one of The Chosen Son, which is all that I had written at that time. Jacqui picks up one copy and promises to read it. After all that had happened in the last twenty-four hours, I have become even more apprehensive about how they will receive it – especially my anti-religious stance and what they may well see as criticism of my saintly parents. I explain that they should tell me if there is anything they don't think is right, and that we can also change the first names of their family members if they want to, although I haven't mentioned their family name anywhere. I explain that I want to publish it, mainly so that white people could understand how those policies had harmed people, even in what seemed like the best possible circumstances where fostered children were treated with love.

On the short ride back to Arthur's place, I comment on the convoluted route he is directing me to take and wonder how he remembered it. He says it is just habit because that's the way the girls walked from Jeannie's place when they came to visit.

'Is it quicker than going on the main roads?' I ask, just to make conversation.

'No,' he says, 'it's so they won't get stopped by police.'

*

When I arrive back at my nephew's luxurious home in the shadow of the Adelaide Hills, I decline emphatic invitations to join their guests at the dinner table, preferring to install myself in the downstairs guest room with my voice recorder to get down as much as I can recall about the day's events. My nephew's wife Libby leaves their dinner guests to join me for a while and surprises me with her line of conversation. Although I have not involved any other family members in my quest to reconnect with Arthur, clearly the reason for this visit to Adelaide has become a talking point. She tells me my nephew often speaks about Len and 'thought the world of him'. There is no reason to expect otherwise, but since not a word has ever passed between Matt and me on this topic, it's surprising to hear that Len has stayed so prominently in his thoughts. I knew that my sister's other child, Jenny-Lea – named after my mother and me – had missed her Uncle Len terribly and had often felt him watching over her in moments of vulnerability during her adolescent years. I did not expect to hear anything remotely similar from her businesslike brother.

But it's the next thing that Libby tells me that most surprises me. She says that Matt has sometimes voiced his suspicion that Len had been pushed from that bridge by police. I calculate that Matt would have been only ten years old when Len died. He must surely have heard that theory from my mother. It's confronting to contemplate how these thoughts could have survived for so long within the family without being properly aired and either acted on or put to rest.

How ironic, I think later that evening, as I become more and more embroiled in Deep Thinking about the past, that my new project to build a bridge between my own guilt-ridden past and a more constructive future, should rely metaphorically on the same kind of structure that had brought my brother's life to an end.

*

Back at work in Melbourne a few days later, I find myself in the office of Professor Lynette Russell AM, a celebrated scholar of Indigenous history who has published a memoir about her own family's colonisation story.[102] She is one of a small coterie who knows about my project and understands what I am trying to do, possibly better than I do. I'm recounting to her the most surprising aspects of my visit to Adelaide, as something of a debrief. As I repeat Arthur's words to her – 'Peter and Jean did nothing wrong' – I see her eyes fill with tears. When I'd first gone to her office several years earlier, tentatively seeking her approval, I think, for the story I was struggling to write, I'd been the one who had sat with tears streaming down my face. Lynette had been understanding, but she'd remained composed and professional; had not displayed any outward emotion. So her teary reaction on hearing my exchange with Arthur puzzled me.

I ask her why she is upset.

'It's the incredible generosity of Aboriginal people,' she says.

This was pause for thought. What I had interpreted from the perspective of my own insatiable need for reassurance as a hurtful rejection of my understanding of the past, Lynette had seen from Arthur's point of view as an act of grace.

As we continue to speak about my hopes of building a positive relationship with Len's relatives, I tell her about the possibility of reviving the family's run-down four-wheel drive, since I know it would make their lives so much easier.

Lynette advises me against trying to be a rescuer. 'That never works,' she says, speaking from bitter experience.

It is the same kind of tough love she dispensed when I'd first told her about my memoir and she warned me to expect 'pushback' if it were ever published. I had expected that would mean from white folk, but I now understood it might come from Aboriginal people as well who saw things differently. I could see that I still had a long way to go at both a personal and a political level, to understand the many strands of everything. But at least I was beginning to see the path I needed to take and to build up the resolve to continue.

A reality check

I telephone Arthur a few weeks later to tell him I've found out that we can't just put another line on the plaque after all, but that I haven't given up on the idea. Because it was cast in bronze, all the words must be stamped onto the plaque during the manufacturing process. They can't be added on later. I will need to speak with my siblings about ordering a completely new one and find out how much it will cost. The conversation is difficult because Jeannie has answered her dad's phone and is acting as a go-between since Arthur is finding it increasingly difficult to hear.

Without any probing from me, Arthur offers his appraisal of the first part of the memoir, which Jeannie relays to me without embellishment. 'Dad says he's disappointed with the book.'

My heart sinks to a place so deep inside that I fear it will be irretrievable. This story was supposed to connect our families – to unite us by coming to a shared understanding about the insuperable difficulties of Len's life with us. That is how I had seen it. But my attempt to write us into the same story has clearly backfired.

Perhaps I should have been ready. After all, this was an ambitious goal and things were never likely to just fall into place. But I am being consumed by that lifelong feeling of being inescapably, existentially wrong. I know we can't grapple with matters of that complexity over the phone, not to mention the added difficulty of this tag-team communication style. But it will be months before I can get to Adelaide again, and I feel that I can't survive without some idea about where things have gone wrong. I summon the composure to ask Jeannie in the cheeriest voice possible if she can find out why her dad is disappointed. She relays something cryptic about Aboriginal people being citizens now.

So maybe it's the part about historical policies, I think. Perhaps he thinks I approve of that treatment, or am being too negative and dwelling on the past? My mind is racing. Does he believe in just getting on with things? That's possible, I suppose. I shouldn't have assumed he would see things the same way as me.

'And there's something wrong you have said about his mother,' Jeannie explains. 'She was never a drinker.'

I am horrified for causing offence but also puzzled because that's what my own mother had told me.

'That's why I wanted your dad to read the book,' I say, 'so I can fix up anything that's wrong.' I know, even as I say it, that there would be some parts I might just have to try to explain, that I couldn't change without betraying myself and the story. 'Please explain to your dad,' I add, 'that I was only a baby when Lennie came to live with us,' —in fact, I was only an embryo, but there is no need to be so precise – 'so there are many things I'm still trying to understand.'

'She was just a baby,' I hear Jeannie relay to Arthur.

No response.

'Can you ask him to mark the places in the book where he thinks things are wrong,' I continue, 'then I'll come to Adelaide as soon as I can, and we can talk them through. And if Arthur wants to tell his own story, then I could write that down as well.'

It was a confronting conversation and continued the trend of things not going at all as I had imagined. But I think afterwards that Arthur's engagement with the content was in some ways preferable to the howling silence that had come from my own siblings. On the one hand, it had been a huge relief that neither of them had protested outright about my portrayal of our family, as I had feared they might. Some of the events I discussed had happened after they had left the family home, and others were such personal observations that they couldn't possibly have known about them. But in that case, wouldn't they want to find out more? I wondered if they had really seen me, even then, after I had offered myself up, so uncharacteristically, to outside scrutiny. While I was pleased it had not caused a rift, it seemed that what I had written had not been a revelation for them and they never offered an opinion about any of it. When I had felt able to ask them some factual questions that might fill a few gaps in my knowledge, they had both submitted graciously to my questioning, but much of the time their memory of events had been no better than mine. I felt our relationship had changed a little. I was no longer the sweet but headstrong baby sister who had grown into an inscrutable and uncompromising woman (at least that's how I thought they might see me). I had revealed to them something about my life and had at least not been rejected outright; had felt some of the burden of the isolation I felt within the family lift. But that was still quite a way from the connection I had hoped to feel that comes through shared experience.

*

Four months passed before I was able to visit Arthur again in Adelaide. His 'disappointment' had played on my mind the whole time, and I wasn't confident that I could get to the bottom of it, let alone make amends. I had managed one trip to Adelaide in the interim but my efforts to contact Arthur had come to nothing. This had made me fear the worst – that his disappointment had become terminal, and he no longer wished to have anything to do with me.

But this time Arthur is in his flat when I arrive at the agreed time. He explains that he'd been very sick with flu last time I was in town. So that was why I had not been able to get in contact. He has indeed lost a lot of weight. He seems a little wary, but at least has agreed to see me. I know I have a lot of work to do to try to reach some level of understanding, that I can't just blunder straight in and risk making things worse. I've brought a cake from the same bakery as last time, but with Arthur's diabetes in mind. A plain fruit cake with no icing. It looks a little dry. He cuts a slice and picks at it distractedly while we attempt some small talk. It turns out that Jeannie has sold the unroadworthy vehicle, so I no longer need to wrestle with the conundrum of whether to offer to help. I ask after Arthur's sister Judy, who's just been diagnosed with a serious illness. The conversation spins around in circles for a while as I await my chance to broach the question of the memoir.

The discussion takes a sudden turn towards Aboriginal politics. Arthur speaks with conviction and insight about some of the major achievements and conflicts of the last few decades. I begin to think we might find a point of connection after all. He lists many of the key legal and political events from Terra Nullius and the Mabo judgement to Prime Minister John Howard, who he holds responsible for wiping out many of the gains in self-determination made by Aboriginal people. But he explains each point as if I were hearing it for the first time and need persuading. I nod to show my agreement but am baffled that he feels the need to explain these things to me.

He concludes, 'And then you write all those things in the book.'

'What things?' I wonder, unsure what to say. 'But Arthur, I wrote about all those bad policies you are talking about,' I finally say. 'I agree with everything you are saying and tried to put that in the book.'

Arthur goes quiet, in a way that reminds me of Len.

Then, trying to indicate my solidarity in a more personal way – and possibly sounding a bit desperate – I add, 'It broke my heart to grow up knowing that Len was facing all this prejudice. And I know it's continuing – you told me yourself that the girls still get stopped by police for no reason.'

I can see Arthur letting my words filter slowly through his mind. But he responds by taking the conversation in a different direction, drawing a line under that discussion. It seems he's decided to tell me some of his own story. I feel my spirits lift. I ask if I can turn on the recorder, so I won't forget what he has said, but he looks at me with alarm and I hurriedly put it away. Clearly, I am not out of the woods yet and am still mishandling things. To my relief, though, he carries on regardless. As he reminisces, I learn that Arthur had toured in his youth with the band Coloured Stone and is related to some of the members. He tells me that one of their most popular songs includes the line 'Black boy, black boy, the colour of your skin is your pride and joy'. I look up the band on the internet later, assuming that its heyday was well before the internet was invented, but still hoping there might be some kind of record. I am surprised to see the band is still active. There are YouTube videos and a Wikipedia entry that records the band's origins at Koonibba, and describes the lyrics of 'Black Boy' as a 'somewhat revolutionary sentiment for Aboriginals of Australia in the 1980s'. I am really starting to like where Arthur is coming from.[103]

Suddenly Arthur drops another bombshell. 'Anyway, I didn't even read the book.'

I'm completely broadsided. The academic in me had foolishly assumed that Arthur would have his marked-up copy of the manuscript on hand, ready to discuss the disputed passages with me. Instead, he has not done his homework. After some initial confusion, I feel relieved that at least his disappointment with the book, real as it may be, wasn't based on having read it. It turns out it is Jacqui who has read it, and her report to Arthur had not been favourable.

'Jacqui reckons it said lots of terrible things about our family,' he says, 'and that Peter and Jenny would roll over in their graves.'

I try desperately to marry that up with the fragments I had already gleaned from the phone conversation curated by Jeannie. There had been an issue about Aboriginal history and citizenship, and incorrect statements about Clara having a drinking problem. I feel like the story is once again in fragments and would have to be pieced back together all over again. I didn't want to launch a defence. In fact, that's not really an option when you're not sure exactly what there is to defend. Also, some of the criticisms might be completely reasonable, if I only knew what they were exactly. So I explain again, apologetically, that it was mainly the policies that took Aboriginal children away from their parents that I had criticised in the book, that I had certainly not meant to say anything negative about their family, and that I could change anything factual that was not correct. Even as I was speaking, I knew that Arthur and his girls would not agree with my rejection of my own parents' religious outlook and the role I thought that might have played in the whole affair, but there was not a lot I could do about that.

I was starting to suspect that constant harping on by white Australians about the hardships inflicted on Aboriginal people by colonisation could be just as irritating as outright hostility or might be considered misplaced. A new generation of Aboriginal activists had emerged who preferred to tell their own stories of survival and resilience and were not interested in expressions of white guilt. Perhaps that had been my mistake. Another possibility was that Jacqui had read my accounts of colonial policies, and the little I had managed to find out about her family's circumstances, as a personal affront rather than a political statement. Being accustomed to being unfairly treated might predispose anyone to expect criticism rather than solidarity. We seemed to have arrived at an impasse: me not understanding the specific concerns the family had about the memoir, and Arthur trying to assess whether anything I had said should change his opinion.

At that point, two teenage girls burst through the door, filling the flat with youthful energy. After minimal greetings and with a sense of absolute entitlement, they head straight for the kitchen and rummage around in the fridge and the cupboards. Arthur politely explains their relationship to him for my benefit, but they show no interest in being introduced to me. It is as if I am not even there. As if the chair where I'm sitting is terra nullius in miniature. When they bounce back into the room, disappointed at not having found anything of interest in Arthur's kitchen, he offers them some of the crumbly cake. They look at it with disdain. No icing. No chocolate. Not interested.

They leap back into the kitchen, take a bottle of water from the fridge and hold it aloft. 'Can we take this, Uncle?'

Arthur barely has time to nod, and they are gone.

When I think about this interlude later, I realise how wrong my first impression about Arthur's life had been. When I first visited his tiny flat, it had seemed like a place of isolation. An ageing man living alone, devoid of material comforts, a photograph of his family mounted on the wall. Perhaps it had brought to mind my own father's situation after my mother had died. He'd been left alone then, insisting that the charity-run hostel where he had lived for several years with Mum had become his home; that he did not want to move in with one of his children and 'be a burden'. He had pared down his possessions to almost nothing, showing no interest in keeping anything beyond a couple of mugs and a spoon, so he could make a cup of tea for himself and a visitor. People were all that he cared about then, and possibly that had always been the case. And now I could see how wrong I had been about Arthur's spartan flat as well. I could reimagine his place now as the epicentre of a lively network of human activity, his girls and other relatives coming and going freely. The place full of life. A spirograph image made up of exquisitely overlapping circles.

*

During the teenage invasion, I had taken the opportunity to unearth from my bag copies of some of the archival documents I'd relied on to piece together aspects of Len's family background. I wasn't trying to privilege these accounts over anything that Arthur might tell me but was keen to show him that I had not simply made things up. Perhaps the documents might help to clarify some points of contention, or at least provide a basis for discussion. I also thought that Arthur might take a personal interest in such things, as I knew he was conducting his own family research. But it was also risky. Pointing to colonial records might only inflame things.

But Arthur accepts the paperwork and glances at it, maintaining his usual inscrutable expression. More silence. But when I hand him a poor quality photocopy I had made many years earlier of the advertisement in the Adelaide Advertiser about two-year-old Lennie needing a home – the one I had found so distressing – Arthur breaks into a broad smile. He tells me he has never seen a picture of Len as a child. He had not laid eyes on his brother at all until he'd come to Adelaide as a young adult and their lives had begun to intertwine. This prompts a major realisation for me. Arthur knows virtually nothing of Len's life from the time he was taken away to hospital as an infant, an event that Arthur would have been too young to remember. It was obvious once you thought about it. I wonder if he and his daughters knew anything about Len's mental distress. Had I made it seem, in my writing, that I was blaming Len for what we had all gone through? The running away. The alcohol abuse. The trouble with police – most of which involved no crime at all. The violence towards himself, and sometimes towards us. I know that I would not be able to resolve these things today but make a mental note to send Arthur some digital copies later of the few family photos I have of Len. I know he would prefer digital to paper, so he can add them to the impressive collection of family photographs stored on his phone.

Arthur then opens up the sensitive topic of Clara's reputed drinking. Finally, I thought, we were focusing on something concrete, the thing that was probably the most contentious point of all. He reiterates that he had never seen his mother take a drink. She had cooked for shearers and been a hard-working woman, he said. I explain that I had included that observation only because my own mother had said it on more than one occasion, and I thought it might help to explain how things had unfolded. But, of course, that could be wrong. In any case, given my personal experience of witnessing Len's demise, I would never see problems with alcohol as a personal failing.

In response, Arthur starts to wonder aloud about whether his mother could have been exposed to alcohol in Adelaide. Perhaps it's Arthur's respect for my own mother that makes him believe, as I did, that she wouldn't have lied about that. There had been no alcohol on the mission, where the rest of the family had stayed. But Clara had been separated from her family for a long time when she had followed her baby son to Adelaide. It comes as a revelation to me to learn that Len's mother had stayed nearby right through his institutionalisation and through his fostering with us, sacrificing precious years with her family on the mission to maintain her vigil. How had I never known that? That time long ago when she had visited our house, I'd assumed she had travelled from that faraway place called Koonibba where I knew my brother had been born.

'Her heart must have been broken,' I say.

Arthur says nothing. And that's where it sits for a while.

Feeling emboldened now that Arthur has broached such a sensitive topic, I decide to do the same myself. I ask if he knows whether his parents tried to get Lennie back after his medical treatment was complete. Arthur is quiet again and I worry that my persistent digging might be stirring up questions he would rather not contemplate. But Arthur's own pronouncement at our last visit, that Clara had 'given Lennie up' was playing on my mind. Perhaps it had just been clumsy wording, and I was offering up a chance to reassess that, just as I was willing to reassess what I had always been told about Clara's supposed problems with alcohol. The Stolen Generation Inquiry is full of accounts of outright trickery and choices made in conditions where none of the available options worked in favour of Aboriginal parents and I wasn't ready to accept that Len's mother had willingly handed her child over to be placed in foster care.

When Arthur had mentioned at our first meeting that he was raised by his older sisters, I had wrongly taken this as possible confirmation that his mother had been unable to care for her children, and had mentally slotted in the 'drinking problem' story as a possible explanation. But now it had become clear that Clara's absence from Arthur's early life was because she had gone to Adelaide to watch over Len, an act of devotion not at all suggestive of a mother who had willingly given up her child. In any case, what mother on the planet could have cared for a child born with club feet without specialist help? That must surely have been what Arthur had meant to convey, that his mother had consented to Len being taken to Adelaide for treatment. But having a child with special needs did not automatically mean having to give him up completely, even in the 1950s, if the parents were white.

I began to wonder why Len's mother had not become a regular part of our family life, since she had been living in Adelaide all along. Our parents were normally so open and welcoming to others, so Clara's exclusion from Len's life was a puzzle. I had always assumed that the long journey from Koonibba to Adelaide, and possibly her indisposed state, were what had prevented more contact with her son. Far from having abandoned him, as Len had apparently believed, or giving him away, as Arthur had put it, Clara must surely have continued to harbour hopes of getting him back. This had been such a blind spot for me. Right now, as it was shaping up in my head, it seemed that Clara had even sacrificed time with her other children in order to gamble on getting Lennie back, or at least make sure she was nearby as he grew. The injustices were beginning to accumulate against this tenacious woman I had been so wary about as a small child.

As my mind raced with all these new perspectives, Arthur continues to tell me about his early life. His sister Nora had come back to Koonibba to look after him, leaving her job with our family to take over from his older sisters while their mother remained in Adelaide. Whereas Western psychology might warn about the lifelong insecurity that could arise from such a changing array of caregivers, Arthur recalls feeling loved and cherished precisely because each of his sisters had contributed to his upbringing. There, once again, were those overlapping circles of kinship and care.

'When Nora returned from Adelaide,' Arthur says, 'that was the first time I realised I had a little brother.'

And whereas I had always felt awkward about Nora's stint as a paid helper in our home, Arthur claimed the episode as a source of family pride. In the context of strict government control over the mobility of Aboriginal people, Nora had used the domestic service system as a passport of sorts. Consequently, Len's family had seen Nora's employment in the distant city as an achievement and an act of independence. One after another, my readings of past events were being unsettled. And it occurred to me, for the first time in my life, that perhaps it had also fallen to Nora in large part to care for me.

I ask Arthur what it was like to grow up at Koonibba – focusing carefully on using the correct pronunciation. I am wondering whether the depiction of hardship I had set out in the first part of my memoir was justified. Perhaps that had been another point of contention. I had since read first-hand stories of happy lives growing up on other missions where the material deprivation was often balanced by the secure sense of identity that comes from shared culture and kinship.[104] At first, Arthur recalls only pride and happy memories. That the mission had established the first AFL football club in Australia. That his father had entered the world way out in the bush, forty kilometres away, but had later come to live on the mission. That as a child Arthur would accompany his dad to round up the sheep on the mission farm. And that later Arthur himself had worked as a carpenter, then a mechanic, then a cement worker. It sounds almost idyllic, apart from the scar Arthur shows me on his hand from an altercation with one of the cement mixers.

I ask about the living conditions growing up on the mission. Arthur says that in his time the children's home was used mainly for kids brought down from the APY lands who'd been displaced by the Maralinga nuclear tests. Arthur's family, long established on the mission, had lived in a tin shed about the size of a garage. The implication seems to be that their situation was far better than many others. At least they had their own space. One side of the shed was reserved for sleeping. The other side was the kitchen. Arthur observes that there are more houses in Koonibba now, bitumen roads and more jobs, but the farm his father used to work on is long gone. He wouldn't mind going back there to live out his days, he says, if he could just get some money.

After a while, Arthur turns his mind to aspects of mission life that had not left such good impressions. He recalls that laws prohibited mission residents from travelling to Ceduna. One family member was allowed to live there because he was a qualified motor mechanic whose skills were needed by the white residents. It makes life on the mission akin to being locked up in prison, complete with curfews. But he insists that it was not the fault of the Lutheran Church that ran the mission. The blame lies squarely with the government. There must have been some residents who thought differently. I later read on a website about a walk-off on Koonibba in 1958 in protest at a lack of consultation by mission administrators.[105] This was just after Lennie had come to live with us. At that time, Arthur would have been a very small child, unaware of mission politics.

Arthur goes on to recount an historical tragedy that he says is remembered by all west coast people: a massacre where his people had been driven over cliffs. I am not sure of the exact time or location, but Arthur speaks about it as if it occurred within living memory. I'm thinking it must be those same cliffs along the Great Australian Bight where tourists go these days to see the migrating whales. He is moving so fast, recounting all this history for my benefit, that I don't get the chance to ask him for the details. I make a mental note to find out more about this atrocity when I get back home.

The conversation then flows from mission life to religion. Arthur identifies himself as Lutheran, calling it 'the religion I was born with'. That had been the religion of the mission, and of my father's German forebears. While I had shunned the religion I'd been born with, Arthur had embraced the one that had been imposed on his forebears. Arthur then produces some old sepia photos stored on his phone, which had come from Pastor Weiblich. I already knew from my visits to the Lutheran archives in Adelaide that the church had assumed a custodial role over documents relating to this aspect of Aboriginal history, and that many individual pastors continued relationships with Aboriginal people whose families were once formally under their control. Arthur reiterates his view that the bad mission policies were the responsibility of the government, not the church, and that the church had supported Koonibba people by giving back the land.

Not one to readily attribute progressive motives to religious institutions, I later read on a government website that in 1931 'the Lutheran Church decided to sell the Station, without consulting residents'.[106] The church reportedly struggled to find a buyer, and despite protests by Aboriginal residents who petitioned for rights to work the land independently, farming on the station where Arthur's father had toiled was abandoned in 1933. Whatever the truth about that detail, it seems that an early opportunity to cede the land to the traditional owners and other occupants had been lost. According to the same source, the mission was taken over in 1963 by the South Australian government, which eventually ceded control to the Koonibba Aboriginal Community in 1975. Whatever roles the church and government played in the transition towards Indigenous control, the narrative ends with the people of Koonibba having to buy back their own land. According to this historical record, Koonibba was finally purchased by the community in 1988, eight years after Len's death.

Arthur's account then moves on to his adult interactions with his younger brother. He speaks about family members travelling to Adelaide to try to stop Len from drinking. He remembers being with Len in the Carrington Hotel, a well-known gathering place for Aboriginal people at the time. I ask him if he recalls my dad coming to collect Len from there but he says he doesn't. I suppose it was only when Len had no other family members with him that he called home for help, so that would make sense. Arthur links Len's drinking problems to his confusion over 'whether he was a blackfella or a whitefella'.

'That's something I was trying to say in the book,' I intervene, trying to claim some common ground, 'that even though Mum and Dad were good people, and we all loved Len very much, we couldn't teach him how to be an Aboriginal man living in a white society.'

Arthur doesn't respond to that directly, but instead observes how all Aboriginal people can recognise other Aboriginal people, regardless of their skin colour. I recall that matters of recognition, and failed recognition, are central themes in many of the stories I had just been reading in Anita Heiss's anthology, Growing up Aboriginal in Australia.[107]

Arthur embellishes the point by identifying the nationalities now incorporated into his own family – Germans, Italians, other assorted white Australians. 'We are all multicultural now,' he says, with obvious delight.

The conversation then moves from Len's life to the circumstances of his death. Arthur tells me he had gone with his older brother Colin to the place where Len had fallen, soon after hearing about his death. It was more than I could ever bring myself to do, and I had never even been sure of the exact spot. Perhaps I would have been more able to confront these realities if I had been in Adelaide at the time. Arthur explains that the bridge near the Old Adelaide Gaol was gone now. But he and his brother had found a place where a wire railing had come loose and had wondered if it was there that Len had fallen. I can't quite work out what that might mean. Did they think it was an accident – had he tripped on that wire? Or could it have been evidence of a struggle? But I don't dare to ask.

Arthur then says something that has never entered my mind – that Len's death had not been properly investigated. He tells me that witnesses had seen Len get into a taxi to head back to our home, but no one knew how or why he had come to be on the bridge. Their family, and possibly mine as well, had asked questions of the police. The police had said there was nothing suspicious.

Arthur adds, 'That was the attitude of the police at the time.' He had seen his people being killed in prison all his life, he says, and no action was ever taken.

I wonder then if he had shared his suspicions with my mother. Why had we never discussed any of it as a family?

It had been an exhausting afternoon, but we had come a long way.

As I prepare to leave, Arthur says, 'I hope I've given you enough for the book.'

It is so reassuring to hear that's what he understands we've been doing. It felt as though there was still quite a way to go until I had fully earned his trust. And yet, despite all my clumsy mistakes, he had given me his blessing.

*

Several months later, I began listening to the voice notes I'd made after the meeting with Arthur. I had been so tense at the time – self-monitoring relentlessly in case I said something that would ruin everything – that I had not fully appreciated the richness of what Arthur had been telling me. As well as the insights into his own life and family, he had told me several things that seemed to warrant further investigation. I always found it reassuring to have something I could research and analyse, something that would distract me from endless, speculative Deep Thinking. That is probably why I had ended up as an academic – although not until quite late in life, having managed to resist growing up properly until then. As Jonathan Safran Foer wrote in Extremely Loud and Incredibly Close, 'I think and think and think, I've thought myself out of happiness one million times, but never once into it.' But thinking with a purpose, and following up actual leads, was a different matter.

The first line of inquiry was the lack of investigation into Len's death. It had been a long time since I'd thought about it. My mother's shock declaration all those years ago that she thought the police could have pushed Len from the bridge had not sparked any resolve on my part to investigate, although if true it would have added Len's name to the long list of Aboriginal deaths in custody. Perhaps I had not been ready then to think about Len's death in that way. It was too emotionally raw, and I would not have felt empowered to do anything about it anyway, or to demand anything from anyone. Perhaps I was also prone to discounting things that my mother said, and she had not provided any observations to support her view, or made any overtures, as far as I was aware, towards finding out the truth.

But Arthur's observations had been different. He and his brothers had gone to the place where Len died. They had spoken with eyewitnesses from the pub who had seen Len get into that taxi and who could have been interviewed. It made their suspicions more concrete. I now realised that the taxi driver should have been located and questioned. I thought again about the notes I'd made from the coroner's report about the strange positioning of Len's body and wondered why I had never queried that, albeit long after the event. Len's family, on the other hand, would have been aware from the outset that the quality of a police investigation was closely correlated with the colour of the deceased person's skin.

I then did something I have never done before – something that is actually at odds with my newfound identity as a 'serious' criminologist. I submitted an online form on the website for the ABC radio program True Crime. I am not a regular listener to such podcasts. In fact, I had never indulged in them at all. But I had followed recent media reports about the death in 1988 of Gomeroi teenager Mark Haines that had centred on this program. I set out some basic details about the circumstances of Len's death without revealing any names – mindful that I had not yet discussed this step with Arthur – and asked to be put in touch with the investigative journalist responsible for reviving interest in that unsolved case.[108]

As I read the reports, it seemed that Len's death had some superficial similarities with the death of Mark Haines, although I'm not suggesting they are linked in any way. In both cases, the bodies were found on railway tracks, and the crime scene – in the words of the ABC program description – 'didn't make sense'. In Mark's case, there was an absence of blood at the discovery site and the strange addition of a towel under the young man's head, which suggested that his body had been placed there. In Len's case, there was nothing quite so striking, other than the haunting description in the coronial record about Len's body being found lying straight, with his limbs well aligned. I recalled that I was not allowed to photocopy the official document at the coroner's office and wondered if I had just substituted my own wording about that in my furtively scribbled notes; had perhaps got it all wrong.

In both cases, there are also unanswered questions about how the young men came to be in the locations in which they were found. In relation to Mark Haines, there are numerous witnesses who can account for his movements on the evening when he died. Some of them have provided information that calls into question the official version of events. There seems to be some advantage, in his case, that the events occurred in a small community, in which people's movements are more easily observed. In contrast, the circumstances of Len's death offered up fewer leads.

A few days later, I received an email from the program saying they had passed on my query to the journalist. I had a little panic at the possibility of Len's story appearing in a future episode of True Crime, even though the paucity of detail would make that unlikely. What I was hoping for were some tips perhaps from an award-winning journalist about possible avenues of inquiry, or maybe some feedback about whether he knew of similar, unexplained deaths in Adelaide around the same time that Len had died. But I never heard back from the journo. Perhaps there were just too many reports of suspicious deaths of Aboriginal people for it to be possible to follow up each one.

With no other leads to follow, I decide that I will need to revisit the South Australian coroner one day and ask to see Len's file again. At the very least, it will put my mind at rest about the accuracy of my notes. Perhaps Arthur will come with me. If the access rules have changed, and they do not recognise me as a close member of Len's family who is entitled to see his records, then maybe the request could come from him. The thought that I am no longer alone with this consoles me.

While I am in detective mode, I decide to pursue the other revelation from Arthur about the cliff massacres. I look up the confronting new website being pieced together by an academic team in Newcastle – Colonial Frontier Massacres in Central and Eastern Australia 1788–1930.[109] The map has yellow dots for Aboriginal deaths and blue squares for events that also involve settler fatalities. The vast majority of the entries are yellow. They are clustered tightly throughout the eastern states, layered on top of each other in some places in sinister circles.

A table elsewhere on the site shows an overall tally of 216 settler fatalities and 13,345 Aboriginal deaths that had been confirmed by the team at that time. This, of course, will be a significant undercount of total deaths in the frontier wars. But the huge disparity between settler and Aboriginal deaths during this period is striking, and is clearly a robust finding, since settler deaths would surely have been more readily recorded. The notes explain that the researchers who constructed the map had not yet included data from Western Australia, or massacres that occurred after 1930. It was sobering to think that massacres could still be taking place even as Aboriginal men and women began volunteering to defend the nation in World War II.

Out of curiosity, I clicked on each of the eleven blue markers where settlers had also been killed. Some of them were pairs of records. Nineteen non-Aboriginal people were killed at Cullin-la-Ringo station on 17 October 1861, followed on 25 October by thirty Aboriginal deaths at nearby Nogoa River. Eleven settlers were killed at Hornet Bank station on 27 October 1857 followed by eighty deaths of Aboriginal people throughout November. These were reprisal killings; punitive expeditions where one settler life is paid for by many Indigenous ones. If eighty settler deaths had occurred in one place, there would be a monument there and schoolchildren would learn about it in their history lessons. I click on the blue square for the 'Maria massacre', which I had heard about, since it happened in the Coorong not far from Adelaide. It is one of the few cases where the colonist deaths outnumber the Aboriginal ones. The narrative explains that Milmenrura warriors attacked survivors of the shipwrecked Maria with spears and clubs, killing twenty-six people. Soon after, six Milmenrura men are recorded as being killed by a 'police party'. It is not clear whether they were amongst the group who had attacked the ill-fated ship – whether their killing followed the logic of law or of war.

The massacre map records fewer fatalities in South Australia than in other states, but I notice several sites marked around Eyre Peninsula. I didn't know the date or the exact location of the event Arthur was talking about, but surmise that if there were cliffs involved it must have been somewhere along the Great Australian Bight around Ceduna. None of the map entries in this area seem to match the description Arthur gave. I notice a form on the website where it is possible to alert the research team about apparent errors or omissions in the data. I fill it in with the little I know about the massacre on the cliffs and send it. There is an explanation on the website about the research team being small so there could be a long delay in replying. While I am waiting to hear back, I do some simple Google searching of my own and realise that the events Arthur had related to me were known as the 'Waterloo Bay massacre'. The deaths had occurred at Elliston, not far from Ceduna, in May 1849. It turns out that the massacre is depicted on the Colonial Frontier Massacres map, but records only ten deaths by shooting, not the hundreds of people driven over cliffs that is the oral history handed down by Arthur's people. Here is how Kokatha elder and author Iris Burgoyne recorded her people's memories of that fateful event:[110]

> [T]his story was passed to me by my people. Their spoken words were always the truth. As young girls at Koonibba, we sat and listened to the old people like Jack Joonary, Jilgina Jack and Wombardy. They were well over a hundred. They shared many of their experiences. They told us about how they survived the Elliston massacres in about 1839 and 1849. Jack Jacobs from Franklin Harbour, old lame Paddy and Dick Dory spoke about it as well. That day they escaped death as they tricked the European horsemen and ran into the bushes. They stood and watched in horror as their people were driven off the cliffs into the sea.

I began to wonder whether Western conceptions about the nature of historical truth had trumped customary knowledge. I contacted the website team again to let them know I had connected Arthur's oral account to the record they had of events at Waterloo Bay. I could tell from what I had read online that the account they had used on the website is the one that can be corroborated from written records. I understood the necessity of observing these scholarly rules, but it seemed that the result in this case was that Aboriginal people were, once again, disbelieved. I expressed this disappointment in my email to the researchers, and soon received a sympathetic reply from the team leader, Professor Lyndall Ryan. She explained that the chair of the SA Heritage Council was 'very confident that the massacre took place and that the perpetrators went to great lengths to cover it up', no doubt through selective inclusions in the official record. This is how Australia's 'secret history' is maintained.

A few weeks later, this vying over historical truth was brought home to me in a chance encounter with a Radio National program, The History Listen. I had turned on the radio as a diversion while doing some tasks in the kitchen, then wandered out to the garden and left it on. As I returned, I heard the words 'Waterloo Bay' and realised they were talking about the massacre of Arthur's people.[111] Coincidences such as this often shake the foundations of my essentially rationalist core – when I suddenly become a magnet for important information about something I have only just heard about. There was a settler woman explaining why she opposed the term 'massacre' being inscribed on the memorial that had recently been erected at the site, asserting that the number of Indigenous deaths had been inflated. When asked what led her to that view she replied, 'Have you heard of Chinese whispers?'

Other contributors treated the Indigenous account with more respect. An anthropologist who has been widely consulted about these events confirmed that the police records from the time could not be considered reliable and said he had formed the view that around twenty Aboriginal people were probably killed, both by shooting and being driven over cliffs. His account resembled the one recorded on the massacre map. One community leader explained that the original killing of a settler that is said to have sparked the reprisal had been a punishment required by law, due to his abuse of Aboriginal women and girls. I resolved to visit the monument myself some time. Perhaps that is something else that Arthur and I might one day do together.

The final piece of research arising from my discussion with Arthur fell into place quite by accident. It turns out to be the most significant revelation of all. I had been trying to read as much as possible by Indigenous authors in order to immerse myself in the profoundly different perspectives these books convey. I was reading a memoir by Ngarrindjeri/Kaurna woman Veronica Brodie about her early life on Raukkun mission,[112] then her time spent in Adelaide under the strict protectionist laws of the 1950s and 60s, when I stumbled on a simple sentence that floored me. It read, 'Women also drank a lot less then –

so how could non-Indigenous people tell their adopted children they were adopted out because their mothers were drunk?' A light bulb went on in my head. How could I not have seen this?

Until that time, I had assumed my mother had formed her opinion about Clara's supposed alcohol problems on the basis of personal experience; that she must have seen Clara in an inebriated state, or heard first-hand reports from reliable sources, perhaps from Len's own family. Like most daughters, I could readily list all my mother's failings, but telling lies was not among them. It had blinded me to the now-so-obvious explanation that she had been a victim of the legitimating myths told to adoptive parents by authorities intent on justifying their practices.

Setting this new understanding alongside another unsettling view held by my mother, that Len had believed that his mother had abandoned him, I felt convinced now that Clara – alongside everything else she had suffered – had been a victim of an outrageous slander. I was starting to learn how Aboriginal mothers had been doubly wronged – first by having their children taken away, then by being blamed for being incapable parents. Worse still, these harsh judgements could infiltrate the thoughts of the very children who had been taken away. A contributor to Anita Heiss's anthology Growing Up Aboriginal in Australia expressed this well:

> Later in life, when I sought out counselling, a practitioner identified that I had a long history of suppressed anger and, in assisting me to work through my issues, we discovered that all these years I've held great anger towards my mother for leaving me that day. I was finally able to resolve my negativity towards her and understand that it was not her fault that she could not hug me or take me home.[113]

It is not surprising then, that critical criminologist Chris Cunneen has argued that one of the most devastating legacies of colonial policies has been the wilful construction of Aboriginal parenting as incompetent, through techniques ranging from exaggeration to outright lies.[114]

I took a photo of the 'light bulb passage' from Veronica Brodie's memoir and sent it to Arthur by text, explaining that I now thought it likely that it was how my mother had formed her erroneous view. Arthur texted back to say he would think about it. I already knew that he was not one to rush to judgement. I felt so sorry that I had put his family through this hurtful process but hoped it would be an enlightening experience in the end, especially for me. It was how the policy that took Lennie away had operated and had implicated unsuspecting people like my parents in its wrongdoing. I would never have questioned my mother's statements had I not read that passage from Veronica Brodie. After a lot of thought, I opted not to simply remove my mother's belief about Clara's supposed drinking from the first part of the memoir, but to recount instead this journey towards what I now thought to be the truth. After all, setting the record straight was an important part of the story.

An act of atonement

Once I'd received some quotes from the stonemason, I contacted my siblings about the plan to erect an entirely new headstone on Len's grave. Neither of them objected, but my sister really embraced the project. I had never been sure what she thought about what I had written, which concerned her as well. So her support for my expensive plan meant a lot, and she even offered to share the cost, as did my brother eventually.

'I don't expect you to pay half,' I'd said. 'I know it's just another one of my crazy ideas.'

Whether she went all the way with me and saw the corrected wording on the headstone as an act of atonement, I can't be sure, and I didn't feel the need to ask. I have never expected others to share in my burdensome habit of Deep Thinking and the associated compulsion to set things right. I was just grateful to feel that I was not entirely alone on this part of the journey.

After checking the wording with Arthur and his daughters, I placed the order for the new plaque. Following a long wait, punctuated by the Christmas break, I was notified that the newly cast plaque had arrived from the foundry. Under the original entry that said 'Beloved chosen son and brother of Peter, Jean and the Weber family', a new line had been added that acknowledged Len's birth family in the same way. The effect, I hoped, would be to modify the proprietorial statement about Len's place in our family and convey that he was never ours alone. Some might question whether we should have stuck to the story that Len was chosen by us, rather than stolen from his first parents. Chosen son had an air of finality about it, giving no hint about Len's original family who had remained a presence in his life and had exercised no choice in the matter. Still, the term coined by my parents came from a place of love, and I now knew that Arthur accepted and valued that.

The new wording couldn't change what had happened, but at least it recorded that Len had been loved and wanted by two families. It occurred to me too late that, by rights, Len's own family should have been listed first. They had, after all, been the first presence in his life. But I consoled myself with the thought that causing the least disruption possible to the wording my parents had selected was a show of respect for them. Ultimately, Arthur and his family appeared more than content with the changes, and that's what mattered the most.

As happened so often during the course of constructing this memoir, I stumbled on some information at that time that seemed to confirm the wider significance of this act of atonement. It was an opinion piece written by a team of archaeologists who had been working with a Northern Territory Indigenous community to identify the occupants of the many unmarked graves in their town.[115] The local people had previously had no tradition of erecting headstones, since underground burial was not a cultural practice. But Northern Territory law, while imposing unfamiliar burial practices on remote communities, failed to mandate the keeping of official records. The authors pointed out that this history of structural racism had left a legacy of loss and confusion. The aim of their project was to determine not only the identity and location of the lost generations, but also to record each person's moiety, clan and kinship relations. To try to restore what had been lost. On Arthur's own admission, their family had long ago accepted the rituals and rites of Christianity. And both Len and his family had been content with the general arrangements for his burial. But the failure to create an accurate historical record of Len's kinship relationships now stood out for me even more clearly as an egregious oversight that had to be rectified.

Once I'd been notified that the plaque was ready, it seemed the right time to contact Arthur to see if he wanted to be part of what I was planning – a commemorative gathering around the grave that would be open to any members of both our families. I now knew that there would be no cultural elements, but I hoped that just coming together in that context would constitute a ceremony of sorts, reconnecting our families in a meaningful way through our mutual love for Len. I was thinking we could have some lunch together afterwards, ideally a picnic in a nearby park. That would give us time to get to know each other in an informal setting where the youngest members of both families could run around and play. As I imagined what might happen, I realised I was idealising again, that I could not presume that other people would align themselves with my agenda, and that I should lower my expectations. I already knew that Bev and her daughter Jen were keen to come. It was time to find out if the idea appealed to anyone else.

Jacqui answers Arthur's phone this time. I am aware now that it had been Jacqui who had objected to what I had written in the memoir. I sense some hesitancy in her voice but at least she doesn't hang up. I ask whether her dad is able to come to the phone but she explains, as Jeannie had done the previous time, that he can't manage now because of his hearing loss. I try to convey what I have in mind as succinctly as I can, tell her the possible dates I could make it to Adelaide, and ask if she could find out what Arthur thinks about it.

After a while she comes back and just says, 'Yeah.'

That's excellent news, but doesn't instil the degree of certainty I am after, given the arrangements that have to be made.

'Does your dad need a bit of time to think about it?' I ask, and when Jacqui agrees, I say I will text him the dates so he can get back to me himself.

It would have been easy to leave things as they stood at that point, but instead I decide to grasp what might be my only chance to repair the harm I have done to our relationship. 'Jacqui, I'm so sorry that you were upset by things I wrote in the book. I never meant that to happen.'

'Yeah, well, I've read it a few times now...'

As her sentence tails off, I wonder whether Arthur might have discussed our last meeting with her, and that perhaps Jacqui has decided to give the book another chance.

Shamefully, I don't really give her the space to find out. My anxiety is making me babble nervously and I talk right over her. 'I was honestly trying to explain how bad these policies were and how much harm they did even when white families loved their adopted children.'

'Yeah, well…'

Her tone is sounding conciliatory, but maybe I'm still afraid to hear what she has to say, so I cut her off again before I can make myself stop. 'If anything doesn't seem right in the book,' I babble on, 'I can change it. I don't want to say anything that hurts your family…' (a brief pause now, but still not enough to let Jacqui get a word in) 'and about writing that your grandmother was a drinker. I am so sorry that distressed you. My mother honestly believed that, and it wasn't meant to be judgemental in any way.' I explain to her the passage I had found in Veronica Brodie's memoir, in case she hadn't seen the text I'd sent to Arthur and reassure her again that I would not let anything stay in the book that said anything wrong about their family.

Although I have barely allowed Jacqui to speak, we part, I hope, on better terms, with the business of organising the gathering left to be conducted via sms.

Next, I send an email to my siblings and their adult children, inviting them to a gathering to commemorate Len, and explaining for the benefit of the nieces and nephews about the need to change a headstone most of them have probably never seen. My brother had predicted that his children, who'd been either very young or not yet born when Len had died, would probably not want to be involved. But it is Neil's youngest child Lucie who is the first to respond, pledging to fly from Sydney to attend. The wife of one of Neil's sons replies soon after, with a commitment that their family will be there too. The rapid buy-in from female members of the family confirms what sociologists, psychologists and anthropologists have always said, that human relationships have a central place in the lives of most women. Whatever their individual reasons might have been, there seemed to be a hunger to do this thing that I was proposing. It was shaping up to be a significant family event; the first occasion since the death of our parents when the whole extended family would come together.

I launched into action, making lists and calculating how many quiches and barbecued chickens I would need for the picnic. I sent Arthur an excited text telling him that many of the younger generation in my family wanted to be there and wondering whether his sisters and their children might like to come as well. I didn't hear from him for a while and began to kick myself for being too pushy. Perhaps he had not bargained on dealing en masse with the whole Weber clan. It would be understandable if that were a daunting prospect.

Coming up to a week before the designated date, I still hadn't received the final thumbs up from the guest of honour. After a few nail-biting hiccups, the stonemason had finally confirmed that the plaque had been installed on Len's headstone, so that was one less thing to worry about. Lucie and I had our flights booked – she from Sydney, me from Melbourne, where I would be working in the lead-up to the big weekend. The Adelaide-based family was on stand-by for final instructions, but I was becoming ever more apprehensive that we might be gathering around Len's grave on our own.

*

On the day before the gathering, I fly into Adelaide through a glorious blue sky. During the flight, I've been engrossed in reading Growing Up Aboriginal in Australia.[116] Something makes me look up just in time to see that we are tracking along a magnificent stretch of the Coorong on our approach to Adelaide airport. For me, this is the place in Australia that resonates most viscerally with a sense of pre-European habitation. My partner and I camped there several times when we still lived in Adelaide, crossing the shallow waters in our trailer sailer – Tony at the tiller, and me most of the time kept busy below winching up the swing keel, then winding it down again, to prevent us from running aground. Once we had reached our isolated camping spot, we would walk to the ocean beach through pristine sandhills. We might have felt that ours were the first footsteps laid down there had it not been for the middens that filled every open space, a testimony to a communal life of plenty that had once been lived there. Although neither of us was susceptible, as a rule, to this way of thinking, we could both sense that the place was drenched in spirituality. One evening as we sat naked in total contentment around our campfire at the water's edge, we'd looked up and seen the graceful silhouette of an emu as it moved slowly across the top of the dunes, head held high and regal, framed against the afterglow of sunset. It felt like an encounter with something sacred. The unexpected glimpse of this magical place from the air is the best arrival I could have wished for, and I take it as a good omen that everything will go well, despite all my fears to the contrary.

I am standing at the luggage carousel at Adelaide airport when Arthur's response to my latest query about the meeting at the cemetery arrives by SMS. It is characteristically brief – 'Yes' – but I literally jump for joy on seeing it. With one eye on the lookout for my suitcase, I begin texting as quickly as my inept baby boomer phone technique will allow, letting family members know that we are definitely on for tomorrow, and that Arthur, at least, will be coming. I'd warned them a couple of days before that I couldn't be certain that Arthur's family would be there. My niece from Sydney had decided, sadly, not to fly after all, since arrangements were uncertain. But the Adelaide-based family had been willing to go ahead either way.

Now that we were back in business, it seemed a shame that Lucie would not be there. Her commitment had been so genuine that she'd ordered several dozen cupcakes from her local vegan bakery in Sydney to bring to the picnic, topped with thick slabs of icing in the colours of the Aboriginal flag. She'd been unsure about whether they would be an appropriate offering for the occasion, but when she asked me whether I thought that Arthur would approve, I had said I was sure, either way, that he would understand her good intentions. When she heard that Arthur would be there after all, she'd sent me a photograph of the cupcakes lined up in rows with their tricolour icing, looking assertive and rather magnificent. I promised to show the photo to Arthur with an apology for her inability to attend. The cupcakes themselves would be consigned to Lucie's freezer, but their image might fill some of the gap left by her last-minute absence.

I spot my bag then and head out of the terminal to collect a hire car. Meanwhile, texts are flying to and fro about how many people would be coming from Arthur's family, and would they all need a lift, and whether it is too hot for a picnic afterwards, and if so, what would we do instead? I feel like I'm swimming in uncertainty. A quick phone check before starting up the hire car reveals a forecast max in the mid-thirties for the next day, which does put the picnic in serious doubt. Even so, I decide to execute my original plan of scouting for suitable picnic spots before heading to my sister's place, just in case we opt to brave the heat, and also for the sheer pleasure of driving around some of my old haunts.

Without too much trouble, I find a suitably shady spot in the North Adelaide parklands, just a five-minute drive from the cemetery. It offers lush green grass, a playground for the kids and picnic tables that are actually in the shade. (Why do they always put picnic tables out in the blazing sun, I have often wondered. To stop them becoming encrusted with bird poo is the only answer I can think of, or perhaps to cater for winter picnics when the warming rays are welcome.) The space is right next to the Adelaide Aquatic Centre, so there are toilets that I can see are accessible from outside the complex, and also a café where folks could go for a cuppa or ice cream. I can imagine us having a pleasant and peaceful time there. I take a video on my phone to show my sister and niece in case proof of adequate shade and amenities is needed, then continue around the ring road that skirts the north parklands to check out the second candidate.

Botanic Park, where Womadelaide is held every March, is a glorious place ringed with giant Morton Bay fig trees that are thriving, despite being thousands of kilometres away from their more tropical homeland. I've attended the famous music festival a few times and always felt sorry for the artists scheduled to perform in the searing daytime heat, when most of the audience takes refuge in the shade of the trees, leaving only a few crazy dancers to leap about in front of the stage. I decide that the trees would do nicely for our picnic as well, although there are no tables at all and the toilets and café in the adjacent Botanic Gardens are a longer walk away, which could be a challenge for some of the older ones. The parking ticket I find on the windscreen when I return to the hire car is the final factor that tips the balance in favour of the Aquatic Centre. But I make a mental note to return to this spot one day for some quiet contemplation under those gigantic boughs.

The next step in the picnic catering plan would have been to order quiches from a fancy bakery that is on the way to my sister's place in the leafy eastern suburbs, for collection the next morning. I'd planned to buy barbecued chickens, drinks, snacks, fruit and salads along the way as well, so I could prepare some picnic platters and chill the drinks overnight. But the lingering doubt over whether the picnic will be viable makes me shift gears and head straight for Bev's house instead. By the time I reach her driveway, Arthur's verdict has arrived by text.

'Perhaps too hot for a picnic.'

So that is decided. More texts and emails with my family members ensue, interspersed with googling of possible venues for a sit-down lunch. But in the end, that idea seems too formal, not to mention indeterminately expensive with the full attendance list still unknown, so I decide to embrace contingency and just leave everyone to decide at the cemetery what they want to do. All that remains is to determine how many of Arthur's family will need a lift in the morning and figure out where I will stop on the way to buy flowers for Len's grave.

I wake up the next morning in the narrow Queen Anne bed that is just like the matched pair my sister and I had slept in at our parents' home before she was married. I'd slept in that single bed at my sister's place many times on lone visits home to Adelaide. As I emerge out of a deep sleep, a family of magpies is warbling contentedly in the trees that line the creek alongside the house. It reminds me of the time almost twenty years before when I'd been staying in this same room, in this same bed, after I'd returned from England for our mother's funeral. I'd been woken on the first morning by the raucous cries of kookaburras. It had been a treat to hear that unmistakable sound after almost a decade living overseas. But the novelty soon wore off, and I would gladly have traded another hour of sleep for the cacophony that erupted each morning before dawn. The sound of magpies occupied an altogether different place in my affections. Their melodic singing had been the soundtrack to my youth, drifting through the bedroom window in our family home near the bird-filled park that ran alongside the River Torrens. It was the sound I had missed the most while living overseas. Waking up on the morning of Len's memorial gathering to the sound of magpies seems auspicious.

I still haven't managed to sort out transport for Arthur and his family, so after breakfast I text him to ask how many people will need a ride from his place. If necessary, I say, we can bring two cars. I'd assumed that my sister's car would be available as a second taxi, but when I go down to breakfast, I'm confronted with my brother-in-law Bruce pacing about in the kitchen with his to-do list, impatient to get to Bunnings.

'But this is the most important day of my life,' I say sotto voce, but also intending him to hear. I know it sounds melodramatic, but also it is true.

A reply comes in just then from Arthur's daughter Jeannie. It would just be Arthur, herself and her son Jayden. Aunty Judy and her daughter Priscilla would be meeting up with Jacqui and her kids at Jacqui's house. This is the first confirmation that one of Arthur's sisters will be coming, plus it means I can do the pick-up on my own in the tiny Toyota Yaris – the type of car that I had always thought of as a bubble car – that I hired at the airport. Bruce is duly despatched to collect his DIY necessities and our second reserve driver, my niece Jen, who had the misfortune of inheriting her grandmother's lupus, is able to stagger back to bed for the extra hour's rest she needs before facing the debilitating heat of the day.

I calculate that if I leave in the next thirty minutes, I will have plenty of time to stop for flowers on the way to Arthur's flat. Just as I think it is all falling into place, a second text arrives from Jeannie asking if I can collect Aunty Judy and the others from Jacqui's place. I have never been there, but I know it is some distance from Arthur's place. I can't do both now that I've dismissed the back-up fleet.

'Can you get to the cemetery by taxi' I text back, unable to think of another solution. I start to remonstrate with myself immediately for letting them down but what can I do? I decide to just pick up the car keys, start driving and hope to clear my head.

Another surprise awaits when I arrive at Arthur's place. Both his daughters and their kids are there. Six people in total – too many for the bubble car. It seems Aunty Judy and her daughter are on their way by bus, all the way from the opposite side of the suburban sprawl. We are going to need a plan B.

'I'll do two trips,' I say, as we pack one of Arthur's daughters and three small grandsons into the Yaris. The others agree to wait at Arthur's place for Aunty Judy and Priscilla to arrive. A sensible person might have ordered an Uber, but I didn't think of that, switching under pressure to my habitual mindset of just doing things myself. On the way, Jeannie is relaxed and easy to talk with, which helps to calm my nerves. She tells me she is training to be a community worker.

'You'll be a really good community worker,' I say, meaning it. 'You are so good with people.'

As we make the final turn towards the cemetery, I notice some unfamiliar words amongst the boys' chatter.

'They're talking in language,' says Jeannie, smiling. 'They only know a little bit. That word' – she repeats it – 'means house.'

I try to remember the word, but it slips clean through the rickety connections in my ageing and currently overtaxed brain.

When we arrive at the cemetery, we are well ahead of the appointed time, but my nephew Nathan and his family are already pulling into the car park. After a quick introduction, I explain to him that I need to do another pick-up run, so we will be late getting started. They decide to drive off in search of somewhere air-conditioned while Jeannie wanders off contentedly with the boys to wait in the shade until I come back. I begin to realise that members of my family would soon be converging on the cemetery to find neither me, nor Arthur, the guest of honour, in attendance. Mortified at that prospect, I dash off some garbled texts before I leave the car park explaining we'll be around thirty minutes late.

As I head back to Arthur's place, I field numerous replies – making fumbled clandestine responses in my lap at traffic lights, typing gobbledegook like 'sion', which is intended to convey that Arthur and I will be arriving at the cemetery 'soon'. I juggle an actual call (no Bluetooth in the budget bubble car) from my sister and niece, who have inexplicably got lost along the way, although they have visited the cemetery many times before, throw in several illegal U-turns after making silly navigational errors of my own, do some strategic speeding trying to make up time, then arrive back at Arthur's place feeling flustered, only to find that Aunty Judy and her daughter have not yet arrived.

On the inside, I am beginning to feel a bit like Basil Fawlty, turning completely apoplectic while things fall apart around him. Of course, nothing is really very wrong. But my deep anxiety about feeling solely responsible for the success or otherwise of the day is stretching my coping mechanisms to the limit. Of course, various family members are late as well – that has been the gist of most of the texts. But Aunty Judy and Priscilla's absence is still a complication.

'Do you know where they are?' I ask – and Jacqui, who has been speaking with them on the phone at the time, relays the question.

'They're on the bus,' she says, 'and it's just turned into Torrens Road.'

Ironically, that is very close to the cemetery, but they are not to know that. They could get off at the next stop and walk there alongside the railway line if they knew the way.

Glancing anxiously at my watch, I have a sudden brainwave.

'Maybe you could tell them to get off somewhere on Torrens Road and we can pick them up along the way.'

'Get off at Arndale shopping centre,' says Jacqui decisively.

And, after some more explanation about where they should wait, it seems we have a plan.

Back in the car, taking that now-familiar route along Torrens Road towards the city, another text comes in. My sister and niece have found their way to the cemetery now and want to know the row number for Len's grave. This time I feel more like an out-of-control John McEnroe screaming 'You CAN'T be serious!' My method for finding the right spot has always been to head towards the outer fence where it begins to slant downwards from the horizontal, then check all the graves towards the end of the rows in that vicinity. Texting those instructions at the next stop at traffic lights is beyond my capabilities, and I'm not happy anyway about being drawn into the nefarious ranks of clandestinely texting drivers. To avoid a meltdown, I simply text back '?' just as Arndale shopping centre comes into view.

Being used to making do without the convenience of a car, Jacqui is something of a public transport expert, which is fortunate because it is not obvious where the bus stops. She directs me confidently around the back of the car park to the place where Aunty Judy and Priscilla are waiting under a tree. A perfectly executed rendezvous, engineered by cooler heads than mine. After a quick introduction, they squeeze themselves into the back of the bubble car. I am starting to wish the surprise upgrade to the more luxurious car from my previous visit had happened on this trip instead when we could do with the extra space. But no one seems to mind being a bit cramped, even with the heat, and we are finally off on the last leg of our journey.

As I drive the last few kilometres, I berate myself inwardly about my time-obsession, and assess my emotional state: suppressed panic. All that restorative yoga and meditative breathing seems to have fallen by the wayside. Arthur's family, in contrast, are the epitome of calm in the face of events that I'm responding to as if they are incipient catastrophes. I calculate that by the time we gather everyone together, we will be about an hour late getting started, which is really of no consequence, but is triggering a deep-seated stress response in me. Left to my own devices, I would not have cared if we didn't get to the cemetery until sunset. But at this point it feels like inconveniencing my family – some of whom, I fear, might have sustained heatstroke by now, or decided to give up and go home – would be unforgivable. I have no faith whatever that their commitment to my project will survive being tested and fall into that old habit of expecting disapproval.

As I pull into the cemetery car park for a second time, I see that everyone is there, except my nephew and his family, who had been the first to arrive. Other than that, there is no sign of the expected mass mutiny. My relatives are mingling under trees chatting amiably, while Jeannie has found a tranquil spot in the children's cemetery where her son and his cousins are entertaining themselves spotting turtles in the pond. I open the boot and take out the flowers I bought earlier that morning: Australian natives for Len, something more delicate, possibly lupins, to put on Mum and Dad's grave later. After some more hellos, we all make our way towards Len's grave, forming into smaller groups travelling at differing speeds, and taking slightly different routes. One of my great-nephews, Josh, keeps stopping at strategic points along the way to ask whether this person is 'buried in a coffin' or 'burned up to ashes'.

'You can't say that, Joshie,' whispers his twin brother Luke, directly into his ear. They are non-identical genetically, in appearance and in just about every way imaginable.

As we gather around Len's grave, I make a few more introductions, am pleased to see some cross-family conversations starting up, then go back to my interminable texting to determine whether Nathan and his family will be arriving soon.

It is only when I overhear admiring comments from others that I realise I've been so busy stressing about arrangements that I haven't even glanced at the headstone – the very reason we are all there. I peer at it through the sea of bodies and am relieved to see that it reads as intended. The bronze plaque has a different surface from the previous one and is flecked with shiny particles that catch the sun. That makes it difficult to read the inscription from some angles, but the consensus seems to be favourable, that a bit of sparkle is no bad thing, even where the serious business of commemoration is concerned, that the new lettering is clear, and the sentiments it expresses appropriate.

There is no shade in this part of the cemetery, and by the time we have lined up for some group photos and Jeannie has placed the flowers on Len's grave, I am beginning to worry people might be about to wilt when I spot my nephew, his wife and son making their way towards us.

With everyone gathered, it is finally time for my speech. My family would have known I could not let the occasion pass without one. I've resolved to say some simple words that will at least acknowledge, if not rectify, a historic wrong, while trying not to get unduly emotional. I thank everyone for coming, acknowledge the Kaurna people as custodians of the land where we are gathered and pay my respects to their elders past, present and future. I hear one of Arthur's daughters say the word 'Kaurna' and wonder if I've mispronounced it, or perhaps she is just repeating it for someone who hasn't heard. I had meant to acknowledge our Gran Weber as our own family elder, so that she was not ignored in the proceedings, but have forgotten to do so. I realise too late that it would have been respectful to also acknowledge the Indigenous people who were in our presence and express my respect for their (non-Kaurna) elders. But that opportunity is lost forever. Next, I explain for the benefit of the younger ones, and for Len's family, that our parents had called Lennie their chosen son to indicate their love for him, but that all along he'd had another family who also loved him. The new plaque now recognised that truth: that Len had only ever been shared between us. This joins our families together in an enduring way, I said, and the coming together of both families today to remember our beloved Len was proof of that. And that was it, although so much remained to be said.

Far from being overcome with emotion, I find I am feeling strangely detached. I ask if anyone else wants to say something and can see Jeannie jabbing her dad in the ribs with her elbow. Eventually, Arthur succumbs and utters a few shy words about knowing that Lennie loved our family. Outgoing Jeannie joins in with an anecdote about her fond memories of Papa Pete teaching herself and her sister to play carpet bowls. I wonder for the first time then if she and Jacqui had even been born at the time Len died. Not knowing their birthdays, I have never done the maths. Perhaps she has no personal memories of her Uncle Len that she can share. My brother Neil then offers up the uncomfortable story about someone suggesting that our mother should just give Lennie back, when our lives had started to become complicated. In my version of the story, it had been the ladies at the church our parents attended who had said that, but Neil attributes it to one of Mum's sisters. It didn't seem to matter now.

When everyone has said their piece, I suggest, for want of a better plan, that we head for the nearby picnic spot I'd picked out the day before, although we were no longer having the picnic. We could at least get some drinks and snacks from the aquatic centre, and people who didn't want to be outside in the heat could sit inside the café.

On our way back to the cars, we make a quick detour to my parents' grave. Along the way, Josh persists with his questions about coffins versus cremation, listening with interest but not alarm to the answers provided by various relatives.

'Does it hurt to be burned up to ashes?'

'No, Joshie, you can't feel things after you're dead.'

'How do they do it?'

Silence and audible deep breaths.

'And will they go to Heaven?'

I leave my pious sister to deal with that one. Then comes an even more confronting question.

'How come the police pushed Uncle Len off the bridge?'

I exchange a quick glance with his mother Libby, who had told me that her husband Matt sometimes mentioned this theory. I hadn't expected it to have filtered down another generation. Maybe some family discussion of it had been part of the preparation for today, although I doubted that a public airing had been intended.

'We don't really know what happened, Josh,' I say, which seems to satisfy him.

When it is time to leave, Jeannie and the three boys happily distribute themselves into other people's cars.

I feel confident enough to risk a joke and call out, 'Watch out with those kids – they might not give them back!'

Jeannie rewards me with a broad smile.

By the time I arrive at the pool with Arthur and the older members of his family, the others have all gone inside. Thinking we would be outside having a picnic, I hadn't done my recognisance on the café very thoroughly the day before, and it turns out that you must go right into the swimming centre to access the seating. Fortunately, it's possible to pass through the turnstiles without buying a ticket for the pool. The others are already inside, perched at the high plastic tables enjoying the air conditioning, chatting happily and sipping cool drinks. Gregarious Jeannie is in the centre of the action, and I can see she is making a big hit with younger members of my family. Arthur's grandsons are at the same table with my two grand-nephews, who are around the same age. They seem to be getting along well.

It isn't until after I've bought the snacks and drinks Jeannie and the boys have selected that I notice that Arthur, Jacqui, Aunty Judy and her daughter have not followed me in. I go back outside and see them gathered around a picnic table under a shady tree. They seem relaxed and comfortable. I recall how my sister had told me that Len's family had stayed outside in her garden at the gathering after Len's funeral, and how I had worried that they had felt excluded. It feels like history repeating itself, but I understand this time that they have made a deliberate choice; it is so much more pleasant out here, away from the noise of the pool and the stale smell of fried food and chlorine. Perhaps they are shy about coming inside as well. It makes me wish we'd been able to have our picnic after all, when we could have all stayed together. I take a second round of orders for food and drinks and return sometime later to deliver them to the outside contingent. Eventually, people start to wander outside from the café, preparing to go their separate ways. My brother agrees to run Jeannie and the three boys back to Arthur's flat, with me to follow with the others in the Yaris.

We find plenty to talk about as we make yet another trip along Torrens Road. I've begun to let myself believe that Arthur and I might be putting the disappointment over the book behind us and starting to rebuild trust. The family is chatting in an easy manner, between themselves or with me, not seeming to mind my presence. Thinking about Len's death prompts Jacqui to mention her sister Lenora. Arthur had spoken that name to me before, explaining it had been a combination of Len's name and the name of Arthur's sister Nora. He had assumed I would know who he was referring to, but I'd struggled at the time to remember. I had said it over and over in my mind. Lenora. It was a beautiful, haunting name that I knew I'd heard before. But I couldn't be sure who it belonged to. I'd even asked Bev over the phone after I'd first made contact with Arthur, hoping she could confirm a fading memory of mine that Arthur and Elizabeth had lost a daughter in a tragic household accident. It's not the sort of thing you should forget, but Bev was just as hazy about it as me, and I hadn't wanted to ask Arthur outright. But here is Jacqui, speaking openly now about her lost sister Lenora. I feel that I have been let in, to some extent, to the family fold. It is a powerful thought that we are remembering both Len and his namesake on the same day; both taken way too early.

When we are not far from his flat, Arthur asks me how much snow there is in Jindabyne.

'None right now,' I explain, 'but there'll be a lot of snow higher up in the mountains in the winter.'

I'd mentioned on my first visit to Adelaide that I lived in a beautiful place in the mountains and that he should come to visit some time.

I'd even shown Arthur pictures of Lake Jindabyne, which is right on our doorstep. Part of me felt ashamed that my circumstances were so much more comfortable than his. And I felt even more ashamed that it had only recently occurred to me to find out that I was living on stolen Ngarigu land. But another part of me wanted desperately to share some of what I had with him and his family. I surmise that by asking about the snow Arthur must be probing to see whether the invitation to visit still stood. If so, that would be a sign of an accord between us, and an outcome that was beyond my wildest dreams.

'Would you like to come and visit some time,' I ask, trying to sound nonchalant.

'Well, I would like to see the snow,' Arthur replies.

I resolve then and there to make sure that Arthur and his family do see snow. It would be my next project, even though I knew the transport challenges would be considerable. We talk for the rest of the journey about the relative merits of flying and driving, knowing that cost would be a major factor, although neither of us mention it.

'I think it would be good to drive,' says Arthur, 'and see a few things along the way.'

I speculate about hiring a people-mover that could carry them all, knowing there is a question mark about who could drive it. Arthur was waiting for a medical exam to try to win back the licence he'd had to surrender due to failing health. His daughters had only just obtained their learner's permits, and I wondered who would be in a position to steer them through all the obstacles these days to obtaining a licence. In any case, driving all the way from Adelaide to Jindabyne would be a challenge for freshly minted drivers, especially with small children in the car, even if they did get their licences in time. I would worry the whole time I was waiting for them to arrive, that something might have happened; just like my mother, I realise with horror. Making the gathering at the cemetery happen seemed like child's play compared with this, but I am certain we can find a way. I feel happy and determined. Arthur's visit will be a sign that he has accepted me as almost-family.

The foundations have been laid for that bridge, although there will be plenty of building to come.

When we get to Arthur's place, Priscilla and Aunty Judy decide to linger for a while. They have faced considerable transport challenges themselves that day and want to make their trip across town worthwhile. I say my goodbyes and hand over the book I brought from home to leave with them – My Side of the Bridge, by Veronica Brodie. I knew the author was not one of their own community's elders, although the family was now living on her country. But it was the book that had helped me understand the lies told to our family about Arthur and Lennie's mother. I thought they might like to have it. I pass it to Jacqui, saying that I know she's the reader of the family, thinking that will please her. She smiles and says she recognises the cover from the photo I'd attached to the text I'd sent her dad. I show her the passage I've marked with a highlighter pen that talks about the misrepresentation of the drinking patterns of Aboriginal women – a rare book desecration that had seemed justified by the enormity of the truth it recorded. I feel as I hand over the book that I am making a peace offering.

*

After I leave Arthur's place, still glowing with excitement about the prospect of their visit, I drive back along Torrens Road one last time to meet up with my brother Neil, his wife Rae, son Nathan, daughter-in-law Libbey and little grandson Julian. They have decided to have a late lunch at the Bombay Bicycle Club, which is very close to the aquatic centre where we had all gathered earlier. I know it by reputation as an old pub that had been done up in full Raj regalia, although I have never been there. I couldn't think of anything more at odds with what we had just been through together than visiting this homage to colonialism, but I decide to put my Deep Thinking aside and prioritise the rare opportunity to spend time with extended family. I find them tucked inside a quiet room that is quite understated compared with the wildly ornate decor I walked through to get there.

The rooms are decked out in different styles, from lush jungles with faux stuffed tigers lurking behind the greenery, to formal dining rooms draped with burgundy velvet held back by gold tassels and walls lined with wooden temple carvings and elephant-foot tables that I fervently hope are made of plastic. It is vulgar and garish but arguably forgivable if viewed through the lens of irony. The ladies' room turns out to be nothing short of phantasmagorical. Every inch of wall is covered with blue and green tiles in a multitude of swirly patterns, and the view upwards from the cubicles extends into a towering glass dome festooned with tropical plants. I wonder how they keep them so healthy and well-watered, but later realise that all the indoor plants are high-quality silk replicas. I make a mental note about how disorientating it would be to be drunk or tripping in this overstimulating environment, although that is very unlikely to happen today.

The vegan curry the others had ordered for me just as the kitchen was about to close is delicious, and there is no doubt that the food and the surroundings are excellent. But in my new spirit of openness, I decide to share my thoughts about the contradiction of following up an act of decolonisation (I don't use that word) by immersing ourselves in a celebration of colonialism. I have finally learned how to say things like this calmly without sounding aggressive (to cover up underlying distress or insecurity), so I manage to cause only mild annoyance to my brother. He looks around at the sepia photographs of men in pith helmets accompanied by natives of various social stations and agrees that it is an overtly colonial theme, but that he prefers to focus on the aesthetic.

'That's always been the difference between us,' I press on, good-naturedly, I hope. 'I can't help but see the politics in everything.'

My time as a mature age postgrad in Cambridge had brought that home to me. Whereas many other people from humble origins, given that opportunity, might have chosen to associate themselves with one of the older colleges that promised history, status and sumptuous surroundings, I had ruled out every college that still had a high table and insisted on the wearing of academic gowns – especially the one where they still dined by candlelight – and had opted for down-to-earth Darwin College. It had turned out to be a perfect choice for me. Firstly, it accepted only graduate students, who were serious about their studies, hailed from a wide range of countries and had generally made their way to Cambridge due to academic merit and commitment. It contrasted with the elite undergraduate colleges where many students were there due to birthright and extreme privilege. You could pick them out on Cambridge streets where they idled about in huddles speaking loudly in received pronunciation, radiating entitlement and whipping out fat chequebooks (which actually still existed in their world) that were linked to their daddy's bank accounts, which they used ostentatiously to make even the most trivial purchase.

Darwin College was a world away in a modest, but still historic, building built on land that had once been owned by a member of the great scientist's family. Its greatest asset, in my view, was that it occupied a prime location for punting on the River Cam – a point that had featured prominently in my selection criteria. Although I felt relatively comfortable in college, as I'd walked around the cobbled streets in awe of the ancient buildings, my admiration had always been tempered by reminders of the scandalous history of town-and-gown inequality. That the old colleges had diverted the town's water into their fountains, sometimes grudgingly installing a single tap outside their walls for the townsfolk to use. That they still employed 'bedders' to fill the role of the maids-cum-nannies to which many of the students were accustomed. My time in Cambridge had been memorable, but fraught with disturbing contradictions.

After the meal at the Bombay Bicycle Club, I linger a while in the hotel car park talking with Neil and Rae. Just like research interviews, where it's often the case that the most interesting things are said once the recording device is off, we seem to have kept the most penetrating subjects as an afterthought to lunch. It turns out that Neil has no idea, or at least no memory, of Mum's allegations about police having caused

Len's death. This disturbing theory had somehow made its way down the generations to my great-nephew Josh but seemed to have bypassed his great-uncle. It was becoming clearer to me, now that I was actually talking to members of my family, how family history is distributed in a kind of patchwork – a conversation here, an experience there, that may or may not be transmitted across or down the line. I tell Neil about the strange information I had gleaned from the autopsy report and, to my surprise, he does not dismiss it, but agrees that it sounds suspicious.

Just as I am thinking of breaking off the conversation, Neil drops an even greater bombshell which shows that this time I am the one who has been in the dark. Neil tells me that our dad had confided in him towards the end of his life, although without further explanation, that if they'd had their time again, he and Mum would not have taken Lennie into their care. I'm sure they did not regret for a minute the love that he had brought into our lives or begrudge any of the hardships that had accompanied it. But it seems they had come to understand something about the wider implications, or at least appreciate that they had been unable to give him what he most needed. I am sure that I had never heard this from Dad. Is it possible I could have forgotten such a major disclosure when this was the very thing that I had always felt divided us?

I was beginning to feel like a character in Mike Leigh's masterpiece Secrets and Lies. What else did I not know about our family? For the entire time I'd been writing this memoir, in fact right from the time of Len's death, one of the themes I kept returning to was the isolation I felt at believing I was the only one in the family who felt there was something amiss about Lennie coming to live with us: who had felt, right from childhood, an inchoate sense that somehow things were not as they should be. It seemed, in that split second after Neil told me what our father had said, that writing the memoir had been worthless. That all along, I could have found what I was looking for by simply speaking to my dad; by discovering that point of agreement. It seemed like hubris now – despite the emotional pain it had caused me – to have thought for all that time that I was in a category of one.

*

Back in my narrow Queen Anne bed at my sister's place that night, there is time to reflect on what happened that day. I feel like it had all rushed by in a frenzy and I had barely experienced any of it. I had spent most of the day stressing about organising things – allowing the practical to triumph over the emotional. Biblically speaking, I'd been a pragmatic Martha, when it was so much more desirable to be her curious sister Mary, anxious to soak up everything that could be learned from the occasion. In terms of the ceremony itself, there had not been any grand revelations, emotional outbursts or lavish gestures made by anyone, least of all me. To my surprise and relief, there had been no weeping, not even a tremor in my voice as I said the words I had been rehearsing in my head. No one had felt the urge to stand in a circle around the grave and hold hands, as I had imagined in my more sentimental moments. Nothing overtly transformative had happened. But I had a sense that I had got it done, something important that had set the record straight. And more than that, my family had supported me by being there, by not complaining about the heat and about being late getting started, and by genuinely embracing Arthur and his relatives. And Arthur and his family had willingly done the same.

When I arrived back at my sister's place that evening, we had stood around in the kitchen talking – my sister, niece and I – conducting a post-mortem on the day's events. Just as I had found out with Neil, there were so many things that each of us knew or didn't know that we had never discussed before. The gathering had provided a chance to say what had gone unspoken for so long. We talked about how Matt's kids had responded – how they had interacted so well with Arthur's grandsons, and how Josh had put the cat amongst the pigeons by pointing the finger of blame for Len's death at the police.

'I suppose I should have done something at the time when Mum told me that,' I'd said, 'but I was just immobilised and incapable of even discussing it with her.'

My niece looked confused. It did not align with the adventurous and outspoken young aunt she remembered from her adolescence who seemed to be on top of everything. 'What do you mean immobilised?,' she'd asked.

'By grief,' I said, 'and childhood trauma after everything that had happened.'

She still looked incredulous. It occurred to me then that she still did not know much about what had happened, outside her own less complicated memories of her beloved Uncle Len. The complications would have to wait for another day.

My sister weighed in with her own confession. 'I've always worried that I didn't do enough.' She looked as if she might cry. 'Len used to come to our house late at night sometimes when he'd had too much to drink. I wanted to help, but the children were young, and Bruce…'. Her story tailed off.

She had told me this before, and I had taken it as a general comment. But now I was left wondering if she was also talking about events on the night Len died, or close to that time. I could see that she had carried her own unspoken burdens too.

Tucked up in bed later, looking back over the day, I am surprised to realise that what had meant the most to me was Arthur's desire to visit me in Jindabyne. He had held out a hand to me. I wonder if he knew how much power he held over my happiness at this point in my life. It would be best if he didn't. The whole thing felt not so much like an act of closure, as people often say. It was more like an opening up to something new. Something wholly unimagined until then. I felt that things could at least be right with Len's family from now on, even if we couldn't change the past. Even if we did not exactly agree on what it had all meant. I knew it would still be difficult to maintain and develop our relationship with so much distance between us, both social and geographic. But this was the sort of challenge I could take on as an adult, although I had been way out of my depth as a child. Now perhaps I could finally let go of my grief for my brother, and at the same time hold onto him by embracing his family.

*

The next morning, my final hours in Adelaide are spent going through my sister's boxes of old photos looking for any images of Len that I don't have at home. My niece Jen has in mind a particular photo of herself with her uncle that she is hoping to find. When we have almost given up, we both find what we are looking for in a faded old album. There is the black and white photo I have always loved of a teenage Bev and Nora, side by side, dressed up to the nines. Some studio portraits of all four of us – Bev and Neil as young adults, Len and me as children – and one of a beaming Len on his own, aged about eight. By the time we get to the little square coloured photos taken on the family's Polaroid camera at Len's twenty-first birthday, his expression is very glum. There is not a single photo in which he is smiling, on what was supposed to be his special day. We find amongst that series the one that Jen had remembered of her Uncle Len holding her as a baby. Len looks serious but loving. Baby Jen is playfully reaching out her hand towards the camera, clearly feeling safe and happy in Len's arms. I pull these photos out of the album, lie them flat on the floor and photograph them for myself, and to send to Arthur later.

By the time I have hauled my suitcase into the hire car and driven away from my sister's house, I am running out of time for the final stop I planned to make on my way to the airport. Although the beaches in Sydney, where I lived for a while, are celebrated for their surf and spectacular rocky settings, I have always preferred the long stretches of flat sand and calm waters of Adelaide's suburban beaches. They speak to something deep inside. I try to spend an evening at Henley Beach whenever I visit my hometown, sitting in a café or on the grassy promenade watching the sun go down over the sea. That is one sight I have missed while living away from the sea, or on the eastern seaboard where the sun rises, rather than sets, over the ocean. The sunsets in Adelaide are truly magnificent: the arid plains to the north radiate dust particles into the sky that regularly generate technicolour pinks, golds and purples.

This time, I settle for a quick lunch of fish and chips and some people-watching in Henley Square. The area has been gentrified and is landscaped with shade sails, outdoor cafés and fountains. My dear old uncle and aunt, long gone now, used to live in a bungalow just around the corner right on the waterfront. Auntie Jean's stories were always about their passion for fishing and their adventures at sea. There was the time Uncle Chook ate the burley that she kept in the fridge, thinking it was savoury mince, and the not-so-funny time their outboard motor failed. That house would be worth well over a million dollars now, and there is nowhere within any proximity to it or the square to find a place to park the car. It's a hot summer's day on the weekend, and the place is heaving. By the time I arrive in Henley Square, having found a park several blocks away, I have about thirty minutes in which to buy my greasy treat and stuff it down while sitting cross-legged on the lawn in the last available patch of shade. It's disappointing, but it's something. Despite leaving Adelaide long ago in search of something I didn't think I could find here, I still love this place and feel a certain sense of belonging.

As I lick the salty grease from my fingers, memories flood back about things I haven't thought about since childhood. Of the many days we enjoyed here as a family in the blazing heat of summer. There was no trouble parking then. It was nothing fancy, just a few delis, the obligatory fish and chip shop and a couple of pubs, and the vastness of the beach that stretched unbroken as far as the eye could see to the north and south. Len and I used to burst out of Dad's FJ Holden, affectionately dubbed the 'Bluebird', and clamber down the boulders that were piled along the foreshore to prevent erosion. Mum would shout at us to go further along the footpath to the stairs, that there were rats and snakes in the rocks, or that we could fall and skin our knees, but the urge to feel the sand on our feet was too great and we had to take the shortest route possible. Len and I would swim like fish all day long or paddle together between the jetties at Henley and Grange on the family's prize possession, a lacquered wooden surf ski. If the mood took me, I would turn endless cartwheels along the beach until I was dizzy or play beach bats or throw a tennis ball back and forth with Dad. Even then, my throwing arm was deadly.

In the evenings as it began to cool down, the Greek and Italian families would arrive with their elaborate picnics that seemed to be just the same as the meals I imagined them eating at home. They would arrange a selection of large saucepans in the middle of their rugs and eat the contents from proper dinner plates. I don't know if I've imagined it, but sometimes in the summer holidays I think there might have been an old-fashioned funfair in the evenings for the kids. Not with big mechanical rides. Just a strip of sideshows laid out higgledy-piggledy along the footpath. I remember being entranced by an old man in a tattered suit and hat with some tiny monkeys, probably marmosets, performing tricks. I wouldn't approve of that now. And another old chap (they all seemed old) with a flea circus. I had looked and looked but couldn't see any fleas. On the drive home to our working-class suburb, you'd often see a trailer parked on the side of Henley Beach Road piled high with watermelons. Sometimes, Dad would stop and buy an enormous one from the Greek vendor to have for afters with our tea. Those were the good times. I was starting to remember them. And I was beginning to feel an attachment to place that I had not felt for a very long time.

*

A couple of weeks later, my niece Lucie visits me in Jindabyne. It turns out that the vegan cupcakes she had made to order for the reunion had been distributed to her friends in Sydney before they reached her freezer. I'd been hoping she would bring some thawed ones with her. We debrief about the gathering at the cemetery, then she tells me something very curious. Although she is the only one of my nieces and nephews who did not know her Uncle Len, Lucie explains that when my mother – her gran – died, she had felt a strong compulsion to find out all she could about him. A lot of things now made sense. That it had been Lucie who had pointed out the omission of Len's name in the newspaper announcement of my dad's death. And that it was Lucie who'd been the first to respond to my invitation to attend the gathering at the cemetery, even though she lived the furthest away.

But other things about Lucie's revelation did not make any sense at all. I was not surprised at the interest a youngest child might have in tracing events that happened before her birth, being in a similar position as a tail-ender myself. Constantly hearing fragments of family stories that seem disconnected from your own life creates a strong motivation to fill in the gaps. I had come to have a similar curiosity about my Papa Neil, who had been a constant presence in my life through my mother's stories, although he had died when I was just a babe in arms. But Lucie's sudden, and very specific, curiosity about her Uncle Len, precisely at the time of my mother's death, seemed somehow different – bordering on the mystical. The death of someone close can trigger all kinds of responses, so perhaps it was just a coincidence. But the thought persisted that there was some hidden connection. Was it something to do with mum having been Len's self-appointed Protector? Could her passing have finally ruptured that special bond and transmitted a signal into the universe that only Lucie, hungry to connect with the past, had detected? It was fanciful, but it was the best explanation I could find.

After Lucie had gone back to Sydney, my thoughts returned to matters more mundane: the approach of the Easter holiday. Hot cross buns had been in the supermarket since the end of the summer holidays – a marketing onslaught I had managed to resist for several months. Despite my many rebellions, I still maintained an allegiance to many of the rules of appropriate behaviour and self-denial I had learned from my childhood. No presents were to be opened on Christmas Day until after the church service. Hot cross buns were strictly for Good Friday to solemnly acknowledge Christ's suffering, and Easter eggs not before Easter Sunday to celebrate the renewal made possible by the resurrection. Both occasions, I knew, had involved a sneaky grafting on of

Christianity to pre-existing pagan festivals designed to lift spirits and mark the changing seasons. It was a kind of colonial appropriation. Even so, for me they provided a reminder to donate to good causes and a chance to spoil any small children in my life.

So, when the supermarket shelves start to overflow with Easter eggs, chocolate bunnies and bilbies, I begin to contemplate what I could buy for Jacqui and Jeannie's sons that would not get squashed in the post. I send an Easter parcel to Cambridge each year for the children of our 'Nigerian son' Steve, usually containing a few little novelties and chocolate shapes that cost a fraction of the international postage and could just as easily have been bought from a shop where they live. Even so, there's nothing more exciting for a small child than to receive a special parcel by post.

When the family had visited us several years before, and we had spent Easter together in Jindabyne, we were able to surprise them on Easter morning with Easter bilbies, as part of our ongoing indoctrination about Australian wildlife. But it seemed unlikely that these fragile little creatures would survive the rough journey to the other side of the planet. This year, I was contemplating sending them some wooden eggs from Oxfam, painted with beautiful Aboriginal motifs, hopefully produced by actual Indigenous people who were benefiting from Oxfam's fair-trade policies. I would fill them with chocolate eggs of course, otherwise what would be the point for an eight- and a six-year-old. But they would have something to keep after that. That option seemed inappropriate for Arthur's grandsons, so I settled for the standard chocolate fare from Woolies, opting for small solid bunnies and miniature eggs that would survive the bumpy journey.

There are always multiple ways to interpret gestures such as this. A sad, childless woman trying to buy affection? A sanctimonious do-gooder inserting herself into places where she's not wanted? Someone engaging in a small act of love and kindness? I couldn't know which of these reactions my modest gift might trigger in Arthur's family. I knew that, for me, it was simply a small step towards making what I hoped would be a lasting connection. A message that they were now a valued part of my life. I already felt enormous affection for Arthur and his family, and, given the chance, would grow to love and support those small boys and take an interest in their lives. I even dared to think that perhaps one day they might call me aunty. I also knew that the relationship was still fragile and that I must always take care to keep a respectful distance. But now that I had found a living connection to my brother, I was not prepared to let it go.

*

I text Arthur over Easter. Without me asking, he mentions that his grandsons were excited to receive the Easter eggs in the post. I can't resist asking if he is still interested in coming to see the snow. The reply comes back in his usual shorthand – 'Thinking about it girls want go me unsure.'

Since coming back from Adelaide, I'd been thinking about how we could get everyone to us. With six of them, the costs and the logistics of them flying over could be prohibitive. But I'd put those doubts to one side and imagined every detail of their visit. Where everyone would sleep. How I would find enough warm bedding. How we could provide waterproof clothes for the snow for all the adults from our own wardrobes, and for the kids by borrowing and scrounging. How we could go tobogganing, make a snowperson, and ride the ski tube to Blue Cow for free; take sandwiches for lunch to save money, and come home, walk the dogs by the lake, then build a fire in the fire pit and have a barbecue dinner.

It's hard to be nuanced when texting is your only form of communication, so I just ask Arthur outright about his uncertainty. 'Are you not sure if you're well enough to travel? Or maybe thinking about the cost?'

'Both at the moment,' comes back the reply.

So I decide to leave it there for a while. A couple of months later, when the snow comes in early and makes it onto the national news, Arthur sends me an unexpected text saying how beautiful it looks. He wants to come, I think to myself. The idea has lodged in his mind.

Amid all the uncertainty about how our relationship will unfold, it is uplifting to have that prospect to hold onto.

A renaissance

Not long before my act of atonement, I had taken the plunge and set up a Twitter account. My first encounter with social media proved to be unexpectedly therapeutic, bearing in mind this was pre-Musk Twitter (now X). It wasn't technophobia that had kept me out of the Twitter-sphere until then. What had held me back had been a combination of habitual reticence about rushing to adopt the latest trend, an aversion to confrontation – which I associated with social media – and an irrational fear that remains with me still about exposing myself to the gaze of anonymous others out there in the big wide world.

To my great surprise, my trepidation fell away within the first few minutes of starting up my account as I saw followers magically starting to appear. It was exciting, gratifying, intriguing. Where were they coming from? To start with, they were mostly people I knew. But after I sent out my first tentative tweets, the numbers started to build – not to celebrity levels, but enough to keep me checking my phone expectantly to see the latest count, and searching my notifications for Likes from people I knew and others I didn't. For the first time in my life, I knew what it must feel like to be a poker machine player compulsively feeding coins into one of those hungry beasts. I was surprised at my susceptibility to Twitter's self-validating allure but pleased to discover I was not so different from other people. As the same names began to appear regularly in my feed, it felt as though I had found a community based on shared values. Since I had often thought of myself as separate from others, this felt like a refreshing change and an antidote to the relentless individualism of Western society.

I began to tweet my opinions about the inhumanity and illegality of Australian border control, and the economic and social divisions unleashed by neoliberal policies. As I came to feel more accepted, I also tweeted about everyday things like the books I'd loved reading, the beauty of the changing seasons in the mountains, and making jam from what had been left after some unidentified peach poachers had stripped our tree almost bare while we were away. It felt like I was coming out of a long hibernation, as if I had been a dormant seed needing sowing.

Growing Pains

Looking back
my life has been
a gaping wound
slowly healing;
a peeling away
revealing
feelings
again.

Thinking back
my mind has been
a dormant seed
needing sowing;
now growing stronger
slowly
knowing
how.

Casting back
my task has been
an exercise
in unlearning;
of burning bridges,
earnest
yearning
for more.

Looking on
my life will be
a treasure
of my own creating;
a liberating from
self-hating,
hibernating
days.

Soon, the opportunity arose to tweet my thoughts about Australia/
Survival/Invasion Day. I tweeted about my decision to retreat into
the tranquillity of the mountains to avoid stumbling upon flag flying
barbecues. About learning belatedly, after almost ten years living in
Jindabyne, that I was living on Ngarigu land. At my confusion after
fishing out a waterlogged baseball cap from the lake – on this of all
days – embroidered with the name of a battleship, an outdated figure
of a boomerang-wielding native, and the motto 'Courage in Difficulty'.
With my increasing vigilance about colonial assumptions, I had been
suspicious about the intentions behind this iconography. I eventually
tracked down the story about HMAS Warramunga and learned that
the motto was meant to honour the Northern Territory people of the
same name.[117] That didn't stop me writing to the historical section
within the Royal Australian Navy asking whether the Warramunga
people had been consulted recently about the stereotypical way in
which they were being portrayed. They told me they had. Gradually, I
was sensing a kind of connection to the network of Indigenous leaders
whose names I saw on Twitter calling out the entrenched racism and
unreflective privilege they encountered every day. In a small way, I felt
I was beginning to do the same.

On one occasion, I stumbled unwittingly into a Twitter hate zone
targeting asylum seekers. It was after I had posted a positive reply to
one of the regular messages from Abdul Aziz Adam, who had recently
won a prestigious United Nations human rights prize despite being

detained on Manus Island. Happily, he now lives as a recognised refugee in Switzerland. As I fended off the ensuing barrage of abuse, I experienced for a very short time what high-profile advocates for refugees or trans women or people of colour must face constantly. I couldn't imagine the level of courage and self-belief it must take to withstand that. Once I had noticed that the vitriol was being redirected away from me and back towards Abdul Aziz himself, I had felt a wave of relief. Shamefully, I had typed out a rebuttal to one abusive message, pointing out the man's achievements, but hesitated to post it because I knew that would redirect the venom back to me. It seemed that my character was being tested in my new online life. And once again, I had run away and opted to protect myself.

I clearly had a long way to go before I would be able to assume the mantle of even a keyboard warrior, let alone a real-world one. But I was delighted when the Twittersphere delivered a manifesto of sorts right to my laptop on how to be a 'good Indigenous ally'. I thought perhaps that was something I could aspire to. It was an article written by Yorta Yorta woman Summer May Findlay, that contained the following advice.[118]

1. Preference our voices i.e. don't speak on behalf of Aboriginal people.
2. Be OK with not always being part of the conversation i.e. shut up and listen.
3. Be there for the easy and the hard times i.e. don't just engage in a superficial way with the Aboriginal struggles that suit you.
4. Say something when you hear inappropriate statements about Aboriginal people i.e. be prepared to 'make a fuss'.
5. Don't take it personally when we don't agree with you i.e. be resilient, like Aboriginal people are required to be.
6. Don't go it alone i.e. always check with Aboriginal people that you have things right.
7. Understand that Aboriginal people are not all the same i.e. views differ, just like other Australians.

I did a quick mental audit of how well I had kept to these principles during the writing of this memoir. Had I spoken for Aboriginal people? Perhaps in some ways, by using historical sources published by non-Aboriginal writers, at least for the first part of the book. And although I had started out thinking I was writing a book about Len, it had over time become just as much about me. Had I listened to Aboriginal people? Well, I hadn't done too well on the phone with Jacqui when I had sought to explain myself rather than listen to her. That was a fail. On the other hand, I'd been reading Anita Heiss's collection Growing up Aboriginal in Australia, which is a form of listening, and had learned a lot. There were so many variations on how to grow up Aboriginal in this country, and none were without major challenges.

Had I learned to intervene when I heard disparaging remarks about Aboriginal people? Yes, I thought I might scrape a pass on that one. With the help of the EMDR therapy to deal with specific emotional triggers forged in childhood, and the generalised calming effect from my daily Wim Hof practice of breath control and cold exposure,[119] I now felt able to 'make a fuss' without triggering a complete emotional meltdown. Had I taken it personally when Len's family had questioned my interpretations, or elected to go it alone regardless of their feelings? I had to admit that those might have been my first instincts, but I could honestly say that I had persevered. I had listened and incorporated their perspectives as best I could and had shifted some of mine. And I had certainly learned from Arthur not to expect all Aboriginal people to hold identical views. Many of his beliefs had turned out to be closer to my parents' world view than to my own. It was a mixed scorecard but it was clear that writing, and living, the memoir had become more than the setting down of historical events. It was an ongoing process of opening myself up to a new ways of knowing – slowly knowing how.

*

As well as reading Indigenous authors while writing the second part of this book, I have also been curious about how writers from a range of different backgrounds have approached their own memoirs. Not that I think there's likely to be a formula. One of the most powerful was Maxine Beneba Clarke's memoir The Hate Race. It spoke to me in several important ways and lived up to the description the author had in her Twitter profile at the time: 'I try to write beautifully about ugly things.' It seems that whenever I refresh my Twitter feed, some whimsical observation or forthright opinion from her appears near the top of the screen. She has since changed her profile image but the first one I saw – a sort of cartoon – looked exactly like Wendy, the cherished brown-skinned doll from my childhood.

Reading about the torrent of racism directed against the young Maxine by students, parents and teachers was doubly hard for me. I felt heartbreak for that little girl of course. But it also brought to life, more vividly than I could ever dare to imagine, what my brother must have endured outside the sanctuary of our family home. In the early chapters, we meet Maxine's infant school peers. There's Carlita, who makes no effort to disguise her disdain for the colour of Maxine's skin. She is probably a One Nation voter now. There's sweet, lisping Bella, who accepts 'Macsthine' without question, but is the subject of bullying herself, and not able to be the ally Maxine needs. Next, we meet caring Jennifer, who writes kind words on Maxine's 'student of the week' poster and becomes her friend for a time. And sassy Susana, who understands why Maxine's mum has bought her a brown-skinned Cabbage Patch doll and tells Carlita to keep her opinions to herself. I try to place my child self within this cast of characters – hoping I might have been a brave Susana, but fearing I may have been a Bella, but without the lisp or the bullying.

Over time, Maxine's ordeal at school gets steadily worse. A turning point arises in her friendship with Jennifer when Maxine and her brother are playing on their BMX bikes with Jennifer and one of her siblings. Faced with sustained racist taunting from a group of boys, Jennifer runs home to tell her parents, who eventually appear at Maxine's house to make sure all is well. At one level, this might seem like a sensible course of action, and Jennifer expects to continue her friendship with Maxine as if nothing had happened. But Maxine's sense of abandonment by her friend is powerful and irreversible. Jennifer could not be relied upon to back her up, had instead run away from a threat that was not directed at her and opted to protect herself. I felt a pang of shame and realisation as I read this. Clearly, I was a Jennifer. But I felt able to forgive both of us now, as we were only children.

*

One day not long ago, my partner is walking our two dogs in the bushland near where we live by the lake. I have just emerged from the chilly water after my morning Wim Hof swim and can hear him blowing the whistle, trying to get them back.

When they appear on the beach, Tony has a remarkable story to tell. 'Belle was barking and barking,' he says. 'I thought she must have had an echidna or some other critter bailed up. But when she finally came back, she was carrying an injured fox in her mouth. She'd been trying to get me to come to help.'

'How was she carrying it?' I ask, mindful that Belle – a feisty blue heeler – had on one memorable occasion grabbed a chihuahua in her mouth and run around triumphantly, shaking it above her head.

'She was carrying it like a mother dog carries a puppy,' Tony says, apparently reading my mind. 'Very gently. I don't think it was Belle that injured it.'

Over the years, we had each seen Belle, and our kelpie-German shepherd cross Bonnie, interacting with foxes. It was plausible that the fox was one of her friends.

'What do you think happened?' I ask.

'Maybe it was hit by a car,' Tony suggests.

Belle had laid the little fox down gently in a gully, and Tony, fearing that the other dogs that usually join our walks would harass the defenceless creature, opts to leave it there while he leashes up Bonnie and Belle and entices the rest of the village pack to follow him back home. Encountering me on the beach, he decides to recruit me to help lead the dogs away.

When I go back into the bush later to look for the fox at the place Tony had described, it is nowhere to be seen. I choose to interpret that as a good sign that it has recovered its ability to move and has found a place of safety.

I relate this story because it was a major test of my personal transformation, away from a person who felt helpless, and yet responsible, for everything wrong in the world, towards a person who could do what was needed but also accept their limitations. Was this radical acceptance? For the first time, I realised this concept I had resisted was actually the first goal in the Serenity Prayer: to accept with serenity the things I cannot change, but in my case without reliance on the help of god. Previously, I would have worried myself sick for days about the fate of that poor fox, berated myself for leaving it unattended, abandoned the jobs that needed doing and traipsed through the bush for hours in search of it, and phoned every wildlife service and vet in the area to find out what to do should I locate it. If it had died despite my efforts, I would have been thrust into the deepest of torments, as had happened some years before when I failed in my efforts to save that baby galah.

Knowing this pattern, Tony's first words when he had met me on the beach had been 'I don't know whether I should tell you this...' However, this time I'd been amazed by my newfound composure. Had that fox been where we had left it, incapacitated and clearly needing help, I would have done everything I could for it, including accepting that the kindest thing might have been to arrange an early release from its suffering. But, since it wasn't there, I was able to let go and respect its capacity to help itself, which is just as it should be.

The next time I was in Canberra, I went to see my EMDR therapist. She had been hinting for a while that I was pretty close to being 'completely fine' (as in, Eleanor Oliphant is Completely Fine) and I could sense as well that it was time to cut the umbilical cord. Kerry never went in for that Freudian dream interpretation malarkey, but I had just had a dream that I wanted to discuss with her. Apart from being the only time in my life I recall dreaming about my mother, there was nothing special about it. It was set in the house we had lived in when I was a small child, and nothing much happened. But it seemed to be allegorical. It contrasted with my usual brand of anxiety dream where I repeatedly, and inexplicably, derail my own efforts to complete an extremely important but straightforward task. I give a short description of the dream to Kerry and ask her opinion about what it might mean.

'Well…' she hesitates and seems reluctant to go down this contested path, 'there were lots of baby animals, and some allusions to human babies, and that can sometimes symbolise rebirth.'

'Yes,' I think. 'Rebirth. That's exactly what it is.'

*

A few months later, I'm in Adelaide again to see my niece Lucie perform her one-woman cabaret show, which provides another opportunity to visit Arthur and his family. I find him out back of Jeannie's house, tearing away at the dense tangle of weeds blanketing the back yard.

'There's a bike under here,' he says, pulling it out triumphantly.

There was bad news since I had been there last. His younger sister Vonnie, the mother of ten children, has died from a massive stroke. She had left a chasm in all their lives, and I would never get to meet her.

Before I can ask, Arthur tells me he still hasn't read the updated manuscript I posted after my last visit. My heart sinks. I was hoping so much for his approval, but also prepared to use this opportunity to talk through anything that remained contentious.

'I read the first page,' he adds, 'but I got really emotional.'

That puts things in a different light. It confirms my belated realisation – obvious once you start to think about it – that Arthur has no idea what had happened during Len's time with us, and just how emotionally disturbed his younger brother had been. I realise then that I hadn't thought this through from his perspective. I had hoped that if we could talk about the book it might bring us closer. But was I entitled to expect that? He might prefer not to know. I had just been thinking of myself and my precious project.

In Jeannie's kitchen, we talk about lunch. I had offered to take the family out for a meal, maybe to the Pizza Hut – somewhere family-friendly, affordable and hopefully not too environmentally unsound. I had mentally ruled out McDonalds on the latter grounds. Jacqui is hovering about, saying she was going to get chips.

'I thought we might go out for lunch,' I remind them, 'my treat.'

Jacqui walks away without saying anything.

'She doesn't like going to places with lots of white people,' Arthur explains. 'Shame job. Jeannie's different, she doesn't mind.'

Once again, this makes me feel ashamed. It was another trick of colonisation to project the shame of all that was done in its name onto those who endured it. There was so much recurring, festering harm I still had to learn to anticipate. We decide to get Chinese takeaway instead, and Jeannie joins me in the hire car to show me the best local place and pick out everyone's favourites.

When they've finished eating, family members disperse through the house and I find myself alone for a while in the kitchen. As usual, White Boy's gigantic face is pressed up against the glass of the sliding door, his smaller sister Tina beside him, both desperate to get inside for pats. A small tan-coloured dog has also appeared in the kitchen who I know from previous visits to be Binnie, White Boy's sometime companion. When Jeannie's small son appears at the door as well, pulling at the handle to come inside, I go up to help and make sure the big dogs don't come in with him. I slide the door open just far enough for Jayden to slip through, while holding White Boy at bay with the other hand. Unbeknown to me, sneaky little Binnie has taken the opportunity to slip through between my legs, and is at large in the backyard.

Jeannie comes into the kitchen at that point and screams, 'Lucky's outside. Lucky's outside.'

Something is clearly wrong. First of all, it seems this isn't Binnie – who I had seen in White Boy's company several times – but another dog that

208

looks exactly like her. Second, there is genuine panic in Jeannie's voice, so I decide to follow her outside, feeling responsible for creating an incipient crisis. Arthur has also appeared from somewhere and has taken hold of White Boy's collar. For a moment, the three of us stand watching not-Binnie and White Boy facing off. The atmosphere is tense, but I begin to think whatever they are worried about is not going to happen. Then, without warning, the pint-sized canine leaps at White Boy's neck and the fight is on.

Arthur, still holding on to White Boy's collar, is yelling at Jeannie, 'Get Lucky. Get Lucky.'

But she is busy trying to prevent Tina from joining in.

Without stopping to think, I jump onto White Boy's back and grab hold of the other side of his collar. I'm struck by the sheer power of him as he throws Arthur and me around like rag dolls. I can't see what is happening on the other side of his enormous head, but it can't be pretty and I'm imagining Lucky in shreds by now. But it seems the little dog has not given up because Arthur is still shouting at Jeannie to grab him and take him away.

Suddenly, White Boy makes a powerful lurch to the right. I hold on for as long as I can but find myself launched through the air, landing with a thud in a puddle of mud. Just for an instant, I register the wetness seeping through my jeans and coating my grey suede boots, and can see Arthur rolling on the ground looking dazed. My next thought is to return to my post. As I lunge for White Boy's collar, I feel his powerful jaws clamp around my forearm. The words 'there goes my arm' flash through my mind, believing – mistakenly, I now know – that his breed was designed for fighting. Instead, White Boy realises he's made a mistake; that I am a human and therefore entitled to special treatment not accorded to members of his own species. He releases his hold.

Somehow – it's all just a blur now – the mighty David and Goliath battle comes to an end and we all retreat into the kitchen, licking our wounds. Lucky has a limp but, against the odds, is otherwise intact. I am oozing blood from several deep puncture wounds in my forearm and am pacing around with aftershocks of intense pain shooting up my arm. Jeannie is nursing a nasty gash on her palm where Lucky has bitten her, and I understand then why it has taken so long to get the tenacious little creature away. Apart from looking dishevelled and shell-shocked, Arthur seems OK. I put my arms around them both spontaneously and we stand for a while in a circle contemplating the crisis we've just experienced together.

From the other side of the kitchen, I think I hear Jacqui saying in her soft voice, 'Other people would have run away.'

It occurs to me that she must be referring to me, and I realise then the significance of what has happened. That I hadn't run away. That, when tested, I had run towards the danger and had not let people down as I had in the past.

Jeannie and I spend the rest of the afternoon at the emergency department of the Queen Elizabeth Hospital being patched up and interrogated about what had happened, then are sent home with strict instructions to be on the lookout for infection.

The next day, I send Jeannie a text message asking if she is OK.

'A bit sore,' she texts back, 'Aunty Leanne.'

There they are. The two words I had dared hope to hear one day but had never dreamed it would be so soon. I had first become an aunty when I was twelve years old. That was a taken-for-granted and wholly unearned type of aunthood. Aunt by birthright. The aunty who had been looked up to and loved, not because of her age and accumulated wisdom, but because of her relative youth and relatability.

This was something entirely different. This meant acceptance and respect. This meant being trusted not to make trouble for the family. This meant being tested and showing solidarity, just like someone's real family would. This meant being allowed to venture a little way inside the overlapping circles and being truly seen. This meant everything.

A reckoning

After an Australian white supremacist gunned down worshippers at a mosque in Christchurch, Twitter erupted again. The messages of hate and victim-blaming did not come my way this time. I had learned how to stay within my safe place. What I saw instead were strong messages of support for the victims and their communities, many coming from Indigenous commentators. The solidarity cut both ways. Soon after the tragedy, the ABC television program The Drum hosted a panel of Muslim women to discuss the implications of the heinous cross-border crime. The panellists returned repeatedly to the need for Australian society to confront the foundational violence of colonisation before there would be any possibility of tackling broader societal problems of racism and Islamophobia. Although seemingly invisible to the more complacent sections of the settler population, all these women from marginalised communities saw a thread connecting white supremacists and violent nationalists to everyday, unexamined racism. It reminded me of conversations I'd had several years before with young people from migrant backgrounds for one of my university research projects in which an articulate young Hazara woman had made this memorable observation: 'People think this country is theirs. This country belongs to Aboriginal people.'

Speaking at the annual Garma festival in 2018, Booker prize-winning author Richard Flanagan – newly aware of his own Aboriginal heritage – bemoaned the nation's 'determined ignorance of our own country'.[120] The propensity to selectively ignore or reinterpret history is a well-known tactic for nationalists. George Orwell examined the psychological mechanisms driving this phenomenon of intentional forgetting in his Notes on Nationalism, where he writes:

The nationalist not only does not disapprove of atrocities committed by his own side, but he has a remarkable capacity for not even hearing about them... Every nationalist is haunted by the belief that the past can be altered... Events which, it is felt, ought not to have happened are left unmentioned and ultimately denied... If one harbours anywhere in one's mind a nationalistic loyalty or hatred, certain facts although in a sense known to be true, are inadmissible.[121]

One contributor to Growing up Aboriginal in Australia has a simple yet powerful response to those who actively deny the need to confront our colonial past:

When people say to me 'you mob live in the past', I say to them, 'No, the past lives in us, because if I can stand in front of you and talk about segregation and apartheid that I've experienced in my own country, it can't be the past because I am very much living'.[122]

Against this backdrop of widespread denial, the demand for truth-telling and for settler Australians to learn from Indigenous knowledge is breaking out all over. Many Indigenous activists have worked themselves to exhaustion trying to transform our national understanding. In a book about Ngarinyin lawman and visionary Bungal (David) Mowaljarlai, Hannah Rachel Bell explains how Mowaljarlai dedicated himself to transferring Indigenous knowledge to settler Australians through what he called 'The Gift':

The Gift is that of knowledge, that particularly Indigenous knowledge of belonging and identity sourced and sustained in relationship with place and country. He believed it was what white fella culture, the newcomers to Australia, needed in order to awaken in them a deeper sense of respect for and stewardship of the original, the native environment and peoples, so they too could properly belong. This was a lifelong mission.[123]

Despite these valiant efforts, it is up to settler Australians to take that essential step, within themselves and as a country as explained here by one contributor from Growing Up Aboriginal in Australia:

[A]t my age now, I have come to realise there is nothing I can do that will put things right; all I can do is work at helping us towards an understanding with whitefellas through my writing. An understanding that may help achieve some sort of realisation for Australians. And to help them develop some sort of ownership; to the koona (shit) of the past; and towards some sort of respectful inclusive future.[124]

Many questions arise for those who share this ideal about how to bring about that inclusive future. I have always found inspiring the revolutionary words of Thomas Paine – 'We have it in our power to begin the world over again' – but have never believed them to be literally true. In my view, the best kind of change comes through the accumulation of small steps in the right direction that may eventually prove transformative.

One process of walking towards a shared, inclusive future has been under way for a long time under the banner of reconciliation.[125] It's a word that has always made me feel uneasy, so I looked up some dictionary definitions. Several of them read, 'The act of causing two people or groups to become friendly again after an argument or disagreement'. This confirmed my misgivings. Reconciliation seems to place the protagonists in positions of equal culpability. Are the crimes of colonisation really just a 'disagreement' between friends, comparable to a lovers' tiff? On the face of it, the term fails to capture the profound power imbalance established and maintained by colonisation. This is not to deny that many valuable outcomes will have been achieved by dedicated people working within that framework.

Acts of reparation are a more direct way of responding to the wrongdoing of the past. This way of thinking assigns culpability squarely on the shoulders of the colonisers and places a high value on practical action. One real-world example is the demand for financial reparation that accompanied Kevin Rudd's apology to the stolen generations.

I found another example, or rather more of a cautionary tale, in the pages of the novel Taboo by Noongar author Kim Scott. The book is set around a gathering of Noongar people on land where a massacre had taken place within living memory. The story is about the survival of the traditional owners and the efforts of some settler landowners to provide some redress. A public commemoration – the opening of a Peace Park – stands as a symbol of truth and reconciliation throughout most of the plot. One of the key drivers of the project has been Janet, the wife of elderly farmer Dan, who is a direct descendant of the main perpetrator of the massacre. With Janet now deceased, Dan proposes to take the reconciliation process one step further through a personal act of reparation.

He offers to hand over a section of land to Tilly, the young Noongar woman who was briefly fostered with his family as a child. Dan's gesture might seem like a genuinely restorative act, but true restitution would require actual ceding of the stolen land. In nominating his son Doug as co-beneficiary of the land transfer, Dan explains, 'One day, I'd like to leave the farm, just this property, I mean, not the others, just this one, to you, Tilly. You and your people, and my son. Representing us. Partners. Business partners. Real reconciliation, I mean.'[126]

Dan's driving force is his desire to unite the two families that had been thrown together, initially through the wrongdoing of his ancestor, but also at a more personal level through the brief period in which Tilly had lived under his own roof. As with Len's story, there is nothing in Taboo to suggest that Tilly experienced anything but kindness during her time in Dan and Janet's home. However, unbeknown to Dan, his son is a known perpetrator of continuing abuse and exploitation of Tilly and her people. So the pathway towards reparation for past wrongs will not be as smooth as the old man imagines, will not be a simple matter of learning to get along and work together while present-day wrongs remain unacknowledged.

Decolonisation is another word that has come into my lexicon over the past few years, offering a more radical and direct response to the harms of colonisation. I quickly discovered that this can mean very different things to different people. Indigenous Alaskan academic Eve Tuck dismisses any usage of the term that does not align with the goal of recovering stolen lands as mere 'metaphor'. With her co-author, she delivers this powerful message to approaches that sidestep this goal, while appearing to maintain progressive credentials:

The absorption of decolonisation by settler social justice frameworks is one way the settler, disturbed by her own settler status, tries to escape or contain the unbearable searchlight of complicity, or having harmed others just by being oneself.[127]

For others, smaller but potentially transformative steps that offer practical gains for Indigenous people at a political, social and economic level might qualify as decolonisation strategies. My Indigenous friend and colleague, Yorta Yorta/Tharawal woman Robyn Newitt, describes decolonisation as a 'recalibration of power' and Noongar author Claire Coleman in her non-fiction book Lies Damn Lies suggests that working to end Aboriginal deaths and imprisonment, engaging in truth-telling and challenging white privilege go some way towards dismantling the processes that perpetuate colonial domination.

Coleman, along with other participants in these debates, also asserts that decolonisation must start from within by examining entrenched assumptions that maintain colonial relations at an inter-personal level. One Indigenous academic I engaged with online on this topic argued that only Indigenous people could decolonise themselves at this psychosocial level, since they are the ones who have experienced colonisation. But, since decolonisation requires transformative change from both colonisers and colonised, I tend to agree with Canadian Indigenous activist Nikki Sanchez, who argues that 'decolonisation is for everyone'.[128] For one thing, as Claire Coleman explains, colonisation is damaging for all of us who live in a settler colonial state:

You, no matter what 'race' you call your own, will be a victim of colonisation until settler colonialism ends. There are many things that need to be done to end it; I don't even know how it can happen, but the first step is surely destroying the coloniser in yourself. Decolonise your mind.[129]

As it starts to gain momentum on a societal scale, decolonisation will no doubt seem like a threatening politics to many people; one that shakes up settled ways of looking at things and requires us to venture out of the white bubbles in which most settler Australians live. An excellent way to combat the fear of change is for non-Indigenous Australians to open their hearts and minds to Indigenous values and perspectives through immersion in Indigenous art, literature and knowledge of the natural world.

The celebrated soprano Deborah Cheetham recognised in her contribution to Growing up Aboriginal in Australia how individual engagement with Indigenous knowledge can be the precursor to wider social change:

> Just as I have gone from not-knowing to knowing, from youth to maturity, I think it is fair to say that, in Australia, we could all benefit from growing up a little more Aboriginal.[130]

Indigenous activist Celeste Liddle expands on the same point, noting the connections between personal and institutional transformation, for both Indigenous and settler peoples:

> [U]ntil this country finally 'grows up Aboriginal' itself and starts not only being honest about its history and the ongoing impacts of colonisation, but also making amends – for example, by negotiating treaty settlements with First Peoples – I don't feel I will be able to completely grow up Aboriginal myself. I wonder if I will ever get to be able to in this lifetime. I hope so.[131]

This is where decolonisation starts in earnest. White people taking a back seat, being prepared to listen and learn, and in the process 'growing up Aboriginal' to some degree.

*

Unexpectedly, writing the second part of this book has set in train something of a personal process of decolonisation. Part of this has been acceptance that we are all part of the same unfolding story, although we will not all see our shared history in the same way. We can only understand this and build bridges by daring to listen and finding common ground on which to meet. I can see now that Len's placement with my caring parents must have seemed like a blessing to his first family, given their powerlessness over the decisions being made by others about Len's life. In some ways, Arthur's understanding of the history our families have shared is closer to my parents' religious world view than it is to mine. In other ways, Arthur and I seem more closely aligned.

I have seen other shifts occurring as well in my internal compass. When I was writing part one of this memoir, I began by reading as much as I could about the crimes of colonisation, usually relying on works of history and social analysis written by settler Australians. Likewise, the novels I read for solace or inspiration in my spare time were generally authored by white women like me. Over time, I found myself more and more drawn to Indigenous writers and to stories told through fiction and memoir by people of colour. Without knowing it, I was beginning to decolonise my own mind. This was a different, possibly less confronting, way of 'daring to listen'. In case it is helpful to others embarking on a similar journey, I have listed some of the magnificent books I read during this time at the end of this volume and will go on discovering more.

One of the themes that came through strongly in the books I read by Melissa Lucashenko, Tara June Winch and Karen Wyld, in particular, was the idea that the spirits of departed loved ones live on, often in the guise of birds or other natural features, or just as an unseen presence, able to provide ongoing advice, inspiration or reassurance to those who can read the signs. While I've had something of an aversion to spiritual beliefs, this outlook appeals to me as infinitely preferable to a system based on an imagined afterlife in which the bereaved might eventually be reunited with their loved ones, provided they are deemed to be deserving.

After reading these books, I began to reassess the way I looked at these things. Here's one example. After my father died, one of the items I carried back to my mountain home from his room in the retirement hostel was a plant in a hanging basket. I had chosen this living object as a fitting memento of him since gardening had been one of his lifelong pleasures. Under Dad's expert care, the succulent was a spectacular sight, cascading down in a mass of pale green tendrils. The long car journey back had taken its toll, then the first Snowy Mountains winter reduced it to a tiny stick. Horrified at the results of my neglect, I lovingly re-potted it and moved it indoors to the sunniest spot in the kitchen where I could see it and tend to it each day. Through this daily nurture, I managed to coax it back to health and abundance. But I soon realised that I didn't just think of it as my dad's plant; I was starting to think of it as my father. I cherished it, felt Dad's presence when I was near it, and gained comfort from tending to its needs. Was I starting, just a little bit – and very belatedly – to 'grow up Aboriginal'?

Undoubtedly top of my list of transformative Indigenous writing is the late Archie Roach's superb memoir, Tell Me Why. From the moment I turned the cover, I hoped his story of growing up in a white family might fill in some of the many gaps in my account; the places where Len should have been. I was immediately drawn to the words, right after the opening dedication to his Aboriginal family, 'To Mum Dulcie and Dad Alex, the Coxes, *who showed me love*' (emphasis added). So, I'd been right then in thinking that love did count for something, even in this whole sorry business.

There is so much to learn from Tell Me Why about the events that are the subject of my book that I hope you will forgive a protracted recounting of its contents. The early chapters follow the familiar contours of Len's story. An Aboriginal child taken from his family at the age of two, enduring institutionalisation and a failed – and, in Archie's case at least, abusive – foster placement; each of them ultimately finding a loving home with a devout and well-intentioned older couple following an appeal in the local newspaper. Each family was also told a malicious lie about the need for their children to be fostered. In our case, it was that Len's mother was unable to care for him due to alcohol addiction. In theirs, that Archie's biological parents had been killed in a housefire. The subterfuge was deliberate and brazen.

Along with the similarities, there were also notable differences in the set-up of the two families. The Coxes' biological children, apart from the youngest, Mary, who was a teenager still living at home, were fully grown at the time they took Archie into their family, whereas my older siblings spent more than a decade at home after Len and I had arrived. I can attest that where you fit in the family in terms of birth order matters a lot. And whereas the Cox family had already fostered another Aboriginal boy before little Archie, my parents had instead been blessed with my surprise arrival to round out their late-in-life family. But the golden thread that binds both stories together, as Archie Roach put it so beautifully, is the 'surplus of love' that had driven both couples to foster Indigenous children.[132]

As emotional problems began to surface, Len had directed his inner rage onto our kitchen crockery, rather than to us. Similarly, Archie Roach writes in his memoir that none of the confused feelings he felt as a child 'were anger directed against [his foster-parents]'.[133] He claims he was a happy child and that, as in our family, he and his foster-brother Noel were treated no differently by the Coxes than their biological children. But the question of difference intruded into the dynamics of both families when both Archie and Len entered the hotbed of identity politics that is school. The way each set of foster-parents responded to the challenges their children began to face is instructive. When Len began to query his outward difference from us, our father drew on his religious beliefs to assure Len that he was equally loved and accepted by god. I suspect that the love of god wielded a far mightier power for Dad than mere acceptance by peers.

When Archie's schoolmates started to point out the mismatch between his and his parents' skin tone, he had asked, 'Dad, am I black?' His foster-father had responded very differently – with outrage. 'You're not black, Archie,' he had said in his strong Glaswegian accent, 'you are Aboriginal, the first people on this land, not a "bloon awee Pommie".'[134] As a proud Scot, perhaps Alex Cox had some awareness of what it meant to be colonised. And although it soon became apparent that he was no more able to help Archie find his own identity than my own, or any other, white family, I can't help but wonder whether his fighting response may have paved the way for Archie's decision to set out on his own journey of discovery.

Although the first years after Archie left his foster family behind were far from easy, he does find the love and support of his own mob, and eventually his voice and salvation. His ability to merge his growing knowledge about his own culture with his Christian beliefs echoes the path taken by both Len and his brother Arthur. And, like Len, Archie finds strength in the teachings of Alcoholics Anonymous and the Serenity Prayer. But it is the ability to express himself through music and to be accepted, and later acclaimed, by the wider society, along with the unconditional love of his new-found family, that seems to give Archie the strength to survive and prosper. There was no such clean break for my brother. For whatever reason, Len never managed to escape the Love Trap we had unwittingly made for him. We will never know whether his fate would have been different had he been able to sever his ties with us and strike out on his own path.

After he had become a celebrated musical icon, Archie recounts seeing a familiar face in the audience at one of his concerts. It turns out to be his foster-sister Mary, whom he hasn't seen since leaving the Coxes' home. He acknowledges her in front of the crowd, and brings her on stage, introducing her simply as his 'sister'. Reading this unexpected turn of events knocked me for six. On the surface, it seemed like another point at which our stories might intersect, and I felt some sympathy for the emotional effort it must have taken for Mary to make her appearance.

When they are alone after the performance, Mary even delivers her own apology of sorts, saying, 'We didn't know, Archie... We thought we were doing the right thing.'[135] But as she breaks into tears, and Archie begins to comfort her, I'm surprised to find that my reaction to this act of grace and kindness is one of indignation.

'How dare she,' I find myself thinking, 'expect this man who has suffered so much, to absolve her.' She, who needed to hear her brother's powerful lyrics to realise something had been wrong. She, who had been a young adult, not an unborn babe, when Archie had come into her family and could have worked it out for herself. She, who was now shifting her emotional burden onto him and offering an excuse in place of an apology. But Archie's big-hearted response puts me and my uncharitable feelings to shame. He recalls that he 'held Mary as she started to fall apart, this woman who had borne guilt for something she hadn't done'.[136] As I read this, I recalled the words of Professor Lynette Russell about the incredible generosity of Aboriginal people.

As I try to dissect my judgemental response, I'm not proud to realise that it is driven by envy. That I would never have a chance to reunite with my brother and be publicly acknowledged by him as his sister. Would not have the opportunity to explain that I now understood how our Love Trap had damaged him. That I had no one to absolve me of my responsibility 'for something I hadn't done' and was not, in any case, looking for absolution but trying, through my actions, to make amends. That it was my parents, not me, whom Arthur had defended when I'd issued my own, misdirected, apology.

But I also think that perhaps, were Len alive today, he might have shared Archie's conflicted view about his relationship with his beloved foster parents:

> I stopped asking questions of Mum and Dad Cox. I knew it was just as confusing for them as it was for me. While I still trusted that they did what they did because they thought it was the best thing for me, I was hurt… They were wonderful, caring people, and I think of them often and fondly, but I knew they'd never completely understand what I was going through.[137]

I will never know how Len came to view the state practices that had blighted his life or understand our family's part in it; whether he might have come to agree with Archie's appraisal below, had he been granted sufficient time and distance to think things through. For my part, these simple words articulate perfectly a conclusion that it has taken me a lifetime, and a whole book, to reach:[138]

> I thought about how much Mum and Dad Cox had done for me. They were part of a racist and damaging system, but they were caught in the gears of that system, like I'd been; they weren't the gears themselves. Their hearts had just gone out to us.

Moreover, I found that Archie Roach had formed a view similar to mine about the ubiquity of the harm caused by these colonial practices, writing that every Australian 'suffers, at least a little, from the dispossession and disconnection' arising from our colonial past.[139]

Tell Me Why finishes in the place that seems to be the ultimate destination for many people who have experienced sustained trauma, whatever the reason: namely, the healing and unifying power of love. Archie Roach concludes, 'Love is the only thing that will keep us from harm.'[140] To this I would only add, and truth.

*

I was once told by a dedicated young lawyer with the Aboriginal Legal Service in Adelaide that the most confronting part of her work was witnessing the grief that was endemic in Aboriginal communities. It was long ago, and I hadn't fully understood at the time what she meant. I still associated grief with individual loss; as something deeply personal to be locked away inside you, something that was distinct from shared experience. Now I understand grief amongst Indigenous people to be synonymous with the collective experience of colonisation. Grief for the loss and waste of dispossession; for the destruction of Country; for the ongoing taking away of children; for family violence, youth suicides and lives lost in other ways through criminalisation, racism and self-harming acts born of despair. I've taken a step back now from my own consuming grief. I understand now that unresolved grief is just love with no place to go. I want to add my grief to the collective grief of colonisation; to give it meaning by finding a place for it there. And I want my love for my brother to live on through my new-found love and care for the family he was only just beginning to reconnect with when he died.

Over time, I have rehabilitated my view of my parents' actions to some degree. I know now that my judgements about them that seemed so harsh to Arthur and his girls were coloured by my youthful disdain for their churchy ways and the pain of what seemed like our irreconcilable differences. And perhaps I have unfairly projected onto them some of my own guilt that I survived, and eventually thrived, while the world seemed to hold no place for my brother. That persistent sense that he was destined to be sacrificed for me, and for others like me.

I have learned many things from spending time with Arthur. He is patient and economical with his words, and it hasn't always been easy to get to the bottom of our different outlooks. But just observing his family has taught me a lot. I have seen how a family under immense pressure can be held together by love – by the overlapping circles of kinship that I keep coming back to over again – and by the sheer sense of achievement at having survived, without obvious anger or malice, in a system stacked so mightily against them. That there is pride in having established and nurtured a family, a home, a community, a football team under these devastating conditions. And in the fact that Arthur's Koonibba community turned a place of bare survival into a place where younger generations could thrive. Even though I have still never been there, Arthur has demystified for me the remote place where he and Lennie were born and confirmed its complex historical role as a sanctuary as well as a place of confinement.

On the other hand, nothing I have found out has given me reason to change my view about the removal policies that brought Len to live with us. To give Arthur's account its due, perhaps Lennie may not have been literally stolen, since his parents were no doubt prepared to release him into the care of authorities so he could obtain the specialist care he needed. But he wasn't given back either to a loving family that did everything in their power to maintain some connection to him. At best, Lennie was borrowed from them but never returned, as if he were merely an overdue library book. What I have learned has banished any unconscious, lurking speculation, if there ever was any, that Len's placement with us may have been 'for the best'. And surprisingly, I have also discovered that my father, towards the end of his life, came to a similar conclusion.

In her novel The Nightingale, Kristin Hannah's heroine – who has kept secret from her family her role as a World War II partisan – explains that 'I always thought it was what I wanted: to be loved and admired. Now I think perhaps I'd like to be known.' These words struck a chord with me. While I am clearly no heroine – in fact, have believed myself to be the opposite – I have felt all my life that I was keeping a terrible secret. Now I have made the decision, through writing this book, to be known. Not in the sense of attracting fame or celebrity, but to speak the truth about the past to make it possible to heal and to live an authentic life and maybe help others along the way.

I want to be known as someone who had an Aboriginal brother who couldn't find a way to live in a hostile white world. Who felt in her adolescence that something wasn't right but didn't have the language to name it. Who used her white privilege to run away and didn't try to save him. Who spent a lifetime trying to understand what went wrong – why our family's love was not enough. Who tried in all the wrong ways to make things right. Who was perhaps too harsh on her parents and sometimes got lost in her own Deep Thinking. Who has tried to re-connect with her brother by getting to know his first family and has learned so much from them about survival and forgiveness. Who has come to appreciate the difference between individual blame and collective responsibility. Who has learned how to focus on small things she may be able to change and move beyond the immobilisation of shame.

The process of becoming known has been about confronting trauma and guilt, not continuing to bury it. It has been about seeking connection with others, rather than putting up barriers; about openness and acknowledgement where things have gone wrong, and hope for doing better in the future at both a personal and collective level. I may not have entirely forgiven myself for failing to support my brother as his life fell apart but maybe I have reached a place of radical acceptance, where I appreciate that forgiveness may not be either necessary or attainable. And just as Lennie's life and mine played out a small part of a bigger colonial story, now that I finish this book, the optimist in me wants to think that the nation is sitting on the cusp of major historical change; that a slow and painful process of decolonisation may be under way. Lennie will not be here to see it, along with many others who have died too young. But at least through this book, and through the distance I have travelled while writing it, I have found a safer place to keep my Misplaced Love for him.

Epilogue

There is no greater agony than bearing an untold story inside you.
Maya Angelou, *I Know Why the Caged Bird Sings*

When I started trying to build a bridge to link the past to the present, I didn't have much to go on. The only thing I knew about the construction of bridges was that they built the Sydney Harbour Bridge starting from both sides of the harbour. When the two structures aligned in the middle, it was hailed as a miracle of precision engineering. My attempt at bridge-building has been more an act of faith than something set in stone.

Towards the end of 2019, I seized the opportunity to build another span in the bridge. A plan started to form in my mind about how I might realise the promise I'd made to bring Arthur's family for them to stay at my home in the Snowy Mountains. I was to be at a conference in Perth, and worked out that I could fly from there to Adelaide, drive the whole family over in a hired people-mover, reverse the journey a week later, then fly back home from Adelaide just in time for Christmas.

It was a punishing schedule, and I knew it would exhaust me at the end of a busy academic year, but it seemed worth a try. It would be early summer, so there would be no snow, but it would be a start; would break the ice, so to speak. It was quite a logistical challenge, and there were a disturbing number of things that could go wrong, but it seemed achievable. While Arthur remained uncertain about the two-day drive when I had proposed the plan via text message, his daughters were keen. And when I found out that even Jacqui's teenage daughter Monica, whom I had never met, was excited about coming, I knew that it would be worth making the effort. The people-mover was booked, child seats arranged, roomy cabins reserved in different caravan parks for the overnight stopovers in each direction, guest room and extra sofa beds made up at home before I left, and the party fridge in the garage crammed full of barbecue meat and store-bought desserts to make for easy catering. I was only a few hours from boarding my flight from Perth when the news came that Jeannie's son was ill and she didn't think he could come. By the time I had landed in Adelaide, Jeannie and other family members were afflicted as well. We had to call off the whole thing.

Conditions for bridge-building were not ideal after that for compelling practical reasons. The start of 2020 was marked by catastrophic bushfires that raged in the Kosciusko National Park near our place right through the summer, filling the sky with smoke and our minds with dread. As my partner and I emerged from that ordeal, I began to consider reviving the people-mover plan during winter instead, as originally planned, then the arrival of Covid-19 brought life as we knew it to a standstill. I had also begun to contemplate visiting Koonibba and wondered if Arthur might like to accompany me; imagined us along the way visiting the memorial commemorating the cliff massacre of his people that he had told me about. If we went in winter, we might even witness the annual whale migration while standing on those same cliffs. But now this would not happen either, as Aboriginal communities shut down tight to protect their Elders from the pandemic. Bridge-building had to be put on hold.

I texted Arthur a few times as the health crisis unfolded, knowing he would be vulnerable to the unpredictable disease. He said he was fine. He liked being home. And his daughters came by and made sure he had everything he needed. I sent an Easter package for the kids, as I had done the year before, but this time making sure that everything was wiped down with disinfectant or detergent, and sending Arthur an SMS warning him to dispose of the outer packaging in case it might be contaminated. We had not yet learned that the transmission of the deadly disease was mainly airborne, so I was taking all precautions. I stopped talking with Jeannie about the possible trip to Koonibba and started asking her instead if they had enough provisions in the house to prepare for lockdowns, then pulled back when I realised my loving concern might be interpreted as patronising or interfering. I worried that if the schools shut down the family might not have the internet access the kids would need to keep up with their schooling. Should I buy them a laptop? I had to stop thinking like that. I just wanted to help and share, but what seemed so human and simple was actually weighed down with lots of baggage. In any case, the family were strong and supported each other. I didn't know how they got by, but they always did. 'We're fine, Aunty Leanne,' Jeannie had said via text when I was offering to help in some way. I told myself they didn't need my white angst. They were enough for each other. They would never allow me to build a Love Trap for them.

*

One morning, after several nerve-wracking years searching for a publisher for this memoir, I woke up from a dream in which a prospective publisher had received a reader's report expressing misgivings about the book. Just as I had done in real life when Arthur had given me his initial appraisal, I wracked my sleeping brain trying to pinpoint what could be wrong. When the answer was revealed to me, it was not at all what I'd been expecting and came as quite a relief. 'The problem with this book', the imaginary reviewer had said, 'is that it has no ending.'

That is probably not far from the truth. Building a bridge between myself and Arthur's family and dealing with a lifetime of grief and guilt is still a work in progress. I have taken some clumsy steps from my side, and Arthur and his family have reached out with generosity of spirit from theirs. When it fully connects up it will be a bridge built from respect, love and mutual understanding, rising above the wreckage wrought by colonisation. A bridge that we can walk along together, although on paths that could never be completely aligned. Whatever transpires in real life – and who can tell what is lurking around the corner waiting to knock us off course again – one thing is certain. In my imagined ending, Arthur sees the snow.

Questions for discussion

The Chosen Son begins with the statement that love is not all that anybody needs. What does the author mean by this? Do you agree?

The author describes her family's relationship with Len as a Love Trap that harmed him. How could this trap have been avoided?

The author suggests that in some ways Len fitted in to his foster family better than she did. Overall, do you think Len's fostering was 'for the best'?

The author is surprised when Len's brother says their mother 'gave him up' and insists that her own parents 'did nothing wrong'. Can we reconcile these differing assessments?

The Chosen Son says very little about Len's disability. How significant do you think it was in the way his life unfolded?

The author finds out that the case files relating to Len's fostering have been destroyed. Do you think these records should have been kept? Is she likely to have found answers there?

The author's parents called Len their 'chosen son'. How was choice exercised in this case, and by whom?

Len believed his birth mother had abandoned him. How might this false belief have taken hold?

The poem 'Feet on the Ground' contrasts feelings of alienation and belonging. How do these themes play out in the book?

Len's Aboriginal family believed Len was confused about his identity. How was this apparent, and could these problems have been avoided?

The author repeatedly expresses feelings of guilt and remorse about failing to help Len. Is the memoir an example of 'white guilt'?

How do her interactions with Arthur influence the author's thinking about Len's fostering with her family?

While barely mentioned in the first part of the book, Len's mother Clara turns out to be a pivotal figure. In what ways has she been erased or misrepresented?

Throughout the first part of the book, the author comes to understand her family's situation as part of a larger story of colonisation. What is the significance of this?

The author distinguishes individual blame from collective responsibility. What is the significance of this in relation to Australia's colonial past, present and future?

Do you share the author's misgivings about reconciliation as a national goal?

The author notes transformations in her own thinking that she sees as a form of decolonisation. In what different ways can this term be understood?

Do you think it was important for Len's Aboriginal family to be acknowledged on his headstone, or was this merely a symbolic gesture?

Why is it so significant for the author when Arthur's adult daughter calls her 'Aunty'?

Acknowledgements

Although 'First Nations' or 'First Peoples' or 'Indigenous Peoples' is now the preferred terminology in many circles, in part 1 I use the phrase 'Aboriginal people' (but never 'Aborigines' unless quoting directly) because it aligns better with the time period during which most of the events described in the book took place. Increasingly, of course, settler Australians are learning to acknowledge First Peoples with reference to their specific identity and language group, a convention I have followed in the second part of the memoir where possible.

While I want to recognise through this book the incalculable harm done to all First Nations people of this country by colonisation, I pay my respects in particular to the Wirangu and Kokatha people to which I now know my brother belonged.

Andrew Wilson, Senior Aboriginal Project Officer at the South Australian State Records office when I began drafting this memoir, was the first person who understood that I too had been caught up in this great national tragedy and tried to help me find out more about my brother's background. I am grateful for the information and encouragement he provided, and for the discussions that followed with Neva Wilson.

I would also like to acknowledge Bryce Clark, a Lutheran pastor based in Adelaide; Dean Heyne, a former teacher at the Koonibba mission school; and Joanne Pompey of Koonibba Community Aboriginal Health, for attempting to put me in touch with Len's surviving relatives.

Although they had initial reservations about this book, I want to thank Len's brother Arthur for sharing his insights and experiences with me and his daughters and grandchildren (grannies) for welcoming me into their lives. I have learned a great deal, and reassessed many of my own perspectives, as a result. I am grateful for their continued forbearance and acceptance and for their permission to publish this book without the need for names to be altered.

I would like to extend particular thanks to my dear friend and ski buddy Lorraine Mazerolle for her cheerfulness, strength of character and deep intuition, and for sharing with me parts of her own journey towards inner peace. Lorraine read an early draft of The Chosen Son on her smart phone in a single sitting within a few hours of receiving it. When I sent her the full draft several years later, she told me she had already heard it all in instalments while riding with me on chairlifts.

Other valued readers along the way were Tony Kiek, Llew Kiek, Mara Kiek, Beverley Scarce, Neil Weber, Ben Bowling, Rebecca Wickes, Helen McKernan, Julie Evans, Jude McCulloch, Elaine Fishwick, Marsha Wajer, Meg Randolph, Rebecca Powell, Michaella Bangard, Marinella Marmo and Alison Gerard. I want to thank them all for their insights, support and encouragement.

Mif Hudson has also been a sympathetic reader and sounding board in matters both psychological and literary. I am sure she will make a great impact on the world one day, either as a qualified therapist or through the equally therapeutic practice of writing novels. Thank you Mif for your candour and friendship.

Another colleague, Sara Maher, author of the debut novel Blinding the Ghost's Eye, also became a late reader and used her prodigious networking skills to bring the manuscript to the attention of some key people. Thanks to author and filmmaker Malcolm McKinnon for taking the time to read an early draft of the manuscript and providing such constructive feedback.

Professor Lynette Russell, former Director of the Monash Indigenous Centre and author of A Little Bird Told Me, listened with compassion to my story, warned me to brace for pushback, but assured me this was a story worth telling.

Another valued colleague, Tharawal/Yorta Yorta woman Robyn Newitt, provided much needed support and practical help to make this book as useful to others as possible. These two strong Indigenous women are a large part of the reason I have found the emotional resilience to pursue the difficult road to publication.

Lynette introduced me to Phillipa McGuinness, an accomplished writer and former publisher, who generously shared her industry knowledge with me and gave me valuable insider tips.

Other people provided professional support along the way, in some cases well before a single word appeared on a page, without which this book could not have been written.

In just six visits, counsellor Diane Nikro helped me more than I could ever have imagined, through the simple device of making me feel accepted. Without this first step, taken many years ago, I would never have had the courage to externalise the confusion and pain that I have kept inside for so long.

Gail Medbury, a phenomenal naturopath, understood that allowing your body to become an emotional battleground takes a heavy physical toll. She kept me going with her magical potions while I wrestled with this book and pointed me towards EMDR therapy when she realised, without being told, that something major was going on.

Kerry Howard, EMDR therapist extraordinaire, feminist blogger and shocking-pink enthusiast, helped me to rewire my brain and move beyond pain and self-recrimination. She took an early draft of The Chosen Son on holiday to America. Apologies, Kerry, for the Clockwork Orange joke.

Leah Scott was the next amazing woman to come into my life. She shared with me her knowledge and enthusiasm for the Wim Hof method that had transformed her own life. Wim Hof soon transformed my mind and body as well and helped me get back in touch with the resilient warrior who had been inside me all along.

I need also to thank our 'Nigerian son' Stephen, who came to live with my partner and me in England a long time ago, under conditions of great duress, when he was only sixteen, and later brought Bunmi, Grace and Daniel into our lives. The unerring love and loyalty that all of them have given to us has been a salvation.

I reconnected with my old schoolfriend Marsha Wajer during the writing of The Chosen Son, each of us amazed to learn that we had kept hidden from each other the troubles our families had been going through during our teens. Marsha has used her deep insight into this story and her skill as a professional artist to produce illustrations that so perfectly complement the text.

And finally, to Tony Kiek, my beloved life partner, who read this story with some difficulty, could not be certain whether others would think it was a good book, but said it had helped him to understand a lot of things. There have indeed been a lot of things to understand.

Sources mentioned in the text

Published books and articles

Adams, Douglas (1979) The Hitchhiker's Guide to the Galaxy, London, Pan Books.

Arendt, H. (1987) 'Collective Responsibility' in Bernauer, J.W. (ed.) Amor Mundi, Martinus Nijhoff Publishers, Dordrecht, Netherlands.

Baldwin, J. (1962a) A Letter to My Nephew published in The Progressive Magazine, available from http://www.progressive.org/news/2014/12/5047/letter-my-nephew

Baldwin, J. (1962b) Another Country, New York, Penguin.

Bell, H.R. (2009) Storymen, Cambridge, Cambridge University Press.

Beneba-Clarke, M. (2018) The Hate Race, Sydney, Hachette.

Bird, C. (ed.) (1998) The Stolen Children Their Stories, Sydney, Random House.

Brodie, V. (2002) My Side of the Bridge, Wakefield Press, Adelaide.

Brock, P. (1993) Outback Ghettos: A history of Aboriginal institutionalisation and survival, Cambridge, Cambridge University Press.

Burgoyne, I. (2000). Mirning: We are the Whales: a Mirning-Kokatha Woman Recounts Life Before and After Dispossession. Broome, Western Australia: Magabala Books.

Burridge, K. (1988) 'Aborigines and Christianity: An overview' in Swain, T. and Rose, R. (eds) Aboriginal Australians and Christian Missions: ethnographic and historical studies, Adelaide, Australian Association for the Study of Religions.

Butler, J. (2010) Frames of War: When is life grievable? New York, Verso.

Cohen, S. (2001) States of Denial: Knowing about atrocities and suffering, Cambridge, Polity.

Coleman, Claire (2021) Lies Damned Lies: A personal exploration of the impact of colonisation, Sydney, Ultimo Press.

Coleman, Dylan (2012) Mazin Grace, Brisbane, Queensland University Press.

Commonwealth of Australia (1997) Bringing Them Home: Report of the National Inquiry into the separation of Aboriginal and Torres Strait Islander people from their families, Canberra, Commonwealth of Australia available at https://www.humanrights.gov.au/publications/bringing-them-home-stolen-children-report-1997

Cowlishaw, G. (2006) 'Collateral damage in the history wars' in Lea, T, Kowal, E. and Cowlishaw, G. (eds) Moving Anthropology: Critical Indigenous Studies, Charles Darwin University Press, Darwin.

Cunneen, C. (2001) Conflict, Politics and Crime: Aboriginal communities and the police, Sydney, Allen & Unwin.

Faulkner, W. (1951) Requiem for a Nun, New York, Random House.

Foer, Jonathan Safran (2005) Extremely Loud and Incredibly Close, Boston, Houghton Mifflin.

Frankl, V. (1946) Man's Search for Meaning, Boston, Beacon Press.

Grant, S. (2019) Australia Day, Sydney, Harper Collins.

Haebich, A. (2000) Broken Circles: Fragmenting Indigenous Families 1800–2000, Fremantle, Fremantle Arts Centre Press.

Hasslett, A. (2016) Imagine Me Gone, Boston, Little, Brown & Company.

Heiss, A. (2016) Barbed Wire and Cherry Blossoms, Sydney, Simon & Schuster.

Heiss, A. (ed.) (2018) Growing up Aboriginal in Australia, Black Inc, Carlton.

Herman J. L. (1992) Trauma and Recovery, New York, Basic Books.

Honeyman, G. (2017) Eleanor Oliphant is Completely Fine, Bishopbriggs (UK), Harper Collins.

Horton, D. (1994) Encyclopaedia of Aboriginal Australia, Canberra, IATSIS.

Kelman, H. and Hamilton, V. (1989) Crimes of Obedience: Toward a social psychology of authority and obedience, New Haven, Yale University Press.

Libesman, T. (2021) 'South Australia v Lampard-Trevorrow [2010] SASC 56' in Watson, N. and Douglas, H. (eds) Indigenous Legal Judgements: Bringing Indigenous voices into judicial decision making. London, Routledge

Mattingley, C. and Hampton, K. (1988) Survival In Our Own Land: 'Aboriginal' experiences in 'South Australia' since 1836, Sydney, Hodder and Stoughton.

Mullighan, E. (2008) Children in State Care Commission of Inquiry: Allegations of sexual abuse and death from criminal conduct available from https://www.childprotection.sa.gov.au/__data/assets/pdf_file/0011/ 107201/children-in-state-care-commission-of-inquiry-introduction. pdf

Pascoe, B. (2014) Dark Emu: Aboriginal Australia and the birth of Agriculture, Broome, Magabala Books.

Raynes, C. (2009) The Last Protector: The illegal removal of Aboriginal children from their parents in South Australia, Adelaide, Wakefield Press.

Raynes, C. (2002) A Little Flour and a Few Blankets: An administrative History of Aboriginal Affairs in South Australia 1834-2000, Adelaide, South Australian Government.

Reynolds, H. (1996) Aboriginal Sovereignty: Reflections on race, state and nation, Sydney, Allen & Unwin.

Reynolds, H. (1998) This Whispering in our Hearts, Sydney, Allen & Unwin.

Roach, Archie (2019) Tell Me Why, Sydney, Simon & Schuster.

Rundle, G. (2014) 44: A Tale of Survival, Scoresby, Five Mile Press.

Russell, Lynette (2002) A Little Bird Told Me: Family secrets, necessary lies, Melbourne, Allen & Unwin.

Salzman and Halloran (2004) in Handbook of Experimental Existential Psychology, edited by J. Greenberg, S. Koole and T Pyszczynski, New York, Guilford.

Scott, Kim (2017) Taboo, Sydney, Picador Australia.

Sunday Mail (1956) Lennie Can Walk Now, published 24 November 1956, page 11.

Toews, M. (2014) All My Puny Sorrows, New York, Alfred A Knopf.

Tuck, E. and Yang, K.W. (2012) Decolonization, Indigeneity, Education & Society, Vol. 1(1) pp 1–40

Vincent, E. (2017) Against Native Title: Conflict and creativity in outback Australia, Canberra, Aboriginal Studies Press.

Weber, L. (2002) A Light in the World's Dark Places: the missionary work of E.G. Neil. (This pamphlet and microfilms of the missionary diary of the Reverend E.G. Neil are available through the Pacific Manuscripts Bureau).

Wood, A. H. (1975) Overseas Missions of the Australian Methodist Church Vol. 1 Tonga and Samoa, Melbourne, Aldersgate Press.

Young, Iris Marion (2003) 'Political Responsibility and Structural Injustice', The Lindley Lecture, University of Kansas available at https:// kuscholarworks.ku.edu/handle/1808/12416

Other material

Adelaide Advertiser 'Lennie Will Walk This Christmas', published 8 December 1956, page 3.

Lutheran Archives, Adelaide

South Australian State Records

Personal correspondence from South Australian State Aboriginal Affairs and Family and Youth Services

Some other great books

Here is a selection of some of the outstanding books, mostly works of fiction, that I read while writing this memoir. Most of them were written by Indigenous authors or others grappling with the contemporary legacy of systemic racism and colonialism in Australia or elsewhere. All of them, in their wisdom and brilliance, enriched and broadened my understanding, for which I am immensely grateful.

Paul Beatty, The Sellout

Larissa Behrendt, After Story

Larissa Behrendt, Home

Tony Birch, Blood

Behrouz Boochani, No Friend but the Mountains

Geraldine Brooks, March

Geraldine Brooks, Horse

Claire Coleman, Terra Nullius

Paul Collis, Dancing Home

Tjanara Goreng Goreng, with Julie Szego, A Long Way From No Go

Veronica Gorrie, Black and Blue: A memoir of racism and resistance

Kate Grenville, Searching for the Secret River

Anita Heiss, Bila Yarrudhanggalangdhura

Sue Monk Kidd, The Secret Life of Bees

Sue Monk Kidd, The Invention of Wings

Harper Lee, To Kill a Mockingbird

Harper Lee, Go Set a Watchman

Melissa Lucashenko, Mullumbimby

Melissa Lucashenko, Too Much Lip

Brenda Matthews, The Last Daughter

Bruce Pascoe, Dark Emu

Archie Roach, Tell Me Why

Zadie Smith, Swing Time

Zadie Smith, On Beauty

Kathryn Stockett, The Help

Chelsea Watego, Another Day in the Colony

Amanda Webster, A Tear in the Soul

Tara June Winch, The Yield

Karen Wyld, Where the Fruit Falls

Notes

1. Brock (1993).
2. Notes taken from Lutheran archives, North Adelaide.
3. Raynes (2009).
4. https://guides.slsa.sa.gov.au/ Aboriginal_Missions/Koonibba
5. Notes taken from Lutheran archives, North Adelaide.
6. Op. cit. 1.
7. Commonwealth of Australia (1997) p. 6.
8. Mattingley and Hampton (1988)
9. Op. cit. 3.
10. Vincent (2017) p. 65.
11. Op. cit. 1, 5.
12. Op. cit. 1.
13. Op. cit. 1.
14. Raynes (2002).
15. Op. cit. 1 and Haebich (2000).
16. The Encyclopaedia of Aboriginal Australia uses the spelling Arrentje but I will use both to reflect my parents' use of Aranda.
17. Op. cit. 4.
18. Op. cit. 1.
19. Op. cit. 4.
20. Op. cit. 8.
21. Op. cit. 1.
22. Cunneen (2001).
23. Baldwin (1962a).
24. Vincent (2017) p. 47.
25. The website referred to is no longer in operation, but the community now has a wiki accessible at https://en.wikipedia. org/wiki/Koonibba
26. Faulkner (1951).
27. https://www.creativespirits. info/aboriginalculture/land/ the-1972-larrakia-petition
28. Heiss (2016) p. 13.
29. Op. cit. 7, p. 402.
30. Coleman (2012).
31. Thanks to Neva Wilson for this information.
32. At http://en.wikipedia.org/ wiki/Stanford_marshmallow_ experiment
33. Cowlishaw (2006).
34. For example see https:// newmatilda.com /2017/01/22/ busting- black-myths-the-truth-about-our-first-peoples/ and Bruce Pascoe's historical work Dark Emu.
35. Op. cit. 7, p. 11.
36. Grant (2019) 2.
37. Bird (1998).
38. Brodie (2002) p. 163.
39. Salzman and Halloran (2004).
40. Bebe Backhouse 'It's not over' in Heiss (2018) p. 18.

41. Jason Goninan 'There are no halves' in Heiss (2018) p. 93.

42. John Williams-Mozley 'Split affinity' in Heiss (2018) p. 275.

43. Op. cit. 7, p. 202.

44. Op. cit. 1.

45. Op. cit. 7, p. 152.

46. Op. cit. 3.

47. Op. cit. 7.

48. Haebich (2000).

49. Op. cit. 3.

50. Op. cit. 3.

51. Op. cit. 7, p. 398.

52. Op. cit. 37.

53. Op. cit. 7, p. 5.

54. Op. cit. 7, p. 8.

55. Libesman (2021) p. 206

56. Op. cit. 7, p. 9

57. Op. cit. 7, p. 211

58. See the 2008 report of the Mullighan Inquiry.

59. https: //www.adelaidenow.com.au/news/south-australia/traumatised-victims-of-eden-park-boys-home-abuse-say-the-salvation-army-should-increase-compensation/news-story/6ae091293257b275253aaf32f6f-5d2c
Also Graham Rundle (2014).

60. The dissenting judgement of South Australian Supreme Court Justice Kirsten Gray in declining to overturn a finding of false imprisonment in the case of Bruce Trevorrow who was taken from his family in 1956 in circumstances remarkably similar to Len's placement with our family, found the fostering family – regardless of their actions and intentions – to be 'an extension of the original and ongoing restraint of the state' as a direct result of policies that 'simply did not affect non-Indigenous children'. Op. cit. 55, p. 216.

61. This term is applied to an area in social psychology research spawned by the Holocaust, that explores how seemingly good people can be enticed to commit harmful acts under the influence of experts. Examples include the infamous Milgram experiments https://www.simplypsychology.org/milgram.html My favourite work in this genre is non-experimental and involved large scale surveys and critical analysis of more recent atrocities – see Kelman and Hamilton (1989).

62. Butler (2010).

63. Op. cit. 7, p. 395.

64. Herman (1992).

65. Op. cit. 7, p. 157.

66. Actually, for the pedants amongst us, 'And as you wish that others would do to you, do so to them' (English Standard Version) or 'And as ye would that men should do to you, do ye also to them likewise' (King James Version).

67. Weber (2002).

68. Op. cit. 1.

69. Op. cit. 67.

70. See for example Wood (1975).

71. Burridge (1988).

72. Reynolds (1996).

73. See for example http: //www. americanpopularculture.com/ journal/articles/spring_2005/ aiello. htm

74. Op. cit. 23.

75. Op. cit. 3.

76. Op. cit. 3.

77. Op. cit. 7, p. 147.

78. Op. cit. 48.

79.Baldwin (1962b) p. 131.

80. Op. cit. 23.

81. https://theconversation.com/ aboriginal-traditions-describe-the-complex-motions-of-planets-the-wandering-stars-of-the-sky-97938

82. https: //www.theguardian. com/commentisfree/2015/aug/ 28/forty-thousand-years-of-Indigenous-maths-can-get-kids-into-numbers-today

83. http://www.abc.net.au/local/ audio/2014/03/17/3965103.htm

84. Op. cit. 7, p. 136.

85. Op. cit. 7, p. 133.

86. Williams-Mozley 'Split affin-ity' in Heiss (2018).

87. Adams (1979).

88. Reputedly, '42' is ASCII code for an asterisk, or 'anything you want it to be'.

89. Arendt (1987) p. 50.

90. Thanks to Dr Julie Evans for introducing me to the work of Iris Marion Young.

91. http://www.kooriweb.org/ foley/resources/pdfs/198.pdf

92. Young (2003) p. 11.

93. View the Statement – Uluru Statement from the Heart.

94. Cited by Carmel Bird, op. cit. 37.

95. Op. cit. 79, p. 85.

96. Hasslett (2016) p. 352.

97. Eye Movement Desensitisa-tion and Reprocessing (which I initially remembered with the mnemonic Every Mentally Deranged Robot) – see www. emdria.org.

98. Frankl (1946) pp 109–110.

99. Taken from the title of Mir-iam Toews's beautiful book All My Puny Sorrows, which in turn is adapted from a poem of the same name by Samuel Taylor Coleridge.

100. 1-02KawandillaCPT (ade-laide.edu.au).

101. Op. cit. 48.

102. Russell (2002).

103. https://en.wikipedia.org/ wiki/Coloured_Stone

104. For example, see an account of growing up on Raukkan Mission (also known as Point McLeay) near the mouth of the River Murray by Veronica Brodie (2002).

105. https://guides.slsa.sa.gov.au/ Aboriginal_Missions/Koonibba

106. https://www.findandconnect. gov.au/ref/sa/biogs/SE01358b. htm

107. Heiss (2018).

108. https://www.abc.net. au/ radio/programs/truecrime/ blood-on-the-tracks/

109. https://c21ch.newcastle. edu.au/colonialmassacres/map. php

110. Burgoyne (2000) p. 114.

111. https://radio.abc.net. au/ programitem/pel3NpjN-4L?play=true

112. Brodie (2002) p. 101.

113. Carol Pettersen 'Too white to be black, too black to be white …' in Heiss (2018) p. 188.

114. Op. cit. 22.

115. https://theconversation. com/a-grave-omission-the-quest-to- identify-the-dead-in-remote-nt-100456

116. Heiss (2018).

117. For an explanation see here: http://www.navy.gov. au/ hmas-warramunga-ii

118. https://www.sbs.com.au/ nitv/article/2018/05/28/how-be-good-Indigenous-ally

119. Wim Hof method involves a special breathing and retention technique and regular cold immersion to balance hormones, reduce inflammation and stimulate the production of endorphins: https://www. wim-hofmethod.com/

120. https://www.theguardian. com/australia-news/2018/aug/ 05/the-world-is-being-undone-before-us-if-we-do-not-reimagine-australia-we-will-be-undone-too

121. George Orwell Notes on Nationalism, quoted by Cohen (2001).

122. Kerry Reed-Gilbert 'The little town on the railway track' in Heiss (2018) p. 202.

123. Bell (2009) p. 2.

124. William Russell 'A story from my life' in Heiss (2018) p. 204.

125. Home – Reconciliation Australia.

126. Scott (2018) p. 274.

127. Tuck and Yang (2012) p. 9.

128. See TEDx talk, 12 March 2019 (90) Decolonization Is for Everyone | Nikki Sanchez | TEDxSFU – YouTube

129. Coleman (2021) p. 212.

130. Deborah Cheetham 'So much still pending' in Heiss (2018).

131. Celeste Liddle 'Black Bum' in Heiss (2018) p. 153.

132. Roach (2019) p. 9.

133. Op. cit. 132 p. 24.

134. Op. cit. 132 p. 13.

135. Op. cit. 132 p. 249.

136. Op. cit. 132 p. 250.

137. Op. cit. 132 pp 27–31.

138. Op. cit. 132 p. 180.

139. Op. cit. 132 p. 299.

140. Op. cit. 132 p. 338.

www.ingramcontent.com/pod-product-compliance
Lightning Source LLC
Chambersburg PA
CBHW031121020426
42333CB00012B/170